Detroit United Railway's parlor car Genesee *ran to Toledo in the 1920's.* O. F. LEE COLLECTION.

THE INTERURBAN ERA

BY WILLIAM D. MIDDLETON

A KALMBACH PUBLICATION

Library of Congress Catalog Card Number:

61-10728

First printing, June 1961. Second printing, December 1961. Third printing, April 1965. Fourth printing, March 1968. Fifth printing, March 1971.

To Dorothy,

who was courted with the occasional assistance of the North Shore Line, and who has traveled a good many interurban miles since then with remarkable forbearance.

FOR the great assistance of many individuals in the preparation of this volume the author extends his most sincere appreciation. The magnificent selection of pictorial material within its covers would have been impossible without the generosity of dozens of photographers and collectors, whose contributions are individually credited at the end of each caption. Much of the historical material, which would otherwise have been all but unobtainable, was drawn from the painstaking publications of the numerous railroad enthusiast groups. Of particular help were those of the Electric Railroaders' Association, the Electric Railway Historical Society, the Central Electric Railfans' Association, *Interurbans*, and individual chapters of the National Railway Historical Society. For their kind help in locating scarce material, suggestions and advice of every description, and assistance in compiling the listings contained in the appendix, special thanks are due J. D. Alrich of the General Electric Company, John Baxter, Morris Cafky, E. Harper Charlton, William J. Clouser, H. T. Crittenden, O. R. Cummings, Everett L. DeGolyer Jr., Frank P. Donovan Jr., Hall E. Downey of General Railway Signal Company, Donald Duke, Charles Goethe, William R. Gordon, Ross B. Grenard Jr., Herbert H. Harwood Jr., LeRoy O. King Sr., LeRoy O. King Jr., Randolph L. Kulp, Edward S. Miller, Louis C. Mueller, Foster M. Palmer, Frank B. Putnam of the Security First National Bank, Los Angeles, Robert J. Sandusky, Martin Schmitt of the University of Oregon Library, Robert A. Selle, Donald K. Slick, John Stern, Paul Stringham, Stan F. Styles, Elmer G. Sulzer, Ira L. Swett, Francis B. Tosh, James W. Walker Jr., Robert S. Wilson, and Jeffrey K. Winslow. Particular thanks go to Freeman H. Hubbard, editor of *Railroad* Magazine, for making available valuable material in the magazine's files, and to Stephen D. Maguire, editor of *Railroad* Magazine's Electric Lines Department, whose extensive personal collection was made available to the author and who furnished many excellent suggestions. Special thanks are also due Bill Krueger and John Hogan of Campus Camera Inc., Madison, Wis., for their careful processing of many of the photographs appearing in this volume, and to Bert Misek for his equally skillful handling of negatives from the George Krambles collection.

IN the long history of transportation development in North America the interurban era is little more than a recent incident. In business terms the electric interurbans must be considered a notable failure, and even in terms of public utility their span of useful service was exceedingly brief. Few of them operated much more than two decades before their role of local passenger carrier and light freight hauler had largely been usurped by rubber-tired transport. Yet there was a time when they seemed to hold unlimited promise for the future, and a good number of persons considered the age of universal electric transportation to be just around the corner.

To many adult Americans, now as much slave as they are master of their automobiles, the interurban railways linger among pleasant memories of an unhurried, less sophisticated time in the recent past. My father still recalls the arrival of the first "Crandic" interurbans in Iowa City during his undergraduate years at the University of Iowa. My mother, raised in Framingham, Mass., remembers with pleasure frequent girlhood excursions to Boston on the fast cars of the Boston & Worcester "Trolley Air Line" (the closed cars made her queasy, but the big open trolleys were wonderful). And when Great-Aunt Viola joined the family in Maine for the summer, she invariably arrived from Boston aboard the Shore Line trolley. One of my own earliest memories is of the big red interurbans of the Clinton, Davenport & Muscatine, which raced along the west bank of the Mississippi past my uncle's home in Le Claire with what seemed, to a small boy's eyes, blinding speed.

In attempting to record something of the color-

ful era of the interurbans I have been confronted with the problem of deciding just what was an interurban, for the intercity electric railway existed in almost infinite gradations between what were little more than long streetcar lines and systems that were virtually identical to electrified steam trunk lines. E. D. Durand, while he was Director of the Census, defined an interurban as "a railway having less than half its track within municipal limits." Many electric railway enthusiasts have limited the term interurban to systems meeting rigid standards of high-speed, intercity operation over private right of way, and some refuse to grant interurban status unless the company transported mail and express on the cars. One railroad fan considered a line an interurban only if the cars had railroad roofs and lavatories. None of these definitions have

been adhered to slavishly here, and the occasional appearance within this volume of electric railways meeting none of these criteria represents no more than personal preference. It is hoped that these lapses will be excused by those with more rigid definitions.

Wherever possible I have chosen illustrative material that is previously unpublished or has been but little seen, but where completeness of coverage has occasionally required the use of illustrations that have been widely published in other works on the subject, they have been used without hesitation.

William D. Middleton

Gölcük, Turkey
August 1960

9

The Coming of the Interurban

Splendid in its newness, this Union Traction Company interurban sped through rural Indiana on a Fort Wayne Limited schedule. GENERAL RAILWAY SIGNAL COMPANY.

The Coming of the Interurban

A HISSING SOUND from the copper wire draped overhead, the urgent clatter of whirling steel wheels on rail joints, and a wailing air horn that commanded respect and attention signaled its coming. Shoving a massive arc headlight and a wooden cowcatcher of imposing dimensions before it, the interurban came racing across the countryside, faster, it seemed, than anything else of man's invention. Trackside vegetation bent aside suddenly at its passing; there was the brief odor of ozone and hot grease from the spinning traction motors; and passengers, reclining in plush-upholstered ease within, looked down idly from the Gothic windows of their varnished vehicle. And then it was gone, leaving behind only a dust cloud and a gently swaying trolley wire.

The interurban was an American transportation phenomenon. Evolved from the urban streetcar, the interurban appeared shortly before the dawn of the 20th century, grew to a vast network of over 18,000 miles in two decades of exuberant growth, and then all but vanished after barely three decades of usefulness. But within its brief life span the interurban bridged the gap between a horse and buggy nation and a modern America that rides on rubber over endless lanes of concrete and asphalt. It changed the ways of rural life forever, and frequently set a pattern for metropolitan growth that continues even today.

The practical electric railway was not the invention of one man, or even of a few men. The period of experimentation that ultimately led to electric transportation began about 1830. In 1834 Thomas Davenport, a Brandon (Vt.) blacksmith, built over a hundred model electric railway motor cars which operated by battery power. Eight years later a man named Davidson constructed for the Edinburgh-Glasgow Railway a 7-ton electric car which attained a speed of 4 miles per hour with power from an iron-zinc sulphuric acid battery. In 1851 Prof. Charles G. Page, with $30,000 appropriated by Congress, constructed a battery-powered locomotive that reached speeds as high as 19 miles per hour between Washington and nearby Bladensburg, Md. The contraption was far from practical, however, and some called it the "electromagnetic humbug."

The development of the dynamo, or generator, after 1860 and the discovery that a dynamo could drive a motor proved to be the key to the practical electric railway. Moses G. Farmer operated one of the first cars with a motor and dynamo in 1867, and the subsequent experimentation of such men as Leo Daft and Charles Van Depoele, as well as many others, brought America to the threshold of the age of electric traction by the late 1880's. The construction of the first really successful electric railway at Richmond in 1887 by a young Naval Academy graduate, Frank Julian Sprague, was followed by wholesale electrification of America's animal- and cable-powered street railways.

The interurban, a logical development from the electric street railway, soon followed. What was perhaps the first interurban—although it eventually became no more than a long streetcar line — began operating between the Twin Cities of Minneapolis and St. Paul in 1891 and soon forced severe curtailment of passenger service on the competing steam railroads. What is most frequently regarded as the first true interurban, the 15-mile East Side Railway, began operating between Portland and Oregon City in February 1893. Another of the earliest interurbans, the 20-mile Sandusky, Milan & Norwalk in Ohio, began operation later the same year.

A principal obstacle to the development of long interurban lines was the impracticality of transmitting over long distances the low-voltage direct current used for electric car operation. The introduction in 1896 of distribution systems which employed high-voltage alternating-current transmission lines and substations which converted the power to the necessary low-voltage direct current solved this particular problem, and during the last few years of the 19th century the great interurban railway boom began to gather momentum. The perfection of a multiple-unit control system by Sprague in

Operating over what is generally regarded as the first true interurban line, this big Oregon Water Power & Railroad Company car, with two open trailers in tow, paused at Golf Junction on the Portland-Oregon City line early in the century. STEPHEN D. MAGUIRE COLLECTION.

1898 which permitted the operation of a train of electric cars under the control of a single motorman in the lead car was another important aid to the development of interurban lines.

The origin of the term "interurban" (from the Latin for "between cities") is usually credited to Charles L. Henry, an Indiana state senator and later a U.S. congressman, who is said to have developed the word to describe the intercity electric railways he was then planning after seeing the "intramural" electric railway at the 1893 Chicago World's Columbian Exposition. Henry, sometimes called the "father of the interurban," was a pioneer in Indiana interurban development and completed the state's first 11-mile line in 1897, which he later built into the 400-mile Union Traction Company, serving much of central Indiana.

The interurbans seemed to fill a travel void for much of America. Aside from what slow, infrequent, and grimy local passenger service might be avail-

able from the steam railroads, rural America was pretty well restricted to whatever lay within horse and buggy range. The interurbans were bright and clean, stopped almost anywhere, and ran far more frequently than the steam trains, for one car made a train. Once in town the cars usually operated through the streets and went right downtown. They were almost always cheaper than steam trains, too.

Small-towners and farm folk alike swarmed aboard the new electric cars to spend a day in the city, shopping or just seeing the sights. Equally important, the fast package and light freight service opened up new markets for farmers and made big city merchandise quickly available to the local shopkeeper. The commercial traveler, or "drummer," took to the interurbans with enthusiasm for they carried him to the heart of the business district, often right to his hotel door, and the frequent schedules made it possible to cover more cities and towns in a day than he could on the steam trains.

Among the earliest interurbans was the Sandusky, Milan & Norwalk, which opened in 1893. This photograph was taken in Norwalk, O., in 1900. JOHN A. REHOR COLLECTION.

Indiana lawyer, state senator, and U.S. congressman Charles L. Henry was credited with originating and popularizing the word "interurban" and became known as the "father of the interurban." The first section of his Union Traction Company, opened in 1898, was Indiana's first interurban. Until his death in 1927 Henry remained an indefatigable advocate of interurban railways. HARRIS & EWING, FROM INDIANA HISTORICAL SOCIETY.

Motorized construction equipment was still in the future even during the last years of interurban development, when the Salt Lake & Utah constructed its line into Payson, Utah, on the eve of World War I. FRED FELLOW COLLECTION.

A Milwaukee Northern Railway track gang pushed north into the village of Cedarburg, Wis., in the winter of 1906-1907. The Milwaukee Northern builders, Comstock, Haigh & Walker Company, beat Milwaukee Electric's John I. Beggs to the routes north of Milwaukee. A planned Fond du Lac branch, which would have left the Sheboygan line here, was never built. DAVID A. STRASSMAN COLLECTION.

This hat-waving crowd of "Glendale Boosters" had just arrived aboard the first train into Pacific Electric's new Subway Terminal at Los Angeles in 1925. HISTORICAL COLLECTIONS, SECURITY FIRST NATIONAL BANK, LOS ANGELES.

Milwaukee Northern Railway's big Niles cars reached Cedar Grove, Wis., August 31, 1908, and citizens found out what the humming rotary converter in the brick depot had brought to their hamlet. That all were not awed by the first-day speeches is evidenced by the determined contingent exiting left, no doubt heading uptown to discuss the event over steins of some potent local lager. DAVID A. STRASSMAN COLLECTION.

Indianapolis was among North America's greatest traction centers, and after 1904 electric cars from the 12 routes entering the city used the new Indianapolis Traction Terminal. The adjacent nine-story office building and the great trainshed cost over a million dollars. In 1914, one of the Indiana interurbans' peak years, 7 million passengers passed through the terminal and a daily average of 520 passenger cars and nearly 100 freight cars were accommodated. GEORGE KRAMBLES COLLECTION.

Occasionally interurban promoters, too strapped for cash to string trolley wire or to build power plants, went into business with gasoline motor cars as a temporary expedient until they could round up the necessary funds. One such line was the 27-mile Woodstock & Sycamore Traction Company in Illinois, which started operation in 1911 with three of these fearsome-looking knife-nosed McKeen gasoline cars. Among the least successful of interurban ventures, the Woodstock & Sycamore was abandoned in 1918, before its owners ever did get around to electrification. STEPHEN D. MAGUIRE COLLECTION.

The roadside development often characteristic of interurbans is illustrated here by the West Chester line of the Philadelphia Suburban Transportation Company. The 1914 Jewett interurban shown was junked a few months after this 1949 photograph was made, but the line itself continued to operate for another five years with streamlined equipment. CHARLES A. BROWN.

structed with expectations of immediate and substantial profits. Within cities the interurbans usually followed the tracks already used by street railway systems, and intermediate towns were often traversed in a similar manner. Once out of town the interurban usually took to its own private right of way, sometimes paralleling the rural roads and sometimes striking off across the open countryside, but almost always following the ups and downs of the natural topography to avoid the expensive cuts and fills of steam railroad practice. An extreme example was the Syracuse & Suburban Railway, whose builders decided to follow the existing highway for their 12-mile line to Edward Falls. This decision resulted in what *Brill Magazine* aptly termed an "arduous alignment and profile." Grades as steep as 11 per cent were frequently encountered.

Interurban rail sections were light, and ballast, if it was used at all, was skimpy. The trolley wire was

Los Angeles, too, was among the great traction centers. Pacific Electric Railway's Henry E. Huntington constructed the magnificent Main Street Terminal, Los Angeles' first "skyscraper," in 1904 to accommodate the interurbans of the rapidly growing PE. Even at the time of this 1950 photograph, the terminal was still the center of intense interurban activity. WILLIAM D. MIDDLETON.

21

usually simply suspended from wooden poles. Occasionally the interurban builders adopted construction standards that were equivalent to those for high-class steam railroads, but such lines were in a minority. All of the construction short cuts of the early years, though they helped the interurbans begin operation in a hurry at low cost, proved to be fatal liabilities in later years, when high speeds and the operation of long freight trains became the keys to survival.

Sometimes communities along the projected route of an interurban were so eager for the stimulating effects of electric transportation that substantial grants or subsidies were offered as inducements to the promoters. One Indiana line, the Winona Railway, had to build the last section of its line between Warsaw and Peru in a headlong rush in order to begin operation by the February 1, 1910, deadline date required to collect the subsidy money proffered by counties along the route.

Because the interurbans were almost always small, locally backed ventures, they were usually sensitive to local aspirations and wants, and as a rule, electric railwaymen refrained from the sort of "public be damned" shenanigans practiced by the steam railroad barons of earlier years. There were occasional lapses, however, one of which occurred in 1924 on the Dayton & Western Traction Company. Valentine Winters, the D&W manager, became involved in a squabble with the city officials of New Lebanon, O., over paving between the rails of the electric line, which traversed city streets. Unable to reach a satisfactory agreement, Winters grandly ripped up his rails and built a new line around New Lebanon, on private right of way outside the corporate limits. "New Lebanon Says Winters Is Bluffing" headlined a Dayton newspaper at the height of the controversy, which may have had something to do with the name "Valley Bluff" which Winters gave the new D&W station just outside town. Tempers cooled, and a few years later the station was quietly renamed New Lebanon.

Stung by the competition of the electric cars, which quickly siphoned off their local passenger and package freight business, the steam railroads often retaliated in heavy-handed fashion. Their hostility was manifested in many ways. Some tried to match the frequent service and low fares of the electrics, which proved to be a costly business. Soon after the new interurban line was opened between Cedar Rapids and Iowa City, Ia., in 1904, the competing Rock Island line began offering an hourly steam train service at low fares, with extra trains on Sunday. Similar measures were taken against another new interurban operating between Des Moines and Colfax. So enamored was the public of the new trolleys, though, that the steam trains were ignored, and after only a few months Rock Island retired

Thrusting a rakish wooden pilot ahead of it, a Fort Wayne, Van Wert & Lima interurban moved through the Lima Public Square about 1906, a year after the 62-mile interstate line opened for business. JOHN H. KELLER COLLECTION, FROM STEPHEN D. MAGUIRE.

from the scene, unhappily licking its fiscal wounds.

Other steam lines attempted to freeze out the new competition. In 1906 the West and Central Passenger Association, a steam road group, resolved that it would not recognize its electric competition either by issuing joint tariffs or by making traffic agreements. One Midwest steam road, the Clover Leaf system (now part of the Nickel Plate), decided to buck the majority trend and issued interline tariffs with interurban lines, realizing a lucrative source of new business in the process.

When the interurbans ventured into carload freight business, a similar hostility was usually the rule. In 1915 the Michigan Central Railroad fought all the way to the U.S. Supreme Court before it

finally bowed to a decision of the Railroad Commission of Michigan ordering it to make a physical connection for carload freight traffic with the Detroit United Railway, an interurban, at Oxford, Mich.

Sometimes the steam road measures were more subtle. In 1914 former Utah Gov. Simon Bamberger hinted darkly that the "keen antagonisms of the Gould and Harriman interests" had made it impossible for him to get outside financial aid for the construction of his Salt Lake City-Ogden interurban. Bamberger managed to raise enough local capital for the project and built his electric line anyway.

Steam roads usually placed every possible obstacle in the way of electric line construction, and often the

These two interurbans, typical of the distinguished wooden cars constructed by the Niles Car Works, met in the street at the Lake Shore Electric Railway's Norwalk (O.) depot in 1908. O. F. LEE COLLECTION.

23

En route to Fort Benjamin Harrison, a Union Traction Company of Indiana interurban trundled past the U.S. Court House and Post Office in Indianapolis sometime around World War I. WILLIAM D. MIDDLETON COLLECTION.

The fierce steam railroad-interurban rivalry of earlier years is typified by this view of a Lehigh Valley Transit interurban and a Reading train racing down parallel track near Souderton, Pa. By the time this photograph was taken in 1950, however, there was little traffic left to squabble over, and in the decade since, electric car, steam locomotive, and this particular passenger train itself have vanished from the Pennsylvania Dutch countryside. LESTER WISMER.

interurbans, unable to obtain a grade-level crossing with a steam line, were forced to build a costly overpass or underpass. Sometimes such conflicts were resolved in a more direct manner. One celebrated incident of such a nature occurred in California when rival construction forces of the Northern Electric Railway and George Gould's Western Pacific, both pushing toward Sacramento, arrived in Marysville about the same time. The two routes crossed at a point adjacent to an apiary just south of the Yuba River. Gould's men got their track in first, but the Northern Electric's track gang arrived soon after and on January 12, 1907, the great "Battle of the Bee Farm" took place when a hundred interurban men tore out all of the newly laid Western Pacific rail and put down their own track.

A similar and even more violent skirmish had taken place two years earlier when a Petaluma & Santa Rosa Railroad track gang attempted to install a crossing with the California Northwestern in Santa Rosa, Calif. On March 1, 1905, after several months of legal maneuvering, a P&SR construction crew advanced on the crossing prepared to cut the steam road rails and install the electric line crossing, only to find CNW forces ready and waiting to repel them. Two steam locomotives, specially fitted with

pipes to douse the P&SR men with steam and hot water, moved relentlessly back and forth across the intersection. As rapidly as the P&SR men dug beneath the CNW rails, CNW men filled the excavation with sand and gravel from waiting cars. The electric men then drove two double-teamed wagons onto the rails in an attempt to blockade the steam men, only to have the wagons demolished by the charging locomotives, which played live steam on the panic-stricken horses.

As the locomotives again bore down on the trolley men P&SR Director Frank A. Brush stopped them by flinging himself prostrate on the rails in their path. The two crews then came to grips in a bloody fist fight. Santa Rosa police arrested several of the steam road leaders, but the battle continued until CNW President A. W. Foster arrived from the south aboard a special train bearing 160 hired toughs and two Marin County deputy sheriffs. Before Foster could carry out threats to have Santa Rosa police arrested for not protecting his property, or failing that to carry the day by brute force, P&SR obtained a Superior Court order commanding the CNW to cease its opposition, and the steam men reluctantly withdrew to San Francisco. A few hours later the electric men completed the crossing to the cheers of the crowd that had gathered to witness the excitement, and shortly before midnight the first interurban rolled into Santa Rosa under its own power.

Speeding westward over a freshly built roadbed, a Sheboygan Light, Power & Railway Company car traveled to Plymouth, Wis., shortly before 1910. The trim interurban was built by the Cincinnati Car Company in 1908.

Some steam railroads, notably in New England and the Far West, recognized the electrics as potentially valuable feeder lines and developed extensive subsidiary interurban systems. "I will make connections even though the motive power be only an ox team," declared the Chicago Great Western's outspoken president, A. B. Stickney, who promptly went out and cornered a good share of Iowa's interurban mileage. Exorbitant prices paid for traction properties in an effort to develop a New England transportation monopoly accelerated a trip to the bankruptcy courts for the New Haven. On the West Coast the Southern Pacific Company had better luck with its interurban interests, and even today the SP-controlled Pacific Electric is a major originator of freight traffic.

Most of the early interurbans were projects of rather limited objectives, befitting the modest means of their principally local backers. Later on, men of greater vision and working capital appeared on the scene to weld the profusion of small properties into great traction systems of truly impressive size, often covering entire states in trolley networks.

An Illinois congressman, William B. McKinley, assembled a collection of smaller interurbans, along with the necessary new construction, into the 550-mile Illinois Traction System, the largest Midwest interurban. The West's great Pacific Electric system represented the combination of four major interurbans, each itself the product of previous mergers. During the '20's Midwest utilities tycoon Samuel Insull assembled a chain of interurban systems that stretched from Milwaukee to Louisville. In the early years of the depression, Insull's Indiana holdings were consolidated into the Indiana Railroad System, which briefly operated a total of nearly 800 miles of track before piecemeal abandonments whittled down its size.

Among the most intriguing of all electric railway projects, perhaps, were some of the bold schemes — unrivaled for sheer audacity — which never materi-

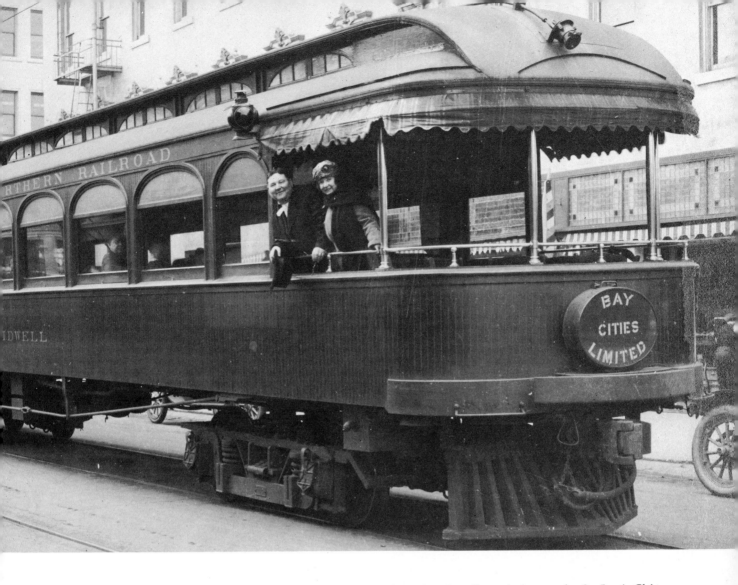

alized. Consider the earliest of them all, an 1893 proposal to build a 252-mile air line electric road between Chicago and St. Louis. Dr. Wellington Adams, the line's promoter, proposed to use a multiphase electrification system, and let it be known that General Electric was prepared to furnish equipment guaranteed to travel 100 miles per hour in perfect safety. The line, to be completed within a year at a cost of 5.5 million dollars, was to be double tracked, with provision for two more tracks at a later date! In publishing reports that surveys were completed, right of way secured, and construction actually under way, the *Street Railway Review* cautiously advised its readers, "Just how much is true is hard to say."

The editors of the steam railroad industry's *Railroad Gazette* were less restrained in their criticism, and worked themselves into a lather over the absurdities of the "electric chicken coops" of the proposed "through by lightning" railroad. After a three column editorial tirade against the project and its promoters, the *Gazette* refrained from belaboring the subject further "out of consideration for the reader."

In view of the state of development of the then infant electric railway industry, the St. Louis-Chicago project was nothing short of fantastic, but probably served well its real purpose of extracting money from the pockets of the gullible.

The Chicago-New York Electric Air Line Railroad, whose plans were unveiled to prospective investors in a series of full-page newspaper ads in July 1906, was even more ambitious. To be straight as an arrow, with maximum grades of ½ of 1 per cent, and free of grade crossings, the projected Air Line would have reduced the mileage between America's two greatest cities to 750 miles of double track "super railroad," fully 160 miles shorter than any steam railroad. Running times between the two cities would be reduced to 10 hours ("10 hours quicker than the quickest") by electric locomotives capable of 100-mile-per-hour speeds, and fares would be "$10 cheaper than the cheapest." Captivated by the enthusiasm of the Air Line's persuasive founder and president, Alexander C. Miller, and by promises of "profits almost beyond calculation," thousands rushed to buy Air Line stock.

If economically unrealistic, the Air Line project was at least within the bounds of technical practicality, and in fairness to its promoters it should be stated that they were men of considerable railroading experience and appeared to be honestly convinced of their project's feasibility.

The first 100-mile division of the 150-million-dollar Air Line, from Chicago to Goshen, Ind., was to be completed within a year; but after seven years of effort, less than 30 miles of arrow-straight track had been finished when the project finally fizzled out, and the Air Line became part of just another minor interurban system. The Air Line's impossibly high construction standards created prohibitive

costs, and stock sales lagged during the severe depression of 1907-1908. Many who had contracted to buy stock on the instalment plan were unable to keep up their payments. Miller's construction crews spent four years erecting a tremendous 2-mile fill across Coffey Creek Bottoms, east of Gary, Ind. Forty acres of standing timber went into a temporary trestle across the valley, and the fill that replaced it measured 180 feet wide at the base and contained a million cubic feet of earth. The job was eventually completed, but it helped to empty the Air Line

Soon after the cars began to operate between Seattle and Tacoma over the high-speed, third-rail Puget Sound Electric Railway in 1902, a train of Brill interurbans rolled past the big totem pole in Seattle's Pioneer Square. WASHINGTON STATE HISTORICAL SOCIETY, FROM ROBERT S. WILSON.

in 10 Hours—Fare $10

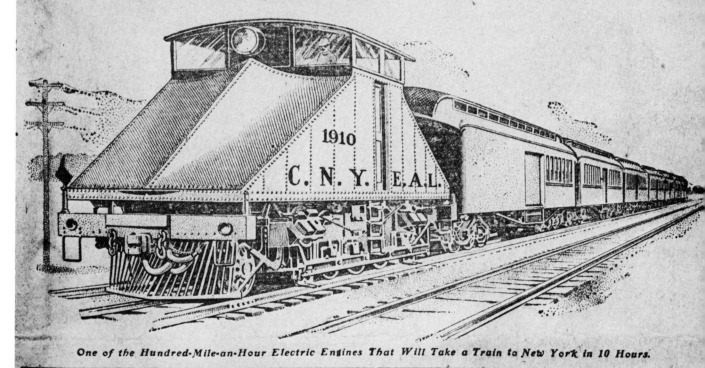

One of the Hundred-Mile-an-Hour Electric Engines That Will Take a Train to New York in 10 Hours.

steam road, it will e-most solidly built high speed of the-aiculations on this ted" with crushed tire length, and 100 d.

fty miles apart and onstantly charged power. Every part n duplicate, so that bly affect the run-

Porte, South Bend, Elkhart, Goshen and many others, it serves a population of 190,000.

It has been shown that electric service through a region of this character yield a gross traffic income of from $10 to $17.50 per capita of the population. Even at the lower estimate of $10 per capita, the gross profits figure up to one million, nine hundred thousand dollars. Our operating expenses will not exceed 50 per cent of the gross receipts, and this would leave net earnings of nine hundred and fifty thousand dollars ($950,000) on a section of road only one hundred miles long. This would enable the road to pay

stock offers. Nothing on earth can wreck its value. From the moment the road begins to run trains, each share of stock will be just as good as money; four times as good if bought at present prices. It will be easy to turn it into instant cash if you don't want transportation, because any ticket broker will cash it at a small discount for brokerage, even in one year from date, when the first hundred-mile section of the road is in actual operation between Chicago and Goshen.

THE EARNINGS OF THE ROAD WILL

vestment, are more largely placed in railro securities than in any other way. The to value of the stock and bond securities railroads in the United States amounts about fourteen billion dollars, which is abo one-eighth of all the wealth of the count

THE TIME TO INVEST IS NOW. NEVE AGAIN WILL THE PRICE BE SO LOW.

Railroad fortunes are the greatest fortun on earth. The men that piled up untold m lions by railroad investments were not m

---

Electric locomotives such as these, claimed promoters of the Chicago-New York Electric Air Line Railroad, would travel between the two cities in 10 hours at speeds up to 100 miles per hour. The Air Line, which proved to be anything but the "proposition with every element of risk absolutely done away with" claimed in an early prospectus, was the greatest fiasco of the interurban era.

---

treasury and to exhaust the stockholders' patience.

Throughout the life of the Air Line project, stockholder interest was sustained and additional contributions solicited by means of such booster organizations as the "Kankakee Air Line Stockholders' Association of the World," and the monthly *Air Line News,* which dramatized every development in the construction work (*e.g.,* "A huge Vulcan steam shovel is already on the job, taking big bites out of hills that stand in the path of the straight and level speedway that is to be the Air Line").

Despite occasional flops of the magnitude of the

Air Line fiasco and the far more frequent failures of lesser schemes, which normally expired with considerably less notice, the interurbans grew prodigiously, and seemed destined for a future of unlimited promise when all America would be laced together by a splendid electric network. During those golden years of growth and triumph no one could have taken seriously the suggestion that many of the very same people, and perhaps even the same train crews, who attended the gala opening celebrations would one day be present for the melancholy departure of the last car. I

The Interurban Era

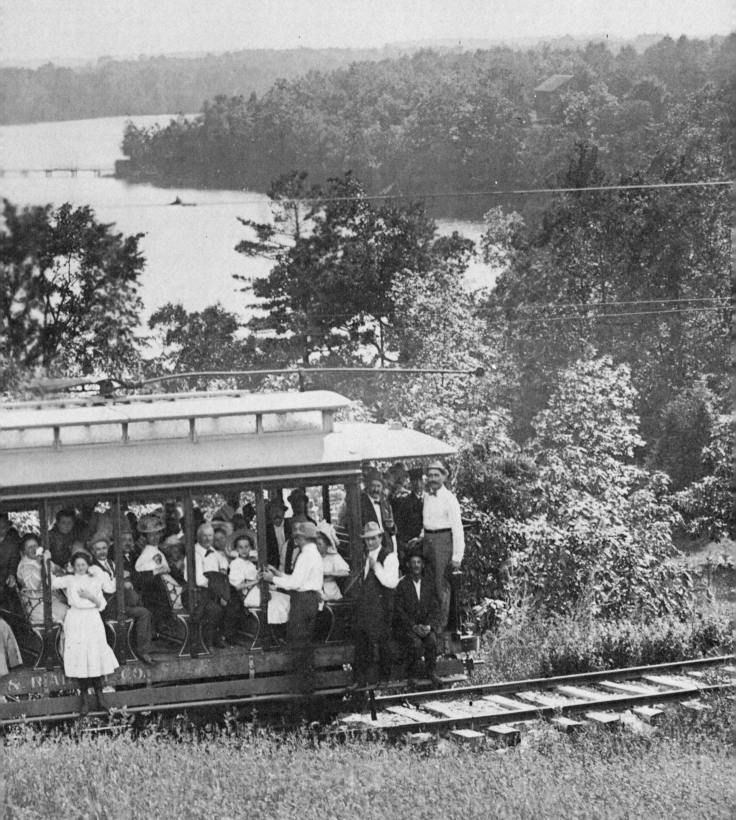

Bound for a summer outing, a capacity crowd rode this Sheboygan Light, Power & Railway Company open car on the company's interurban line to Elkhart Lake, Wis., about 1909. TRAINS COLLECTION.

The Interurban Era

AN infinitely more impressive and elegant vehicle than the urban trolleys from which it evolved, the interurban car was an imposing sight as it rumbled and worried its way through the traffic of city streets, bound for the countryside and the freedom of its own private rails. Once free of the city the big cars hurried along at exhilarating speeds, swaying and "nosing" from side to side on the often uneven track. Windows flung open against the warmth of a summer's day scooped up the rich odors of the countryside, sometimes mingled with the ozone smell generated by the electric traction motors or the pungent odor of grinding brake shoes as the car slowed for a stop. A high-pitched screaming came from the traction motors and gears, and the steady thump and hiss of the trolley wheel overhead was faintly heard. The wheels beat a measured rhythm over staggered rail joints, and now and then, to the clank of loose fitting switch points and frogs, the car lurched through turnouts that led to spurs or sidings. Occasionally the air compressor beneath the car cut in with its characteristic *lung-a-lung-a-lung*. The conductor's signal cord, suspended from the ceiling, flip-flopped back and forth, and there was a muffled creaking from the car's ornate woodwork.

At night the powerful headlight knifed through the darkness ahead, and when the trolley wire was coated with sleet, the countryside was fleetingly illuminated with great blue-white flashes every time the racing trolley wheel, or "shoe," momentarily lost contact with the wire.

Sealed off in his special compartment at the front, the motorman, clad in the cap and pin-striped coveralls of real railroading, busied himself with controller, brakes, bell, and air horn. The blue-uniformed, brass-buttoned conductor collected the fares, chatted amiably with the passengers, and in the wintertime, if the car wasn't equipped with electric heaters, stoked coal into the hot water heater that kept the car comfortably overheated. There was an easy informality to interurban travel. Most of the train crews knew their regular clientele on a first-name basis, and they were not above such homely tasks as running a few errands for a housewife along the line, or seeing to the safe arrival of an unescorted child at his destination.

The interurban was everyone's conveyance in the days before the family car, and it provided far more than just the transportation necessities of farmer, small-towner, or commercial traveler. Whether for business, a family picnic outing, a Sunday excursion to town, or simply the thrilling experience of high-speed trolleying, almost everyone rode the cars.

Resourceful interurban entrepreneurs were rarely content just to accommodate those who had to travel, and many were the ideas employed to lure the public aboard. Few lines of importance were without an "Electric Park" or its equivalent, located far enough from town, of course, to require a trip on the interurban to get there. Typical was the elaborate park that was an integral part of construction plans for the Stark Electric Railway, built in northern Ohio soon after the turn of the century. A pond that was dammed for the line's powerhouse was also stocked with fish, and a fleet of rowboats was purchased for rental. Playground equipment and a picnic pavilion were installed on the edge of the pond, and a dance hall was erected in a nearby wood. Provision for ice skating on the pond made the park a year-round traffic builder for the interurban.

Any interurban such as the Chicago, Ottawa & Peoria, which was fortunate enough to have a Chautauqua Park along its route, could count on heavy traffic when great crowds thronged to the annual camp meeting, which was the occasion for addresses by noted orators and lecturers. Other lines offered such attractions as beaches, salt water plunges, or auto race tracks.

Another form of traffic development, and perhaps the first "park and ride" plan, was tried in 1910 by the Iowa & Illinois Railway, which operated

An amusement park was a sure-fire traffic builder for interurban lines. This was the Lackawanna & Wyoming Valley Railroad's Rocky Glen Park at Moosic, Pa. EDWARD S. MILLER.

between Clinton and Davenport, Ia. As a means of encouraging farmers to use I&I service, the company erected wooden sheds at highway crossings into which prospective rural passengers could put their horses without charge while taking a trip to one of the terminal cities aboard the electric cars. To protect against horse thieves, each farmer was expected to bring his own padlock.

Hardly any interurban of consequence failed to have one or more handsome parlor cars available for charter service, for as an early text on the operation of electric railways commented, "The chartered car appeals to the feelings of exclusiveness, sense of ownership and comfort beloved of most humans."

The trolley car funeral, said to be "vastly superior to a horse-drawn hearse" service, was commonplace too in the early years of the century. Special cars,

equipped to handle caskets and designed to provide privacy for the mourners, were usually employed. For large funerals a charter car followed along behind the funeral car with the overflow of mourners. Sunday visitors were another source of revenue that made a suburban cemetery along the line an asset to any interurban.

Excursion and sight-seeing traffic was intensively promoted by the interurbans. The Lake Shore Electric Railway in Ohio regularly operated "theater specials" into Toledo and Cleveland shortly after the turn of the century. A caterer was usually hired to serve coffee and a light luncheon aboard the cars on the return trip, and on other occasions entertainment, perhaps by a mandolin club or an "orchestra gramophone," was provided. During the '20's the Chicago North Shore & Milwaukee operated "Grand

33

Opera Specials" during the season, and served a light supper to opera-goers on the way home. For those with less cultured tastes Michigan United Railways agents sold round-trip tickets with coupons good for cut-rate admission to a circuit of 25-cent vaudeville theaters, and the Fort Wayne & Wabash Valley did a good business in dancing party specials.

An Ohio line, the Toledo, Fostoria & Findlay, built up its week-end traffic with "Sunday Dinner Excursions," offering a free dinner ticket to any one of several Findlay restaurants with excursion tickets from points 20 or more miles away.

A number of Midwestern interurbans constructed baseball parks to stimulate traffic, and several Ohio lines organized leagues among on-line communities.

The Cleveland & Southwestern Baseball Trolley League included six towns reached by the interurban, and the railway donated a silver cup to the winning team, assisted in advertising, and offered free rides to the players. One of the line's officers even acted as the league president.

Southern California's Pacific Electric system operated what was easily the most extensive excursion and sight-seeing business of all. Every attraction of consequence was reached by a PE excursion, and for the first 20 years or so of the century there just wasn't any other way to see Southern California. The "Balloon Route Trolley Trip" (a "$10 trip for a dollar") took tourists out Sunset Boulevard to Hollywood and the beach cities west of Los Angeles.

The attractions of Monarch Park, midway between Franklin and Oil City, Pa., stimulated traffic aboard the electric cars of the Citizens Traction Company. Twice a day the Monarch Park Concert Band performed at the pagoda, and three nights a week the Goss-Green dance orchestra played under Japanese lanterns and fake palm trees in the dance hall. BOTH PHOTOS: DONALD K. SLICK COLLECTION.

A principal source of income for Utah's Salt Lake, Garfield & Western interurban was excursion travel to the company's Saltair resort on Great Salt Lake, where salt-water bathing, boating, picnicking, one of the world's largest dance pavilions, and all manner of other diversions drew great throngs of pleasure seekers. BOTH PHOTOS: FRED FELLOW COLLECTION.

Among the many attractions were a visit to the Hollywood studio of world-famous painter Paul de Longpré, a stop at Santa Monica's Camera Obscura, and a visit to Venice, which then boasted genuine canals and gondolas.

The "Orange Empire Trolley Trip" carried trolley excursionists on a 150-mile tour of the San Bernardino County citrus areas, and the "Triangle Trolley Trip" offered a look at the beach cities south of Los Angeles. The "Catalina Special" provided boat train service to the docks at Wilmington, where a connection was made with the Avalon steamer service. In earlier years excursions were operated to the Ostrich Farm, near San Gabriel, and to E. J. "Lucky" Baldwin's ranch.

The greatest of all PE's attractions was the famed Mount Lowe line, the "Greatest Mountain Trolley Trip in the World," which carried tourists, by means of the Great Cable Incline and the narrow-gauge Alpine Division, to Alpine Tavern, 1100 feet below the summit of the mountain. Three other hotels, hiking trails and bridle paths, a zoo, a

Holiday-bound for the neighboring Bamberger Railroad's Lagoon amusement park, a mid-'20's employees' excursion from a Utah packing plant rode eight well-filled interurban cars behind a Salt Lake & Utah freight locomotive. FRED FELLOW COLLECTION.

iastic trolley tourist," was of such a time-consuming and arduous nature that it was hardly calculated to cause undue concern on the part of steam railway officials, and was probably more talked about than actually experienced. In 1910 E. C. Van Valkenburgh, in a trip recounted for *Electric Railway Journal* readers, spent just short of four weeks and covered 1643 miles in what was described as a "leisurely outing" between the two cities. Without side trips the entire journey, covering some 1163 miles, was then possible in 45 to 50 hours of continuous trolley riding, or in a week's time by daylight travel, at a cost of less than $20. "A better way of seeing the country at reasonable cost would be hard to imagine," advised Van Valkenburgh.

Five years later, as outlined in the 1915 *Interurban Trolley Guide,* the trip took anywhere from 31 to 45 hours of actual trolley riding, depending upon connections, and covered 23 different electric railways.

The entire journey between the two cities was never actually possible by trolley. The most direct route required the use of steam railroads between Tarrytown and Hudson, N. Y., and again between Little Falls and Fonda, a total of some 120 miles by steam. A more circuitous routing through Connecticut and Massachusetts, which was possible for a period of only about two years around 1917-1918, reduced the necessary steam mileage to about 55.

The practicality of long-distance trolley travel was convincingly demonstrated in 1910 by the 2000-mile "Utica (N. Y.) Electric Railway Tour." A Utica-Syracuse interurban car, fitted with lounge furniture and provided with a porter to attend to the

The practicality of sustained interurban travel was demonstrated by several Indianapolis Trade Association "Booster's Specials," which traveled throughout Indiana to promote the city. This one, made up of chartered Indiana Union Traction Company equipment, was photographed at South Bend in 1910. The most extensive of all such junkets, however, was the 14-day, 2000-mile Midwestern tour made the same year by a group of Utica (N. Y.) "Boosters." GEORGE KRAMBLES COLLECTION.

In a time of unhurried travel, combination interurban-steamer through routings were sometimes available. This Inland Empire System express from Spokane, Wash., made a dockside connection at Coeur d'Alene, Ida., with steamers of the Red Collar Line, which offered service to points on Coeur d'Alene Lake and the St. Joe River. LEROY O. KING JR. COLLECTION.

comforts of the 26 "Utica Boosters," was used throughout the excursion, which spread the news of Utica's business and industrial advantages through six states to points as far west as Indianapolis and Detroit. When the boosters returned 14 days later they were met by a band at the edge of town, and a triumphant parade of pedestrians, streetcars, wagons, and automobiles followed the interurban car down Genesee Street to Bagg's Hotel, where all adjourned for a banquet and speeches.

Throughout the electric railway era interurban travel was predominantly of the short-haul, local variety, and during the early years it was exclusively so. But soon after the turn of the century, as some of the traction systems assumed substantial dimensions and an interconnecting network of traction lines spread across many states, particularly in the

Midwest, interurban traffic men began to develop an interest in the long-distance passenger. Special mileage coupon books good for travel over any line, issued by many Midwestern lines, made long-distance interurban travel inexpensive. The Central Electric Railroad Association, for example, sold a coupon book for $17.50 that was good for $20 worth of fares over any of its member Midwestern companies.

Sometimes the interurbans developed a long-distance business between important points by operating through cars over the rails of two or more connecting lines. Perhaps the first such invasion of the steam roads' long-haul market was the de luxe Indianapolis-Dayton Interstate Limited service inaugurated in 1905 by the Dayton & Western, the Richmond Street & Interurban Railway, and the

Indianapolis & Eastern. Special cars built for the service featured plush parlor seats and heavy Wilton carpeting in the main compartment, while the smoking section was fitted with leather upholstered seats and inlaid linoleum floors. The interior was finished in St. Jago mahogany with "inlaid decorations of the most recent design." A buffet between the two compartments served light meals from a menu said to be every bit the equal of those on Pullman buffet cars. Such de luxe interurban service, it was predicted, would soon become common between points as far as 200 to 300 miles apart.

Occasionally, when direct electric routings all the way were not available, the interurbans joined with other carriers in long-distance through routings. In 1915 the Fort Wayne & Northern Indiana

"Motorman" was by far the most popular title for interurban car operators, but a few lines favored the steam railroads' more pretentious "engineer," and at least one line, the Puget Sound Electric, compromised on the title "motorneer." In French Canada he was sometimes a "garde moteur" and in Cuba (here) a "motorista." WILLIAM D. MIDDLETON.

was selling through tickets all the way to St. Louis, routed over its own line and the Clover Leaf System, one of the few Midwestern steam railroads that would have anything to do with the interurbans. Quite a few years later the Dayton & Western, in company with the Terre Haute, Indianapolis & Eastern, was bidding for Dayton-Chicago business with a through-car routing to Indianapolis, where a steam railroad connection was made.

In 1910 the Grand Rapids, Grand Haven & Muskegon Railway and the Grand Rapids, Holland & Chicago Railway were offering through service to Milwaukee and Chicago via steamer connections at their western terminals. On the West Coast the California Navigation & Improvement Company and the Central California Traction Company were offering the same sort of combination between San Francisco and Lodi with a through routing that involved steamers from San Francisco to Stockton, where passengers transferred to the electric cars for the final leg of the trip.

In 1927 the Chicago South Shore & South Bend was offering a Chicago-Detroit "Golden Arrow" service in conjunction with the Shore Line Motor Coach Company. A limited train took passengers as far as South Bend, where they transferred to a nonstop bus, complete with toilet facilities and an observation compartment, for the remainder of the journey. The combination cut a full 3 hours from the all-bus routing between the two cities.

A year later the Cleveland Southwestern Railway & Light Company began selling through interurban-air tickets to Detroit from points along its lines. Passengers transferred from the trolleys to Ford trimotors of the Cleveland-Detroit Air Line at the Cleveland airport, which was conveniently located beside the interurban's line into the city.

As the long-distance passenger business became more important the larger interurban systems endeavored to provide luxury services that were equal to, or even better than, those offered by the steam railroads. Parlor cars, heavily carpeted, lavishly decorated, and staffed with porters, were frequently installed on the long runs. Light meals were served from buffet sections on many of them, and several lines operated full dining cars. A few of the longest interurbans even introduced sleeping car service.

Bearing such dashing names as *Liberty Bell Limited, Dixie Flyer,* and *Meteor,* de luxe interurban limiteds sped imperiously through the rolling hills of the Pennsylvania Dutch countryside, Hoosier farmland, and California canyon alike, transporting passengers in princely comfort on their errands of importance.

Surely the electric way was the very best way to travel. ⅃

In the earlier years of the interurban era, two-man crews of motorman and conductor were almost universal, and sometimes interurban lines patterned their operating rules after those of steam rail-roading. Among these was Iowa's Fort Dodge Line, which even as late as 1955 still went about the job of running electric cars in the traditional manner. Here conductor F. E. Nunamaker passes up a clearance card from the operator at Fort Dodge to motorman E. J. Berg before their departure with southbound train No. 2 for Des Moines. Both wore the respective blue serge uniform and overalls of their occupations. WILLIAM D. MIDDLETON.

The Interurban Car

Separated by 30 years of progress, these two interurbans bore little resemblance to one another although they served similar purposes in their respective eras. Magnificent wooden 302 was built by Niles in 1907 for the Washington, Baltimore & Annapolis and later was sold to the Rock Island Southern. The Key System articulated unit, in purposeful 1938 styling, covered interurbanlike routes east of San Francisco, yet had automatic cab signals for rush-hour operation on 1-minute headway over the 7-mile fog-shrouded Bay Bridge. WILLIAM D. MIDDLETON COLLECTION (LEFT); RICHARD STEINHEIMER (ABOVE).

The Interurban Car

BORN of an age which took joy in lavish ornamentation, the interurban car of the early years was a splendid sight. The very first cars were little different from the prosaic streetcars from which they evolved, but the skilled craftsmen who fashioned the big electric cars, with the instinctive sense of balance and proportion common to artisans of their kind, soon developed an altogether distinctive interurban car architecture.

With the exception of the shorter length dictated by operation through city streets, the dimensions of the interurbans were more like those of steam cars than those of the city streetcars. Interurban cars were usually anywhere from 50 to 60 feet long, although cars over 70 feet in length were built for a few lines. Car width was often restricted by the width of the "devil strip" between double tracks of street railway properties. For the 4-foot devil strip found in a majority of cities a car width of 8'4" was usually standard, but where clearances allowed, cars were often built to widths equal to steam railroad standards. Interurban cars were frequently designed for double end operation, with controls at each end and reversible seating, which enabled quick turnarounds without the necessity for loops or wyes. Usually, however, interurban operators favored the single end car, which permitted better interior arrangement, eliminated the cost of duplicate controls and fenders, and enabled the use of less expensive nonreversible seating.

Early car construction was invariably of wood and was aptly described as "house-upon-a-flat-car" construction. Heavy timber sills provided the entire structural support, and the carbody simply rested on the sills. As cars became too long and heavy to be supported by the wood sills alone, steel truss rods and queen posts were added under the car. Large turnbuckles made it possible to restore the car to level after it began to sag with the strains of age and service. Some master mechanics even preferred to send a car away from a visit to the shops with a slight arch to its back.

The clerestory "railroad" roof of steam road practice, which provided good ventilation, was widely favored by interurban lines, although some roads later adopted a high arch roof when satisfactory ventilators were developed. The necessity for operation of interurban trains around sharp curves required the adoption of long radius couplings and rounded ends, which resulted in a far more pleasing appearance than the flat ends of steam road cars. The almost universal use of "Gothic" arched windows, fitted with what was variously described as "art" or "cathedral" leaded glass upper panels, gave a dash of elegance to any interurban. So highly regarded was the arch window, in fact, that even later, when some interurbans adopted rectangular, clear glass upper panels — which furnished better interior illumination — a fake arch top, visible only from the outside, was installed above the upper panel in place of the usual letter board. This variation was known as the "Washington" sash after it was first used on an order of cars for the Washington Railway & Electric Company.

The durable, dark "Pullman green" finish of steam railroad practice was favored by many interurban roads, but many others felt that the extra cost of less serviceable but brighter colors was good advertising. Lighter colors also afforded better visibility of approaching electric cars. A variety of red, orange, yellow, blue, and green hues were commonly used, and many lines were widely known by the distinctive colors of their equipment. Interurban cars were usually assigned numbers, and most

The zenith of wooden interurban car architecture was represented by the equipment delivered in 1911 by the Cincinnati Car Company for the Stone & Webster Engineering Corporation's Galveston-Houston Electric Railway. This car is seen in the blue and white "bluebird" colors worn during the '20's, when the Galveston Flyer *won honors as America's fastest interurban.* GEORGE KRAMBLES COLLECTION.

lines gave names only to their more elegant parlor, sleeping, and dining cars. There were occasional exceptions. A few lines named their cars after on-line communities or famous local personages. Portland's East Side Railway gave its cars girls' names such as *Ava*, *Helen*, and *Flora*; and Maine's Portland-Lewiston Interurban named all its cars after flowers.

Interurban car interiors were usually divided into a smoking section and a nonsmoking compartment, sometimes referred to as the "ladies' parlor"; and most of them had a baggage and express compartment, often fitted with folding wooden seats or camp stools for overflow crowds. The carbuilders lavished their greatest efforts on fanciful decorative effects for the car interiors. Fine woods of every description were employed. Ash, cherry, quartered oak, California redwood, basswood, maple, and birch were all popular. Mahoganies were imported from Tobago, Mexico, the African Gold Coast, and South and Central America; and teakwood came from India, China, and the Philippines. When exceptional beauty and richness of finish were desired, vermilion — a heavy, hard-to-work wood of the mahogany family — was used. For particularly handsome effects the dark woods were often inlaid with white holly; and complex color schemes, artistic moldings, and intricate carvings were provided.

Plush upholstery was commonly employed in the main compartment, and the more elegant cars were fitted with heavy draperies and thick carpeting. More durable and easily cleaned materials, such as leather or cane upholstery and linoleum flooring, were favored for the smoking compartments, where the rougher element customarily rode. Interurbans usually had lavatories, and such other extras as water coolers, mirrors, and electric fans. Match scratchers and polished brass spittoons were provided for the smoker clientele, and heavy ornamental bronze was liberally used for luggage racks, light fixtures, hardware, and other trimmings.

With the arrival of balmy summer weather some interurbans rolled out their special open cars. Widely used in New England and California, the open car enjoyed a more limited popularity on interurban lines elsewhere in the U.S. The most common type of open car was fitted with benches running the full width of the car and continuous running boards, so that it could be boarded at any point. Conductors had to negotiate the running boards to collect fares. Waterproof awnings were lowered in case of rain.

The open car was a delight to ride on a hot summer night; nevertheless, it had its disadvantages. Women found it almost impossible to climb aboard the standard single-step open car after the hobble

The impressive dimensions of the WB&A's Niles "Electric Pullmans" are evident in a broadside study. The big cars regularly clocked 66-mile-per-hour average speeds once they got out of town. LEROY O. KING COLLECTION.

skirt became fashionable. J. G. Brill, a leading car-builder, came up with the Narragansett car, a patented two-step design, as an answer to this problem. Boarding and alighting accidents were altogether too frequent on open cars, and the prospect of a passenger inadvertently "joining the birds" in high-speed interurban operation probably kept more than one traction official awake nights. Some lines solved the problem by providing standard center aisles and vestibules, and screening in the lower part of the sides.

On the West Coast, where weather was subject to year-around vagaries, the "combination," or "semi-open," type of car was often adopted, presumably in an effort to please everyone. One end of the car was constructed as an ordinary closed car, while the other was an open section. Usually, it was found, everyone wanted to ride in the same end, depending upon the weather. An earlier variation of the combination type was the California car, which had a closed center section and an open section at each end.

Traction companies found the provision of a duplicate set of equipment for summer operation a costly proposition. An early effort to develop a type of car adaptable to year-around operation was the "convertible" car (or "nonhibernating" car, as one builder described it), which could be transformed from a closed to an open car by the use of removable side panels. More widely used was the

This Northern Ohio Traction & Light Company interurban was constructed with the "Washington" sash, an arrangement which employed clear glass upper sash for improved interior illumination but retained the class of "Gothic" window design with dummy art glass arches in place of the customary letter board. O. F. LEE COLLECTION.

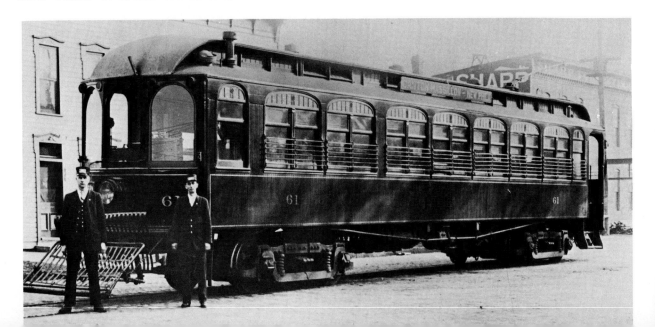

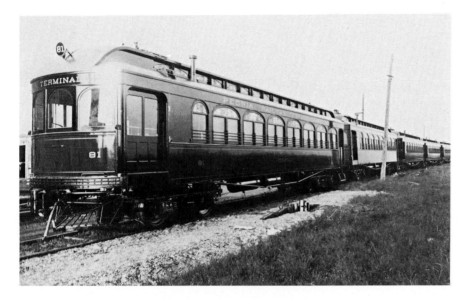

The distinctive architecture of the interurban car had not yet been evolved when J. G. Brill delivered this deck roof car for service on the Washington, Alexandria & Mt. Vernon Railway's new line to Alexandria in 1896. Nevertheless, the car was equipped with such interurban features as train doors for passage between cars, a lavatory, and a water cooler. It was capable of hauling one or two trailers at speeds up to 45 miles per hour. This carload of dour individuals, probably Brill factory workers, simulated passengers for an advertisement that appeared in the February 1896 Street Railway Journal. LEROY O. KING COLLECTION.

"semi-convertible" car, which had window sash that disappeared into either wall or roof pockets for summer operation, while the side panels remained fixed in place. The J. G. Brill Company, which developed its patented roof pocket semi-convertible system in 1899, pointed out in some early hard-sell advertising that the wall pockets used by other builders often became rubbish receptacles and were a dangerous breeding place for germs; one instance

was detailed in which a carelessly discarded cigar had started a fire in a wall pocket.

The interurbans' strength was their ability to furnish an economical short-haul passenger service, a fact which was reflected in the durably furnished coaches that predominated in electric line equipment rosters. But as the interurbans began to edge into the long-distance luxury travel field in the years following the turn of the century, more lavishly furnished equipment was frequently seen. Carpeted parlor cars fitted with cushioned wicker lounge chairs were often provided for the long-distance limited runs, and in the Midwest and West the open observation platform, complete with brass railing, scalloped awning, and a drumhead sign bearing the road's emblem or train name, frequently appeared on the premier interurban schedules, in the manner of the best steam railroad limited trains of the time.

An early example of the ornate parlor cars often maintained for charter service was the pretentiously titled "drawing room car" that was available in 1906 to transport the elite over the 25-mile Augusta-Aiken Railway & Electric Company in Georgia. The car's interior was fitted with handsome rugs,

Typical of the summer cars operated in great numbers by street railways and interurbans was this 14-bench open car built by Jackson & Sharp in 1900 for the Philadelphia & West Chester Traction Company. PHILADELPHIA SUBURBAN TRANSPORTATION COMPANY.

Designed to please everyone in the variable California climate, semi-open cars similar to this one ranged by the hundreds over the rails of Pacific Electric and other California interurbans. Later on, the open section on these PE cars was enclosed up to the belt rail and eventually was closed entirely. Visible in the photograph is the pneumatic trolley base favored by PE over the usual spring base. IRA SWETT — MAGNA COLLECTION.

An interior view of a more severely furnished Youngstown & Southern Railway Niles combine clearly shows such typical electric car appurtenances as the conductor's fare register and the coal-fired stove that fed hot water to the heating system. O. F. LEE COLLECTION.

Interior appointments of this car, built by Brill in 1907 for the West Shore Railroad's Utica-Syracuse electrification, were typical of the early interurbans. The walkover seats were upholstered in figured plush, and the interior was finished in inlaid mahogany. The carbuilder's fanciful decorative touch was evident in the embellishments applied to the full Empire ceiling and the elaborate baggage racks. INDUSTRIAL PHOTO SERVICE.

55

The Holland Palace Car Company hoped to revolutionize the long-distance interurban business with a combination design that converted from parlor to sleeping car through the use of rolling partitions. Only two of them were ever built. STEPHEN D. MAGUIRE COLLECTION (ABOVE); GEORGE KRAMBLES COLLECTION (RIGHT).

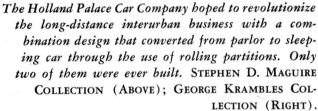

Officers of the Everett-Moore syndicate, which controlled a number of interurbans in Ohio, Michigan, and other Midwestern states, rode over their Cleveland area holdings in regal style aboard the private drawing room car Josephine, *which included two observation compartments, a stateroom, bathroom, kitchen, and a stenographer's office among its accommodations. Only a few years after delivery by the J. G. Brill Company the* Josephine *came to an untimely end in a spectacular fire.* GEORGE KRAMBLES COLLECTION.

kitchen prepared food for a menu said to be almost as extensive as that of a large hotel.

In 1903 a new company, the Holland Palace Car Company, which hoped to occupy a position in the electric railway industry comparable to that of the Pullman Company in steam railroading, appeared on the scene with a pair of ingenious combination cars, the *Theodore* and the *Francis,* that converted from parlor car by day to sleeping car at night through the use of rolling partitions. First tried on the 64-mile run between Columbus and Zanesville, O., too short to make use of the sleeping car feature, the two cars were later placed in overnight service on the Illinois Traction System.

Although the Holland cars were considered unsatisfactory, owing principally to excessive noise and vibration from the power trucks, Illinois Traction's sleeper service drew considerable interest, and in 1910 the company placed new sleepers of its own design in service over the 172-mile St. Louis-Peoria main line. The noise problem of the Holland cars was eliminated by operating the new cars as trailers.

In a time before air conditioning, cinder-free

electric sleeper service offered distinct advantages over steam railroad Pullmans, and Illinois Traction's new sleeping car accommodations were equal or superior to those of Pullman cars in almost every respect. Berths in the electric sleepers were fully 6 inches longer than in standard Pullmans, and the cars featured windows for upper berth passengers, an innovation that didn't appear on the steam railroads until two decades later. A reading lamp and a plush-lined, fireproof safety deposit box were installed in every berth. Porters on the cars served hot coffee and rolls without charge in the morning. Interurban sleeper travel was cheap, too. Uppers and lowers cost only $1 and $1.25, respectively, and porters were not allowed to accept tips. Later Illinois Traction sleeping car innovations included air conditioning and all-room sleepers.

Few other interurbans ever ventured into the sleeping car business. The Oregon Electric Railway operated sleepers between Portland and Eugene for a few years, and the Interstate Public Service Company introduced an Indianapolis-Louisville service in 1926 with a group of handsome steel cars. The

The Oregon Electric Railway employed a pair of these Barney & Smith sleepers, built along conventional lines, in a Portland-Eugene service for several years before selling them to the Pacific Great Eastern steam line in British Columbia, where they continued to operate until recent years. ARTHUR D. DUBIN COLLECTION.

Waterloo, Cedar Falls & Northern line in Iowa, although it never had sleepers of its own, once hauled Pullman cars from Waterloo to Cedar Rapids, where they were attached to Chicago-bound trains of the Chicago & North Western.

Occasionally the officials of some of the larger traction systems operated handsome private cars, which often rivaled the rolling stock of steam road contemporaries in the luxury of their equipment and furnishings. Probably the most magnificent interurban of the entire traction era was the private car *Alabama,* which the St. Louis Car Company turned out in 1905 for Southern California traction magnate Henry E. Huntington. Almost as large as a Pullman car, the 63-foot *Alabama* weighed 103,000 pounds and was driven by four 200-horsepower motors. The *Alabama* was the most powerful, and one of the fastest, interurbans ever built; it was capable of speeds approaching 100 miles per hour, and once covered the 20 miles between Los Angeles and Long Beach in 15 minutes, an average speed of 80 miles per hour. The big car could be coupled into any steam train, and Huntington used it for trips throughout the U.S., as well as over his own Pacific Electric system. The *Alabama*'s interior was finished in figured African mahogany, with inlay work and carvings for decoration, and the two staterooms were fitted with figured Prima Vera silk shades. A dining room, with places for 10, buffet, china closet, and a genuine fireplace, was located at one end of the car, and an observation compartment with a built-in jardiniere was installed at the opposite end.

After relinquishing active control of his traction empire, Huntington sold the *Alabama* to the Sacramento Northern Railroad for service as a de luxe parlor-buffet car. In 1931 a coffee percolator short-circuited in the kitchen and the resulting conflagration burned the mighty *Alabama* to the rails.

The *Elmlawn,* acquired by the International Railway Company in 1905 for the use of funeral parties en route to cemeteries in Buffalo, Niagara Falls, Lockport, and the Tonawandas, was typical of the special funeral cars operated by several interurbans. Suitably finished in a somber dark green, the *Elmlawn* was fitted with heavy green draperies which provided adequate privacy for the party, and a special door and sliding shelf were installed for the casket.

Frequently the interurban carbuilders pioneered important innovations in railroad passenger rolling stock. Several interurban lines, for example, were experimenting with roller bearing journals as early as 1911. The fully automatic coupling, which the steam railroad industry has yet to adopt, was a practical reality on an interurban line in 1914. The

interurbans were a decade ahead of the steam railroads in lightweight car construction, and a wind-tunnel-designed, aerodynamic interurban was in daily operation in 1931, fully three years before the first diesel-electric streamliner took to steam road rails. But in the most fundamental advance of all in the railroad passenger car during the first half of the 20th century, the transition from wood to all-steel construction, the interurban builders lagged nearly 10 years behind the steam railroads. Even a few street railways and subways had steel cars well before they appeared on interurbans.

The switch to steel was a reluctant one, for most of the carbuilders were ill equipped for metal car fabrication. Faced with the necessity of acquiring the expensive heavy machinery required to cut, form, and fasten steel members, more than one builder simply went out of business. Steel was first used only in center sill members, then for side plating which was fastened over wood framing members in what was termed "semi-steel" or "composite" construction. The full advantages of steel construction were not realized until steel side plating was used in conjunction with steel framing members in such a manner that the car sides acted as girders and, along with the center sills, helped to carry the car's weight. Even after cars were being constructed entirely of steel the truss rods of wood construction were sometimes retained, although

Directors of the C. D. Beebe syndicate, whose interurban activities were centered around Syracuse, N. Y., traveled about their traction domain in the incomparable private car 999, delivered by the G. C. Kuhlman Car Company of Cleveland in 1910. A splendid set of builder's views of its richly finished interior reveal scenes of electric car luxury that was not intended for the masses. CHARLES GOETHE COLLECTION (BELOW); WILLIAM D. MIDDLETON COLLECTION (RIGHT).

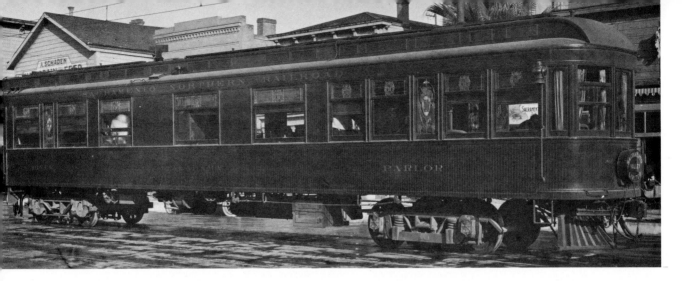

A few years after Pacific Electric tycoon Henry E. Huntington relinquished control of his traction empire to Southern Pacific, his celebrated private car Alabama was sold to the Sacramento Northern Railroad, where its sumptuous furnishings became available to the general public in parlor-diner service on the Meteor and other limited trains. It is seen here at Sacramento waiting to be attached to the San Francisco-bound Sacramento Valley Limited. Like many wooden interurbans, the Alabama met its end by fire. DAVID L. JOSLYN COLLECTION.

Before the automobile hearse became an acceptable mode of transportation to the last resting place, dignified funeral cars such as the Milwaukee Electric's No. 1000 were a common sight on interurban and street railway lines, and an on-line cemetery was considered a definite asset. STATE HISTORICAL SOCIETY OF WISCONSIN.

This special train, which operated over Pacific Electric's Glendale line in 1914, marked the first successful use of couplings which automatically made car, air, and electrical connections. Widely used on electric railways, the innovation was still not adopted for general use on steam railroads in 1961. WILLIAM D. MIDDLETON COLLECTION.

many carbuilders were convinced that the compression introduced into the steel frame when the truss rods were tightened actually served to weaken a car rather than to strengthen it, as its users supposed.

By 1915, all-steel interurban car construction was almost universal. The greater safety of steel equipment in the event of accidents was an improvement of major importance, and the lines which adopted the new cars were quick to exploit the publicity advantages. In 1915 one line, the Toledo, Fostoria & Findlay Railway, went so far as to insist that the builders use round-head, rather than countersunk, rivets wherever possible in its new steel cars, in order to clearly advertise to the public that the cars were not made of wood.

The use of steel was lavish in the first years of metal car construction. Some of the first steel cars, built for the Union Traction Company of Indiana in 1913, weighed almost 43 tons; and some of the heaviest cars ever built, which were turned out in 1914 for the Michigan Railway, weighed over 65 tons. Within a few years, as the builders became more familiar with the new materials, excess weight was eliminated, and cars of comparable size were being built which weighed less than 30 tons.

Soon after World War I, when the automobile first began to make serious inroads upon interurban passenger revenues, many lines started to search for means of effecting substantial operating economies. Some of their most rewarding efforts were in the direction of lightweight car construction. Stronger alloys, lightweight metals, and better design were all used in an effort to reduce carbody weight, which in turn permitted the use of smaller trucks and motors with corresponding economies in power consumption. Ten lightweight cars built by the G. C. Kuhlman Car Company in 1922 for the Western Ohio Railway, for example, weighed only half as

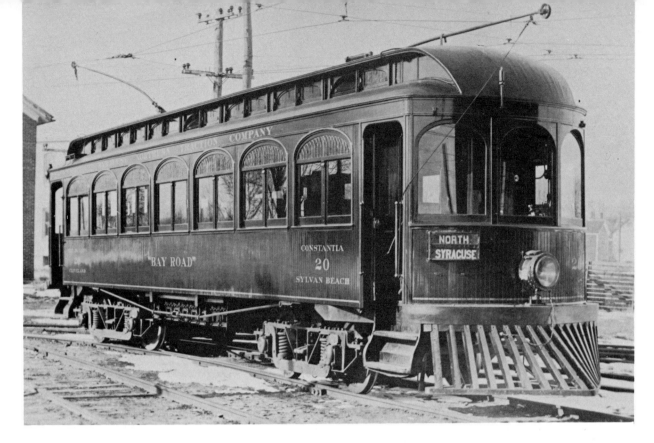

An otherwise conventional interurban of the Syracuse Northern Traction Company was distinguished by the experimental application of roller bearings. Several other interurbans, as early as 1910, made similar applications, far in advance of the adoption of roller bearings by steam railroads.
ROBERT O. WATERS COLLECTION, FROM WILLIAM R. GORDON.

A close-up shows one type of fully automatic coupling, in interurban service on the Baltimore & Annapolis. WILLIAM D. MIDDLETON.

much and consumed only half as much power as the cars they replaced, yet were capable of speeds as high as 50 miles per hour.

A number of builders produced satisfactory lightweight cars, but the most notable of the lightweights was the distinctive curved-side design developed by the Cincinnati Car Company. An important structural innovation gave the cars their unusual "fishbelly" appearance. A reverse curve, introduced into the alloy steel side plates, provided a girder strength much greater than that afforded by a flat plate of the same weight. Vertical stiffeners, cut to the curve of the side plates, maintained the side contour. The roof was built as a unit and was supported by two pairs of vertical posts which rested directly on the body bolsters. The window posts, which were structural members in ordinary car construction, were simply inserts between the side plate and the letter board in the Cincinnati design. A special low-floor arch bar cantilever truck was developed for the car. Aluminum was liberally used for interior fittings to further conserve weight.

The first Cincinnati curved-side cars, a group of 10 built in 1922 for interurban service on the Kentucky Traction & Terminal Company, were nothing less than a revolutionary improvement. Weighing barely 25,000 pounds in working order, the lightest

63

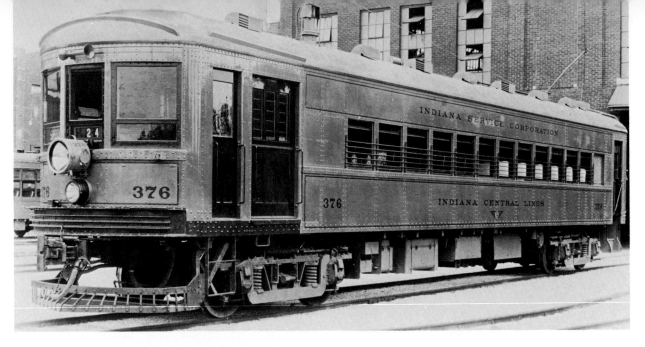

Interurban car architecture of the heavy steel car period tended to straightforward, functional design, and rarely were the results more pleasing than in the case of this Indiana Service Corporation combine, one of five constructed by the St. Louis Car Company in 1926. WILBOURNE B. COX COLLECTION.

cars of their size and capacity ever turned out by Cincinnati, they weighed less than a third as much as the wooden cars they replaced, and the company's interurban power load was reduced by half. Four 25-horsepower motors gave them a free running speed of 36 miles per hour — almost 10 miles per hour slower than the cars they replaced — but improved acceleration and deceleration characteristics made it possible to maintain the same schedules. The reduced power costs, in addition to the economies of one-man operation, enabled the line to reduce its fares. So spectacular was the success of the new cars that within two months a parallel bus operation had been forced out of business.

Even at an early stage of development interurban cars were capable of rather high speeds, often in excess of 60 miles per hour, but over-all running times were usually anything but rapid. Lightly and cheaply built lines, which precluded sustained high speeds, and the almost universal operation through the streets of cities and towns, made high average speeds impossible. As late as 1906 three Ohio interurbans were claiming the "fastest electric service in the world" with limited trains which each averaged only about 32 miles per hour. The deficiency in speed was unimportant in the short haul passenger business, for the steam trains were even slower; but as the interurbans essayed the long haul trade, speed became a matter of great concern.

In 1904 the John Stephenson Company, of Elizabeth, N. J., exhibited a 12-wheeled interurban car, designed for extremely high-speed operation, at the

To provide increased seating capacity in a single unit, a few lines came up with articulated interurbans. The Milwaukee Electric Lines created eight of them in its Cold Spring shops in 1929 from conventional steel cars acquired from the Indianapolis & Cincinnati Traction Company. The resulting "duplex" units seated 84 passengers. STATE HISTORICAL SOCIETY OF WISCONSIN.

64

Louisiana Purchase Exposition in St. Louis. The car, it was claimed, could attain speeds as high as 120 miles per hour, but there is no evidence that it was ever operated at speeds even approaching this figure. Stephenson, however, did produce some remarkable high-speed cars at an early date. In 1903 a Stephenson-built car on the Aurora, Elgin & Chicago Railway managed to cover the 35 miles between Aurora and Chicago in 34 minutes 39 seconds despite the loss of over 6 minutes in stops, and numerous speed reductions for steam railroads, trolley lines, and street and highway crossings.

In 1903 the officials of the Louisiana Purchase Exposition organized the Electric Railway Test Commission to conduct a series of tests to develop a carbody design that would reduce wind resistance at high speeds. A long series of tests was carried out by the Commission in 1905 on the Union Traction Company near Noblesville, Ind., with the *Louisiana,* a special dynamometer car which consisted of a 32-foot carbody arranged to roll freely on rails secured to a special motorized flat car so that the carbody's resistance could be measured independent of that for the entire car. Vestibule sections of different shapes were suspended independent of the carbody, with a dynamometer to measure the resistance of each. Over 200 test runs were made at speeds up to 70 miles per hour with parabolic, wedge, standard, and flat vestibule ends.

The *Louisiana* test results indicated that a para-

bolic-shaped front end reduced wind resistance at high speeds below that of the conventional rounded profile, and a variety of interurban known as the "windsplitter" car subsequently appeared on several lines in Indiana, Ohio, and New York. Although the streamlined front end gave a dramatic appearance to the cars, no significant operating economies were realized, and streamlining was soon discarded for another quarter century.

Interurban lines showed renewed interest in high-speed operation in the face of the increasing automobile competition during the post-World War I period. The first speed-up efforts took the form of heavy steel cars, equipped with powerful motors, which were capable of extremely high sustained speeds. The most notable results along these lines were achieved by the three major Chicago area interurbans controlled by Samuel Insull, which not only operated handsome new steel cars but, even more important, spent millions in reconstructing track and power facilities to enable the lines to fully exploit the potential capacity of the new cars. Top speeds in excess of 80 miles per hour were reached regularly, and station-to-station averages as high as

This builder's close-up shows the "drum" connector employed to connect the carbodies of the articulated interurbans delivered to the Washington, Baltimore & Annapolis by J. G. Brill in 1927. WILLIAM D. MIDDLETON COLLECTION.

Most successful of the lightweight cars produced during the '20's was the Cincinnati Car Company's curved-side design, which was produced in such numbers for both interurban and street railway service that it became known as the Cincinnati "rubber stamp" car. This trim parlor car was delivered to the Indianapolis & Southeastern Railroad in 1929, only three years before the company went out of business. The car itself, however, operated for another 14 years on lines in Tennessee and Georgia. GEORGE KRAMBLES COLLECTION.

70 miles per hour were not infrequently attained.

On other systems efforts were directed to the development of a lightweight, high-speed car that could operate smoothly over the typically light, often rough interurban track, for many of the lines could ill afford the costly overhaul of roadbed and power systems required for satisfactory high-speed operation of heavy equipment.

Late in 1929, Dr. Thomas Conway Jr. and associates formed the new Cincinnati & Lake Erie Rail-road from three ailing Ohio traction properties and immediately ordered from the Cincinnati Car Company 20 radical new high-speed cars designed to win back a declining passenger traffic. The design of the new cars was based upon extensive experimentation begun by the Conway group early in 1929 and carried out in conjunction with the Westinghouse Electric & Manufacturing Company, the General Electric Company, the J. G. Brill Company, the Cincinnati Car Company, and the Westinghouse

A rakish parabolic front end gave the "windsplitter" cars evolved from the 1904 Louisiana *tests a formidable appearance, but the design proved to be no faster than conventional cars and few were built. This steel windsplitter was one of two built by G. C. Kuhlman in 1912 for New York's Utica-Syracuse third-rail line, where they were known as "Arrow Cars." It is seen here on Clinton Square in Syracuse about to depart on a Utica local schedule.* INDUSTRIAL PHOTO SERVICE.

Traction Brake Company. Based upon the test results, specifications were built up under the direction of W. L. Butler, C&LE executive vice-president, for a low-level, lightweight car of steel and aluminum that would be capable of sustained speeds in excess of 75 miles per hour.

Among the major problems faced by C&LE and the manufacturers were the development of a satisfactory low-level truck which would operate smoothly at the extremely high speeds contemplated and the design of motors that were capable of producing the necessary power yet would meet the severe clearance limits of the low-level trucks. Braking presented another serious problem, and from the test program it was determined that something in addition to air braking was required.

The Cincinnati Car Company adapted some of the low-level arch bar cantilever trucks used on its lightweight interurbans and mounted them under a car comparable to the type planned by C&LE for experimental purposes. A design was evolved for a satisfactory 28-inch-wheel, low-level truck, and following prolonged negotiation both Westinghouse and General Electric contracted to supply traction motors which developed 100 horsepower yet were compact enough to be mounted on the Cincinnati truck. The braking problems were solved by designing a magnetic track brake which came into play only after the air brake application approached the safe limits of wheel friction.

The new cars, which made liberal use of alumi-num, went into service during 1930. Eminently successful, they were capable of speeds in excess of 90 miles per hour. In the extensive publicity which surrounded their introduction, one of the cars attained a reputed speed of 97 miles per hour in a race against an airplane staged near Dayton in July 1930 for the benefit of Pathé newsreel cameras. Another of the cars outdistanced a racing car by 15 lengths in a race held on the National Pike between Springfield and Columbus. Soon after the high-speeds went into regular service *Electric Railway Journal* reported, "Certain of the de luxe trains overtake and pass such steam trains as the *Ohio State Limited* to the great amusement and gratification of the interurbans' passengers."

The response to the new equipment was heartening, and C&LE reported increased business at the expense of private autos, buses, and steam trains. Three weeks after the cars went into service the Big Four Railroad was forced to discontinue its Cincinnati-Columbus *Senator*.

A year later the newly formed Indiana Railroad System acquired a fleet of 35 similar cars from Pullman and the American Car & Foundry Company. Somewhat heavier, the Indiana cars had all-aluminum bodies and employed a more conventional type of equalized cast steel truck. Unlike the C&LE cars, they were equipped for multiple unit operation.

In 1930 the Conway group gained control of the Philadelphia & Western Railway, which badly needed new equipment to regain its competitive

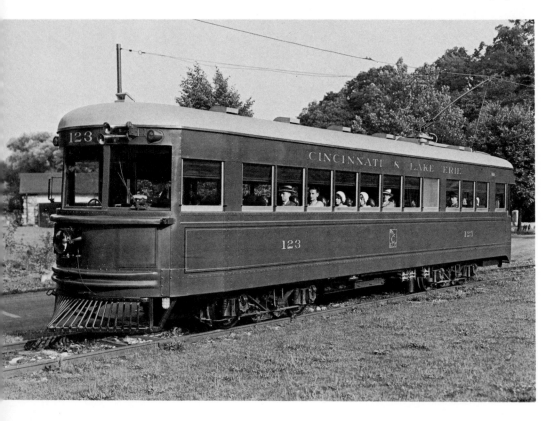

Exhaustive testing produced the phenomenal "Red Devil" lightweight, high-speed car for the Cincinnati & Lake Erie in 1930. Ten were built as straight coaches, and 10 as coach-lounges, fitted with swank furniture and provided with "wrap-around" windshield visibility from the observation section. The 123 was photographed at Moraine Park. BOTH PHOTOS: MAYFIELD PHOTOS INC.

position with newly electrified suburban lines of the Pennsylvania and Reading railroads. Co-ordination of a broad research program and preparation of detailed plans for the new cars was placed under the direction of P&W Vice-Chairman W. L. Butler, who had been largely responsible for development of the C&LE high-speed car design. One of the C&LE cars was shipped to P&W, where a testing program conducted in collaboration with the J. G. Brill Company produced an improved low-level truck design.

An elaborate wind tunnel investigation was carried out at the University of Michigan under the direction of Prof. Felix W. Pawlowski to develop a carbody design which would permit the attainment of the desired high speeds with the lowest possible power consumption. Some 30 types of models were tested and Professor Pawlowski determined that a streamlined car could be constructed which would save 40 per cent or more of the energy required by the conventional type of suburban car operated at speeds in excess of 60 miles per hour.

The 10 Brill-built "Bullet" cars that were the result of the P&W research program represented the finest lightweight, high-speed interurban cars ever constructed. Built almost entirely of aluminum, the big 55-foot cars each had a total weight of barely 26 tons. Wind tunnel research had shown that even such items as roof ventilators had an adverse effect on power consumption, and the roofs of the Bullets were unbroken by vents. Instead, ventilating air was drawn in through louvers at front and back of

Wind tunnel research, along with experience gained with the C&LE cars and the results of still more testing, produced this "Bullet" design for Philadelphia & Western in 1931. The sleek cars not only looked, but were, capable of speeds of over 90 miles per hour. WILLIAM D. MIDDLETON.

The Indiana Railroad's celebrated fleet of 35 high-speed cars delivered in 1931 was similar to the design developed by Cincinnati & Lake Erie. Pullman and ACF divided the million-dollar order. BARNEY NEUBERGER COLLECTION.

the cars and exhausted through streamlined ducts.

The cars were designed for M.U. operation, and completely automatic, self-centering couplers were developed which made car, air, and electrical connections. Four 100-horsepower GE motors were mounted on the new Brill 89-E high-speed trucks. Equipped with field taps, the cars were able to attain speeds as high as 92 miles per hour, and in a test run one of the cars covered the 13.5-mile P&W line from Norristown to the 69th Street Terminal in Upper Darby in just 11 minutes.

The high-speed car development represented virtually the last major effort of the interurban carbuilders, soon to succumb to the combined effects of depression and a rapidly failing traction industry. Aside from a 1932 order for five cars of a modified Bullet design, constructed by Brill for the Fonda, Johnstown & Gloversville, none of the lightweight, high-speed car designs was ever repeated.

With a few notable exceptions, interurban car construction came to a virtual end during the early years of the depression. In 1939 the bankrupt Chicago North Shore & Milwaukee came back from a paralyzing strike and near abandonment with an order for two streamlined, air-conditioned trains that represented an ingenious solution to an almost impossible set of operating conditions. The North Shore wanted a train that could run like the wind and provide all the comforts of a steam road streamliner. Yet it had to operate through the narrow platforms and around the hairpin turns of Chicago's El and, like a streetcar, negotiate major thoroughfares in Milwaukee. All this notwithstanding, builder St. Louis Car Company managed to shoehorn a complete streamliner into the *Electroliner*'s 156-foot, fish-bellied length. Constructed of welded high-tensile steel, each of the *Electroliners* consisted of four articulated units, driven by eight 125-horsepower motors and capable of speeds in the vicinity of 85 miles per hour. Entirely successful, they represented the finest interurban equipment ever constructed.

Another Chicago interurban, the Chicago Aurora & Elgin, purchased 10 new cars from the St. Louis Car Company at the end of World War II. While they featured a number of mechanical and electrical improvements, they were little different in outward appearance from the heavy steel cars of the post-World War I era. The very last interurbans of all were three streamlined trains delivered by St. Louis Car to the Illinois Terminal Railroad during 1948-1949. Clad in corrugated aluminum and trimmed in blue, the three hoof-nosed trains featured air conditioning, reclining seat coaches, parlor-observation cars, and à la carte dining service.

Modifications of the streamlined PCC (Presidents' Conference Committee) streetcar developed in the mid-'30's were used by several interurban systems. Pacific Electric, Illinois Terminal, and Philadelphia Suburban employed double-end, multiple-unit PCC-type cars in suburban services, and the Pittsburgh Railways used PCC cars on its long Washington and Charleroi interurban routes.

Quite often during the interurbans' declining years, equipment improvement took the form of rebuilding and modernization of elderly rolling stock, with sometimes questionable results. Metal plating was often applied over the wood sheathing of an-

Articulated carbodies permitted the North Shore's Electroliner *streamliners to snake around the abrupt curvature of Chicago's elevated and Milwaukee street railway tracks, and a "fish-belly" side enabled them to squeeze between narrow elevated platforms. One of them whipped along north of Racine, Wis., at close to its 85-mile-per-hour top speed on the way to Chicago.* WILLIAM D. MIDDLETON.

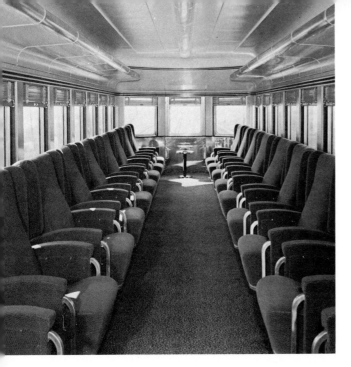

The very last interurbans of all were three of these streamlined trains for the Illinois Terminal Railroad's St. Louis-Decatur and St. Louis-Peoria services. One is shown arriving at IT's subway in St. Louis. Their accommodations included reclining seat coaches, dining service, and parlor-observation sections, and all of these were comparable in every way to those of the finest postwar steam road streamliners. STEPHEN D. MAGUIRE COLLECTION (LEFT); WILLIAM D. MIDDLETON (RIGHT).

tiquated cars in an effort to deceive the public, but this provided no added protection when wooden equipment was involved in collisions. Arched windows and stained glass became anachronisms as America entered the age of streamlining, and the sheet metal that was used to conceal them from view usually destroyed the graceful lines and pleasing balance of the carbuilders' architecture of an earlier time. Garish color schemes with such fanciful effects as wings, swirls, and stripes were often employed in an effort to lend an air of speed and modernity. The North Shore Line went so far as to tediously decorate some of its equipment with aluminum paint and shadow markings in an effort to convince passengers that its 1920-vintage steel cars were really corrugated stainless-steel streamliners.

More to the point, many interurbans concentrated on mechanical improvements and interior renovation of equipment, and a few even added air conditioning. The South Shore Line, which began chopping some of its solid Pullman-built interurbans in two and splicing in an extra mid-section to gain extra seating capacity during World War II, carried the process still further on many cars to add new foam rubber seating, picture windows, and air conditioning, and managed to produce interurbans that rivaled the best contemporary steam road coaches in passenger comforts. **I**

The New England Trolley

Southbound from Naugatuck to New Haven, a Connecticut Company trolley crossed a trestle at Beacon Falls in 1936. WILBUR SHERWOOD, FROM JEFFREY K. WINSLOW COLLECTION.

Bound for Fair Haven, on the New York border, the Rutland Railway, Light & Power Company's Laconia-built combine No. 26 paused in a Rutland (Vt.) street alongside a snappy runabout, while the motorman posed stiffly in the doorway for the photographer. BARNEY NEUBERGER COLLECTION.

THE TROLLEY THAT MET ALL THE TRAINS

Typical of the New England trolleys that met all the trains, and the last of them to survive, was the 8-mile Springfield Terminal Railway, which operated down the Black River Valley from Springfield, Vt., to Charleston, N.H., where a connection was made with Boston & Maine's Connecticut River line. The electric line developed an important carload freight business from industries at Springfield, which was not served by a steam railroad, and the company remains in operation as a diesel-powered freight feeder for the parent B&M. Passenger operation ended in 1947. At upper right, the company's two steel combines, both built by Wason in 1925, are seen on the square at Springfield in 1940; at right, one of them has just met a northbound B&M local at Charleston in 1941. CHARLES A. BROWN (UPPER RIGHT); STEPHEN D. MAGUIRE (RIGHT).

Humming along through the orderly and tranquil Green Mountain countryside, the Mount Mansfield Electric Railway's combine No. 3 rolled past the park at Waterbury Center, Vt. STEPHEN D. MAGUIRE COLLECTION.

80

In July 1907, this group of straw-hatted dignitaries traveled from Springfield to Palmer, Mass., on the first run over the Springfield & Eastern Railway. The exquisitely detailed parlor cars Huguenot *and* Rockrimmon *were provided for the occasion.* BARNEY NEUBERGER COLLECTION.

The 46-mile "trolley air line" of Boston & Worcester Street Railway was among the most important of New England interurbans. With more private right of way operation than most of them, the company was able to provide relatively fast service. This line-up of B&W open cars was photographed about 1905 at the Muster Grounds in Framingham. BARNEY NEUBERGER COLLECTION.

The lightly built New England electric lines were even more poorly adapted to the operation of heavy freight trains than most interurbans, and all but a few of them were confined to handling small shipments in box motors. The early development of good highways in New England brought a quicker end to such operations there than elsewhere. This "Electric Express" train was photographed at Brockton, Mass., on the Bay State Street Railway, one of the most extensive of New England electric systems. Hard hit by truck competition, the company was obliged to give up its freight operation in 1920. INDUSTRIAL PHOTO SERVICE.

Although neither could be classified as an interurban, there were two notable steam railroad electrification experiments in the Boston region. In the late '20's the Boston, Revere Beach & Lynn Railroad electrified its narrow gauge steam suburban line, and coaches were provided with the necessary electrical equipment. Here at Crescent Beach station at Revere Beach, hordes of commuters unload from an outbound train. Abandoned before World War II, much of the former narrow gauge right of way is now used by a new rapid transit line of Boston's Metropolitan Transit Authority. GENERAL ELECTRIC COMPANY.

In 1895 the New Haven Railroad electrified its Nantasket Beach line with trolley, and in 1896 extended the electric operation some 3 miles with center-running third rail. Boasting 200 horsepower, high-wheeled motor car 2510 seated 80 persons, was more heroic in proportions than street railway open cars. INDUSTRIAL PHOTO SERVICE.

The Brockton & Plymouth Street Railway operated through historic Pilgrim ground, and appropriately, the first cars of its earliest predecessor company bore such names as Governor Bradford, Elder Brewster, Myles Standish, *and* John Alden. *The bass drum being carried on this overloaded car at Whitman was bound along with the crowd to Memorial Day festivities at the company's Mayflower Grove park in Pembroke.* CARL L. SMITH COLLECTION.

A few minutes out of Short Beach on the way to New Haven, a Connecticut Company car rolled through lush rural scenery. Although the last Connecticut Company electric passenger services were given up soon after World War II, the trackage seen here is still operated as part of that owned by the Branford Electric Railway museum group. KENT W. COCHRANE.

Northbound from New Haven to Waterbury over one of the fastest Connecticut Company lines, an Osgood Bradley suburban car passed through High Rock Grove at Naugatuck in May of 1937. ROGER BORRUP.

In 1903, under newly elected President Charles S. Mellen, the New York, New Haven & Hartford Railroad began the acquisition of a vast mileage of urban and rural trolley lines in Massachusetts, Rhode Island, Connecticut, and New York's Westchester County, along with Long Island Sound steamship companies, in order to assure a continued New Haven monopoly of transportation in southern New England. By 1909 the New Haven controlled an estimated 1500 miles of electric railways, and ultimately the steam line's electric subsidiaries included eight major properties. Largest of them was the Connecticut Company, which operated some 700 miles of New Haven-owned track in the state. The New Haven's holdings in Rhode Island were similarly grouped under the management of the Rhode Island Company, and the railroad's several Massachusetts trolley systems were held by the New England Investment & Securities Company.

To acquire control the New Haven paid prices that were often far higher than warranted by the electric lines' true value, or any but the most optimistic estimates of their future earnings. The Rhode Island trolley system, for example, was purchased for an amount said to be greater than three times its actual valuation.

The excessive prices paid for the New Haven's electric subsidiaries, combined with their poor financial showing, contributed to the subsequent bankruptcy of the railroad, and by 1914 the Justice Department had brought action under the Sherman Antitrust Act to force the New Haven to divest itself of its electric line interests. Having closely tied the corporate structure of the trolleys to that of the steam line, Mellen stated rather smugly of the Government action, "The result is that now the Department of Justice is in despair. It is a hopeless tangle, as I intended it should be."

Within the year, however, the New Haven was ordered to give up all of its electric line holdings except the New York, Westchester & Boston, and 21 of the company's directors were indicted for violation of the Sherman Act. In Massachusetts state courts found New Haven control of electric lines through its subsidiary holding company to be in violation of state law. **1**

Connecticut Company officers and other distinguished personages rode about the system in high style aboard business car No. 500, built in 1904 by the J. G. Brill Company. The car's interior was finished in hand-carved oak, provided with a lavatory and steward's galley, and furnished with broadloom carpeting and wicker lounge chairs. After the end of Connecticut Company electric passenger service, No. 500 became the première car of the Branford Electric Railway museum, where these photographs were taken in 1959. BOTH PHOTOS: WILLIAM D. MIDDLETON.

Among the least successful of New England interurbans was the Shore Line Electric Railway, which opened a line between New Haven and Saybrook, Conn., in 1910. By 1913, through leases of connecting lines, the company was operating some 250 miles of track extending east to Westerly, R. I., and northward up the Quinebaug River valley almost to the Massachusetts border. Plagued by meager earnings, the company suffered a series of serious reverses beginning with a violent head-on collision in 1917 which took 19 lives and injured 35, and culminating with a strike in 1919 that resulted in bankruptcy and the suspension of operations. Portions of the system later resumed independent operation, and the original Shore Line route between Saybrook and New Haven was restored to operation after four years of idleness — but lasted only six more years. In contrast to its poor financial showing, the original Shore Line route was constructed to some of the highest standards in New England, with extensive private right of way and a 1200-volt catenary trolley system. Shown here operating over the original line is one of the company's wooden, center-entrance cars built by Jewett in 1910. A few of them were sold in 1920 after the suspension of service and one survived into the early '50's on Iowa's Charles City Western Railway. GENERAL ELECTRIC COMPANY.

"Take the Trolley," advised this early promotional folder, which contained a lithographed map of Connecticut Valley electric lines and described points of interest along the way. STEPHEN D. MAGUIRE COLLECTION.

Through Eastern Hills and Valleys
The Middle Atlantic States

Not long after the turn of the century a deck-roofed International Railway car waited at the Lockport depot for a trip to Buffalo. STEPHEN D. MAGUIRE COLLECTION.

Through Eastern Hills and Valleys

The Middle Atlantic States

IN TERMS of total interurban mileage the Middle Atlantic states were eclipsed only by the East North Central states with their phenomenal network in the Midwestern heartland of the interurban. Pennsylvania, if it lacked the integrated traction system of such states as Ohio and Indiana, exceeded all other states in sheer numbers of electric railway properties. The populous cities of New Jersey were linked by the trolley rails of numerous independent companies and the great Public Service Railway system, which operated nearly 900 miles of street and interurban railway. From the Hudson to the Pennsylvania border, broken only by a 31-mile gap between Little Falls and Fonda, upstate New York boasted a continuous web of interurban railways, which followed such earlier arteries of Empire State commerce as the Mohawk Trail, the Erie Canal, and the New York Central through the prosperous cities of the Mohawk Valley and the southern littoral of Lake Ontario.

A considerable traction development was centered about the Upper Hudson cities of Albany, Troy, and Schenectady. South of the capital city third-rail interurbans of the Albany Southern Railroad raced down the east side of the Hudson to Nassau, Kinderhook, and Hudson. In its earlier years the Albany-Hudson line offered summer excursionists a combination trolley-steamer outing for only 75 cents, which included one-way transportation on the interurban and a return trip aboard steamers of the Hudson River Day Line. For those who so wished, an evening stopover for theatrical performances at the company's Electric Park on Kinderhook Lake could be arranged. The Schenectady Railways operated interurbans to Albany, Troy, and Saratoga; and summer travelers to the posh watering places of Ballston Spa, Saratoga, Lake George, and the lower Adirondacks rode the big open cars of the Hudson Valley Railway, which extended from Troy to Warrensburg.

A steam short line, the Fonda, Johnstown & Gloversville Railroad, opened a Schenectady-Gloversville electric division soon after the turn of the century. One of the big wooden St. Louis-built interurbans that provided the initial service, Schenectady Limited car No. 104, paused for this photograph near Johnstown. Its luxuriously appointed interior included a paneled and mirrored smoking room. The banner draped across the pilot advertised a Fourth of July celebration at Sacandaga Park in the Adirondacks, reached by the company's steam division.
FROM WILLIAM R. GORDON.

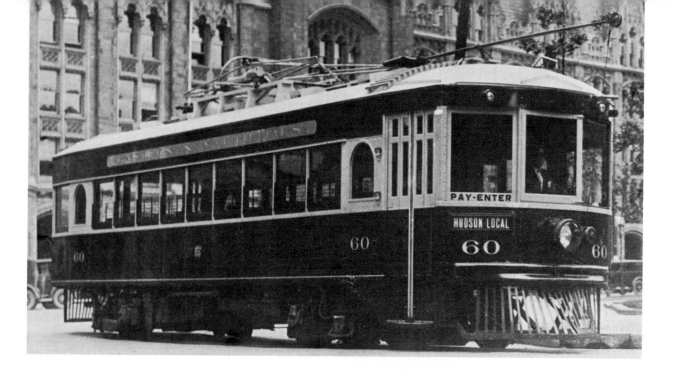

Albany-Hudson Fast Line No. 60 was well equipped for current collection, with trolley poles, pantograph, and third-rail shoes. The Fast Line was abandoned in 1929, but this car rolled up the miles until after World War II, on the FJ&G and on the Portland-Oregon City interurban. JOHN D. MURPHY, FROM WILLIAM R. GORDON.

Past a rambling frame summer hotel, a Hudson Valley open car rolled through a tree-shaded street of Ballston Spa on the way to Saratoga. Like several other New York interurbans, the Hudson Valley was owned by a steam railroad, having been bought out early in the century by the Delaware & Hudson. STEPHEN D. MAGUIRE COLLECTION.

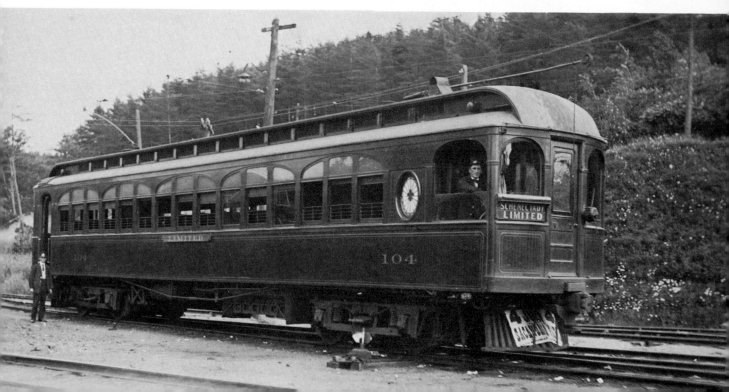

Despite the hard times of depression and declining traffic, FJ&G made an earnest effort to stay in the interurban passenger business with five lightweight "Bullet" cars delivered by J. G. Brill in 1932, accelerated schedules, and reduced fares. Business boomed for a time, but abandonment of electric operation came only six years later and the Bullets found a new home on Utah's Bamberger Railroad. Two of the high-speed cars met at the Johnstown depot on the occasion of a 1936 fan excursion. JAMES P. SHUMAN, FROM WILLIAM MOEDINGER JR.

One of the fastest Empire State interurbans was the New York State Railways' 44-mile route, formerly the Rochester & Eastern Rapid Railway, which connected Rochester with the Finger Lakes region and Geneva. Beyond Geneva, interurban travelers were able to continue as far south as Watkins by means of a Seneca Lake steamship connection. Impromptu races between the electric cars and steam trains on the parallel New York Central Auburn branch, between Rochester and Canandaigua, were common, and in a celebrated contest staged in 1904 an R&E car outdistanced a four-car passenger train. This splendid scene was photographed shortly after a new block signal installation in 1914 enabled the line to reduce running times for the Orange Limiteds to 1 hour 45 minutes from previous schedules of 2 hours or more. During R&E's last years timings were further accelerated when the line, along with other Rochester interurbans, entered the city through a new 9-mile subway, laid in the abandoned bed of the old Erie Canal. But only three years after the interurbans began using the subway in 1928, the last of them was abandoned. GENERAL RAILWAY SIGNAL COMPANY.

Among the lines of the Central's trolley empire was a notable interurban experiment, the 44-mile Oneida Railway, which began operating between Utica and Syracuse in 1907 over the tracks of the NYC-owned West Shore Railroad, electrified for the purpose with a 600-volt underrunning third-rail power system identical to that used in New York Central's New York terminal electrification. Ultimately, it was envisioned, the Oneida line could become part of a New York-to-Buffalo electrification of the New York Central. The electric cars, which supplemented West Shore steam trains, reached downtown Syracuse and Utica over street railway tracks. Fourteen of these wood and steel cars, delivered in 1907 by J. G. Brill, were standard equipment for the line. INDUSTRIAL PHOTO SERVICE.

Soon after the turn of the century the New York Central, in order to forestall the threatened competition of new electric railways in its territory, began acquiring widespread interests in a number of upstate electric lines, consolidating them into the 600-mile New York State Railways in 1909.

For a relatively brief period, from 1911 to 1919, the important Buffalo, Lockport & Rochester Railway was a part of the Beebe syndicate. The line, which operated from Rochester to Lockport, where a Buffalo connection was made, was built to unusually high standards, with 70-pound rail and crushed rock ballast. Shown are two of the heavy wooden cars built by Niles which were operated in high-speed service. GEORGE KRAMBLES COLLECTION.

Second only to the New York State Railways in New York interurban mileage were the five lines, largely centered around Syracuse, operated by the syndicate headed by Clifford D. Beebe. At their peak the Beebe lines included some 318 miles of electric railway, extending from Oswego to Lockport, as well as steamship lines on Skaneateles and Oneida lakes. Pride of the syndicate was the 88-mile Rochester, Syracuse & Eastern Railroad, completed in 1909 at a total cost of 7 million dollars and hailed at the time as one of the nation's finest interurbans. Double tracked throughout, the route was free of grade crossings, and observed a maximum curvature of 6 degrees outside of towns. Much of the line employed heavy steel catenary bridges to support the trolley wire. Driven by four 125-horsepower motors each, the company's limited cars made the trip between terminals in 2 hours 50 minutes.

A Syracuse, Lake Shore & Northern car battled a typical upstate New York winter on the way south from Oswego to Syracuse. The double track, steel overhead bridges, and catenary trolley wire were representative of the high construction standards observed by Beebe lines. FROM WILLIAM R. GORDON.

An elderly Jewett interurban of the Beebe syndicate's Auburn & Syracuse Railroad squealed around a tight curve in Auburn streets on its way to Syracuse in 1922. STEPHEN D. MAGUIRE COLLECTION.

Bound for a Lake Ontario outing at Olcott Beach, three heavily loaded International Railway interurbans paused for the photographer.
STEPHEN D. MAGUIRE COLLECTION.

Extended interurban travel in almost every direction from Buffalo was possible. Interurbans of the International Railway transported Niagara Frontier residents to Lockport and Olcott Beach, on Lake Ontario, and to Niagara Falls. At Lockport passengers bound for Rochester could transfer to cars of the Buffalo, Lockport & Rochester Railway, and for a few years a through car service between Buffalo and Rochester was available. At the Falls connections could be made for Canadian points. So dense was traffic over the International Railway's original "Honeymoon Line" to the Falls, opened in 1895, that trackage was replaced in 1918 with the company's splendidly engineered "Buffalo-Niagara Falls High Speed Line," which cut running time between the two cities from 80 minutes to an hour.

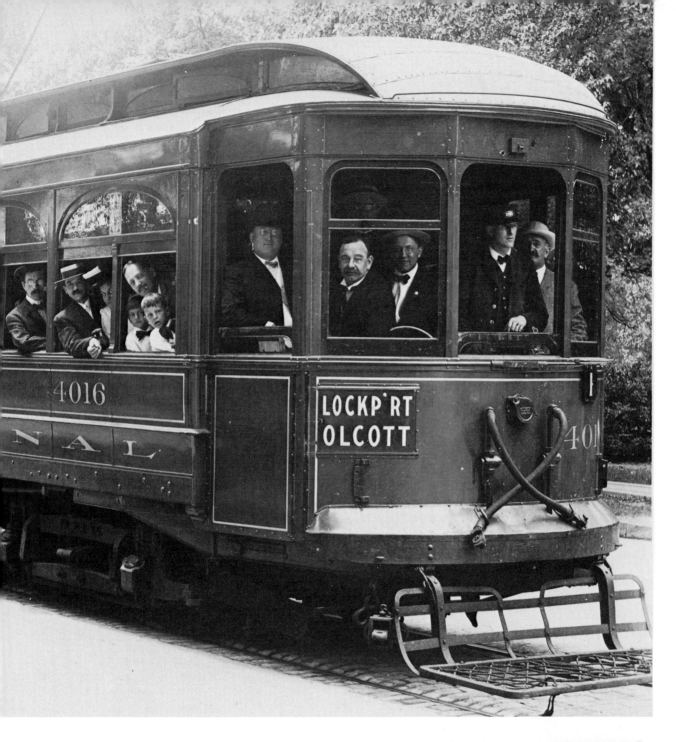

THE GREAT GORGE ROUTE

No visit to the Falls was really complete without a trip through the gorge by open trolley on the Niagara Gorge Railway. Postcard views of "The Great Gorge Route" were mailed home by the thousands. STEPHEN D. MAGUIRE COLLECTION.

THROUGH THE GORGE BY TROLLEY.
NIAGARA FALLS, N.Y.

West of Buffalo the Buffalo & Lake Erie Traction Company tied the Empire State trolley network to the great systems of Ohio and Indiana. Mainstays of the 90-mile Buffalo (N.Y.)-Erie (Pa.) main line were a dozen fast and heavy Kuhlman interurbans of particularly graceful proportions. Two of them are shown here, glistening in freshly applied varnish. GEORGE KRAMBLES COLLECTION.

New York's longest lived interurban was the Jamestown, Westfield & Northwestern, which was created in 1913 by electrification of a bankrupt steam railroad that operated up the east shore of Chautauqua Lake from Jamestown to a junction with the New York Central at Westfield. A phenomenal snowfall caused complications when it came time for the JW&NW to discontinue passenger service in November 1947, as this "last day" scene at Westfield indicates, and the company was forced to precede its passenger cars with a locomotive to break through heavy drifts on the line. ROBERT W. RICHARDSON.

The B&LE emerged from an extended receivership in 1924 with a new management and a new name, the Buffalo & Erie Railway. Fourteen lightweight "fishbelly" interurbans were delivered the next year by the Cincinnati Car Company. The first really fast lightweight cars built, they were capable of mile-a-minute speeds. Weighing only half as much as the big wooden cars they replaced, and designed for one-man operation, the new interurbans reduced the company's operating costs per car-mile by over 25 per cent. Interior appointments included parlor chairs, available at no extra cost, and for a brief period, limited cars were staffed with porters. Shortly after the new equipment went into service a limited from Buffalo rolled through Erie streets in heavy flivver traffic. FRED E. BARBER, FROM HOWARD E. JOHNSTON COLLECTION.

The New York, Westchester & Boston, opened in 1912, was one of the most superbly engineered — and expensive — lines of the electric traction era. Constructed to standards equal to those of the mainline electrification of its parent New Haven, the Westchester employed 11,000-volt A.C. power, a catenary overhead supported by heavy steel structures, a grade-crossing-free right of way, and reinforced concrete stations of truly monumental architecture. Planned to relieve commuter congestion on the New Haven's Grand Central Terminal line, the NYW&B never developed sufficient traffic to pay its high costs or to even approach its tremendous passenger-carrying capacity. Shortly before abandonment in 1937 a White Plains car and a two-car Port Chester train crossed a massive, four-track steel viaduct in Mt. Vernon that characterized the Westchester. GEORGE E. VOTAVA.

The Elmira, Corning & Waverly Railway's route between Elmira and Corning was only a year old when interurbans 107 and 110 met at a siding near Big Flats, on the banks of the Chemung River, in 1912. In pre-automobile days vacation travel to summer cottages along the river furnished a considerable traffic. STEPHEN D. MAGUIRE COLLECTION.

New Jersey's Burlington & Mount Holly Traction Railroad Company was an early Pennsylvania Railroad electrification experiment. The line's One-Spot, a trim combine, towed an open-platform coach belonging to its parent. STEPHEN D. MAGUIRE COLLECTION.

The last New Jersey interurban was the Atlantic City & Shore Railroad, which operated between the resort centers of Atlantic City and Ocean City. After the cars reached the outskirts of the line's terminal cities, trolley poles were hooked down for a fast ride over third-rail-equipped trackage of the Pennsylvania Railroad. In 1947 "Shore Fast Line" interurban 117 traversed the long trestle crossing Great Egg Harbor River, between Ocean City and Somers Point. JOHN A. REHOR.

PENNSYLVANIA DUTCH

More scenic than rapid was the Philadelphia & Easton Electric Railway, whose cars required fully 2 hours to negotiate the 32-mile route between Easton and Doylestown, Pa. The line was part of a route to Delaware Water Gap resorts for unhurried Philadelphians, requiring no less than 6 hours and five changes of cars en route for the 84-mile journey. One of the company's little trolleys rattled through splendid Delaware Valley scenery near Raubsville not many years after opening in 1904. STEPHEN D. MAGUIRE COLLECTION.

The Northampton Transit Company, which wandered some 18 miles northward from Easton to Bangor, Pa., was another link in the leisurely scenic route from Philadelphia to the Water Gap. Passengers were scarce in the line's sparsely settled territory, and the economies of Cincinnati lightweight cars were introduced in 1924. Bright and new, one of them paused at the company's neat station at a park not far from Easton. STEPHEN D. MAGUIRE COLLECTION.

Short Line interurbans were impressive vehicles. Cincinnati-built No. 111, a double-end coach seating 52, weighed almost 38 tons. Trolley poles were used for operation through city streets, but the pantograph was raised for fast running through open country. STEPHEN D. MAGUIRE COLLECTION.

Pittsburgh Railways, which still remains as one of the largest street railway systems in North America, operated a pair of interurban routes through spectacular scenery to Washington, Donora, Charleroi, and Roscoe. These left Pittsburgh through the Mount Washington tunnel, the second longest interurban tunnel in the U. S. St. Louis-built interurban No. 3802, which featured plushupholstered bucket seats and rear-facing observation seats, is seen near Thompsonville on the Washington line. The car was the last word in Pittsburgh Railways interurban equipment until the arrival of radio-equipped, air-cooled PCC interurbans during the late 1940's. UNION SWITCH & SIGNAL COMPANY, FROM ROBERT F. SCANLON.

The conductor on a northbound Butler Flyer did some short flagging while the motorman called the dispatcher for orders. STEPHEN D. MAGUIRE COLLECTION.

ORANGE TROLLEYS ON WEST PENN HILLS

Through wonderfully scenic hills and valleys of western Pennsylvania, studded with coal tipples and beehive coke ovens, wandered the distinctive orange trolleys of the West Penn Railways, a system that at one time operated 340 miles of electric railway in Pennsylvania, West Virginia, and Ohio. The principal West Penn electric lines were included in the company's Coke Region, located in Westmoreland and Fayette counties in the bituminous-rich Allegheny Plateau. ∎

Northbound from Fairchance to Uniontown, West Penn 706 met furious action on neighboring Baltimore & Ohio, where an articulated hurled smoke and cinders into the sky as it fought upgrade with a string of hoppers. LESTER WISMER, FROM STEPHEN D. MAGUIRE.

This is the magnetic track brake employed by West Penn interurbans, which were without conventional air brake systems. To stop his car a West Penn motorman used controller positions that converted the traction motors to generators. The current passed through the spring-suspended electromagnets, drawing them down against the rail and at the same time actuating a series of levers which tightened brake shoes. Once stopped, the cars were held by cranking up a long gooseneck hand brake. ANTHONY F. KRISAK.

A few shirt-sleeved passengers gazed momentarily upon the waters of Loyalhanna Creek as car 711 sped across a bridge on the Latrobe line in 1952. JOHN STERN.

Bridges, sharp curves, and perilous grades abounded on the abrupt profile of West Penn lines. Center-door car 715 traveled across a typical trestle on the Uniontown-Brownsville line in 1949. This interurban was one of 39 identical airless, whistleless cars built by the Cincinnati Car Company and company shops from 1912 to 1925 which performed a majority of West Penn services thereafter. ANTHONY F. KRISAK.

Trolley Sparks in Dixieland
The South Atlantic States

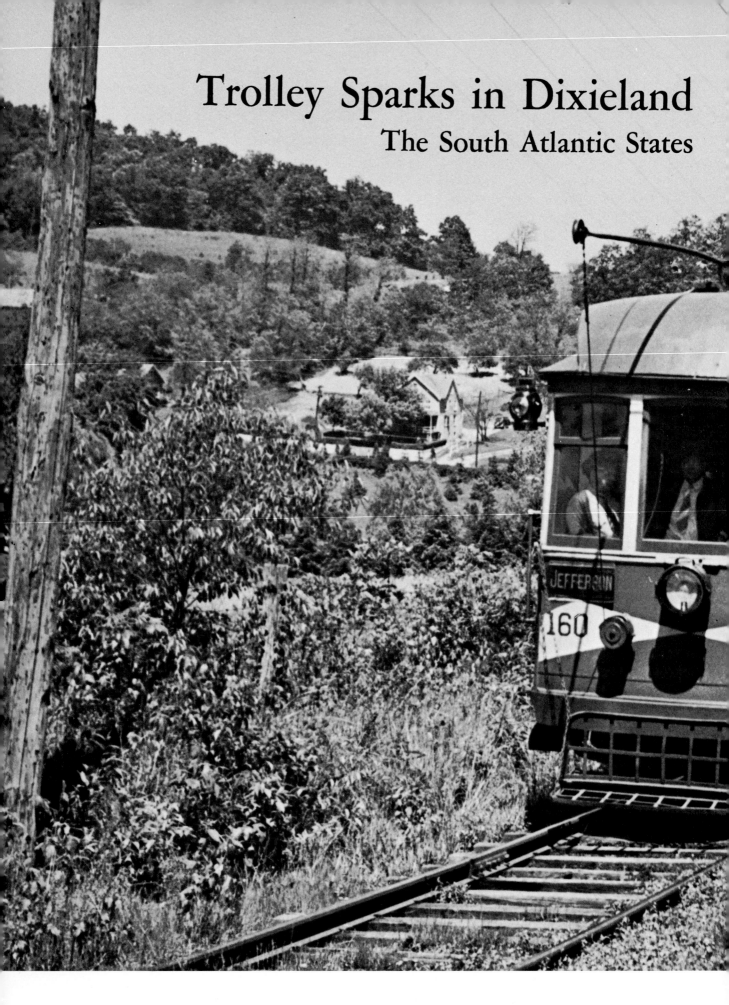

On the occasion of a 1941 excursion Hagerstown & Frederick Railway interurban No. 160 headed for Myersville, Md., on what was left of the company's onetime route from Frederick to Hagerstown. The engaging H&F roamed in roller coaster fashion across the scenic Maryland hills, with grades that often seemed perilous in the extreme. HOWARD E. JOHNSTON.

Trolley Sparks in Dixieland

The South Atlantic States

SOUTH of the heavily populated industrial areas of the Middle Atlantic coast, interurbans became infrequent. In the less populated, less prosperous states of the Confederacy beyond the Potomac there were far fewer opportunities for the quick and plentiful profits interurban developers so often foresaw in other areas. Aside from a substantial electric mileage in Maryland, there were only occasional interurbans which ventured into the country from the larger cities, and in the entire region only a handful of systems existed which could be called of major importance. Beyond the environs of the national capital, sustained travel by the electric cars was not possible.

70 MPH ACROSS MARYLAND

Pre-eminent among interurbans of the South Atlantic states was Maryland's Washington, Baltimore & Annapolis Railroad, which joined the cities of its corporate title with a remarkable high-speed system. Electrified with a 6600-volt A.C. system, the WB&A's double track Baltimore-Washington main line was opened in 1908, and limited service was initially provided with huge 62-foot, 44-ton Niles "Electric Pullmans." Too heavy to permit operation over Washington streetcar tracks, the big cars were soon sold and replaced by equipment of more modest dimensions. Before World War I WB&A, in company with connecting steamship lines, operated an extensive excursion business to such widespread points as Norfolk, Savannah, Boston, and Providence. A round trip Washington-Atlantic City tour, for example, which included interurban transportation to Baltimore, steamship passage to Philadelphia, and steam railroad travel to Atlantic City, cost only $5. At the peak of WB&A operations close to 100 trains cleared the Baltimore terminal daily. Washington limiteds left every half hour, and locals departed hourly. Annapolis trains operated every hour on the South Shore line and every half hour on the North Shore route.

WB&A's finest interurbans were 10 of these two-section articulated cars delivered by J. G. Brill in 1927. Seating 94 passengers in plush-upholstered bucket seats, the 97-foot cars represented a 27 per cent reduction in weight from the company's older wooden equipment of comparable capacity. Despite a half hour spent getting out of Washington over the local car tracks, these big cars were able to operate between the Washington and Baltimore terminals on schedules that were competitive with the steam railroads. On some limited schedules, with 65-minute timings for the 40-mile run, average speeds in excess of 70 miles per hour were maintained over the 24 miles of open track between the two cities. GEORGE KRAMBLES COLLECTION.

Originally the steam-powered Annapolis & Elk-ridge, the WB&A's South Shore line into Annapolis was among America's earliest railroads, having operated its first train on Christmas Day 1840. During the early days of the Civil War its rails were used by Union troops to bypass Baltimore after Confederate sympathizers had cut the Baltimore & Ohio main line. This two-car special operated to Annapolis over the line in 1935. Parlor car No. 100, at the rear of the train, was normally reserved for charter service or such distinguished tasks as transporting dignitaries from the Capital to the Naval Academy. HOWARD E. JOHNSTON COLLECTION.

A three-car Washington-Baltimore train descended into Pratt Street at Baltimore from the B&O overcrossing three days before abandonment in 1935. The two steel passenger cars that headed the train then moved west to the Chicago Aurora & Elgin, where they served for better than 20 years more. JAMES P. SHUMAN, FROM WILLIAM MOEDINGER JR.

By Short Line to the Severn Shore

WB&A's direct North Shore route from Baltimore to Annapolis originally opened in 1887 as the steam-propelled Annapolis & Baltimore Short Line. Electrified by the Maryland Electric Railways in 1908, the Short Line was merged into WB&A in 1921. When the bankrupt WB&A was sold at public auction on the courthouse lawn in Annapolis in 1935, bondholders of the old Short Line bought it back, reorganized it as the Baltimore & Annapolis Railroad, and continued to operate the electric cars until 1950.

On a June afternoon in 1948 B&A combine No. 94 rolled across a placid arm of the Severn River estuary into the Annapolis terminal. The much-rebuilt Wason interurban, originally a center-entrance car, was acquired by the predecessor Short Line in 1914, when SL junked its A.C. system in favor of 1200-volt D.C. power. WILLIAM D. MIDDLETON.

Initial electric service over the Short Line was operated with substantial wooden equipment manufactured by the Southern Car Company at High Point, N. C. Because of the cumbersome transformers and complicated controls required for the company's 6600-volt A.C. power system the cars were remarkably heavy, weighing all of 50 tons. A train, made up of two of the ponderous coaches and a pair of trailers evidently dating from the Short Line's steam days, was photographed at Annapolis in the charge of a handsomely moustachioed conductor. O. F. LEE COLLECTION.

With express and mail piled high on the front platform, B&A car No. 205 approached the Linthicum Heights station in 1949 on the way to Annapolis. WILLIAM D. MIDDLETON.

When the B&A went on its own in 1935 trolley wire was strung over the Baltimore & Ohio main line and the electric cars began operating into the B&O's Camden Station at Baltimore. In 1949 car No. 94 negotiated the specialwork at Carroll Tower to leave the B&O main and head south on single track to Annapolis. WILLIAM D. MIDDLETON.

The clanging of the crossing bell was muted by a wet, clinging snow as a southbound two-car B&A train rolled through Linthicum Heights in December 1948. EDWARD J. MELANSON.

126

Until 1954 the Hagerstown & Frederick Railway, under Potomac Edison control, maintained the last of its once extensive passenger operation, a service which wandered 18 miles north from Frederick to Thurmont, where connections were made with mainline trains of the Western Maryland Railway. Combine No. 171 met the Western Maryland local from Baltimore in 1952 (above) and then headed south to Frederick (below). BOTH PHOTOS: JOHN STERN.

Ready for the 25-mile run to Clarksburg, an orange Jewett interurban peered out from the gloom of the Monongahela-West Penn Public Service Company's interurban terminal at Weston, W. Va., in 1941. Monongahela Valley passenger operation by the company continued until after World War II. HOWARD E. JOHNSTON.

129

In a heavily wooded setting a lightweight Cincinnati interurban and a much older wooden Jewett combine met at Philadelphia siding on Monongahela-West Penn's Clarksburg-Weston line in 1946. By this time the cars were being operated by the City Lines of West Virginia. JOHN F. HORAN.

ELECTRIC CARS IN THE OLD DOMINION

In its time the Washington & Old Dominion Railway provided such amenities as extra-fare, open-platform observation cars and porter service on its trains which operated some 52 miles up the Potomac Valley from Georgetown, D. C., to the Blue Ridge foothills at Bluemont over the rails of a former Southern Railway System branch, acquired and electrified by the W&OD in 1912. Another W&OD line carried excursionists to the Great Falls of the Potomac, north of Washington. Service on this line, it was said, tended to be casual. In 1916 company officials were obliged to reprimand a motorman who carried a shotgun on the front platform and took potshots through the open front window at rabbits which were lured onto the rails by the headlight beam.

An Old Dominion local, having transported mail, express, and a few passengers to the communities along the way, unloaded at its Bluemont terminal in 1937. The crack Loudon Limited *of earlier days stopped only at a few points of unquestioned importance along the line.* E. E. EDWARDS.

To the consternation of motorists on U. S. highways 19 and 21, this interurban made an abrupt 180-degree turn, crossing and recrossing the pavement, to gain access to its bridge across the Norfolk & Western main line at Bluefield, W. Va., on the Tri-City Traction Company's interurban run to nearby Princeton. Beneath the skirting and fanciful striping, car No. 120 was just another curved-side Cincinnati lightweight. The cars continued to operate over the 12-mile line for another seven years after this photograph was taken in 1940. STEPHEN D. MAGUIRE.

CATENARY IN THE CAROLINAS

Carolina utility and tobacco tycoon James Buchanan "Buck" Duke, founder of such diverse institutions as the Duke Power Company, Duke University, the Duke Endowment, and the American Tobacco Company "Tobacco Trust," added a high class interurban to the list shortly before World War I. Duke's electric line, the Piedmont & Northern Railway, actually consisted of two physically isolated divisions, totaling 130 route miles in length, which extended from Greenwood to Spartanburg, S. C., and from Gastonia to Charlotte, N. C. Plans to close the 51-mile "missing link" between the two divisions, and to undertake ambitious extension projects to Winston-Salem and Durham, were temporarily delayed by World War I and the need for major postwar rehabilitation after the disaster of Federal control. Ready to go again in 1927, P&N announced that work was "about to begin," only to be thwarted once more, this time by the Interstate Commerce Commission, which claimed jurisdiction over the new construction under the 1920 Transportation Act and denied permission. Claiming exemption from I.C.C. control as an interurban, Piedmont & Northern fought all the way to the U. S. Supreme Court before finally giving up the fruitless battle in 1930. I

Piedmont & Northern founder and tobacco tycoon James Buchanan "Buck" Duke. PIEDMONT & NORTHERN RAILWAY.

With a uniformed porter in attendance at the step box, this two-car P&N train was ready to roll over the South Carolina Division. The parlor car Catawba, *once a handsome open-platform observation car, had suffered the installation of this graceless solarium rear end in an unfortunate attempt at modernization.* PIEDMONT & NORTHERN RAILWAY.

Headed by combine No. 2101, a two-car train roared through a raw cut near Lyman, S.C., in 1947. CHARLES A. BROWN.

A two-car P&N train rolled into Spartanburg, at the northernmost end of the South Carolina Division, in 1947. CHARLES A. BROWN.

The Interurban's Midwest Empire
The North Central States

For the benefit of the company photographer, one of Cincinnati & Lake Erie's new lightweight cars posed at Springfield, O., in 1930 in a classic tableau of trainside activity. MAYFIELD PHOTOS INC.

The Interurban's Midwest Empire

The North Central States

THERE WAS, it has been said with but little exaggeration, an interurban line wrapped around nearly every Indiana county courthouse. The Midwest was the heartland of the interurban, and here it grew in its greatest profusion and purest form. Within the five East North Central states of Ohio, Indiana, Michigan, Illinois, and Wisconsin was concentrated some 7540 miles of interurban railway — better than 40 per cent of the U. S. total. Ohio had a greater interurban mileage than any state in the Union, and Indiana was not far behind. There was hardly a major city in either state that was not reached by at least one interurban line. The population centers of southern Michigan were laced together with an equally extensive trolley network. Illinois ranked fourth in national interurban mileage, with a network of major lines radiating from Chicago and the greatest of all Midwest interurbans — Congressman McKinley's Illinois Traction System — slicing through central Illinois from St. Louis to the Indiana border. Wisconsin alone among Midwestern states east of the Mississippi lacked broad electric railway development, but among the few Dairyland interurbans was one of the finest systems of the entire Midwest. West of the Mississippi Midwestern interurban development was less frequent, except in Iowa, where flourished some of the most successful of all U. S. interurbans.

An early nighttime photograph at the Springfield (O.) interurban depot recorded in dramatic fashion the dashing front end of the Indiana, Columbus & Eastern Traction Company's interurban No. 93. Formed in 1906 from several financially distressed lines, the IC&E became part of the great Ohio Electric Railway system in 1907, went its own way after dismemberment of the OE in 1921, and finally became part of the Cincinnati & Lake Erie Railroad. O. F. LEE COLLECTION.

Among electric railway historians are some who regard the Akron, Bedford & Cleveland Railroad as the first real interurban. Certainly the company's 35-mile line between Cleveland and Akron, opened in 1895, two years after the pioneer Oregon City interurban, was among the earliest of the major interurban systems. Shortly after the turn of the century the AB&C became part of the Everett-Moore syndicate's Northern Ohio Traction & Light Company that ultimately expanded into one of the major Ohio electric railways, with street and interurban railway operations throughout much of northeastern Ohio. Workmen at the Canton carbarn posed about 1910 with an assorted line-up of Northern Ohio city and interurban equipment.
STEPHEN D. MAGUIRE COLLECTION.

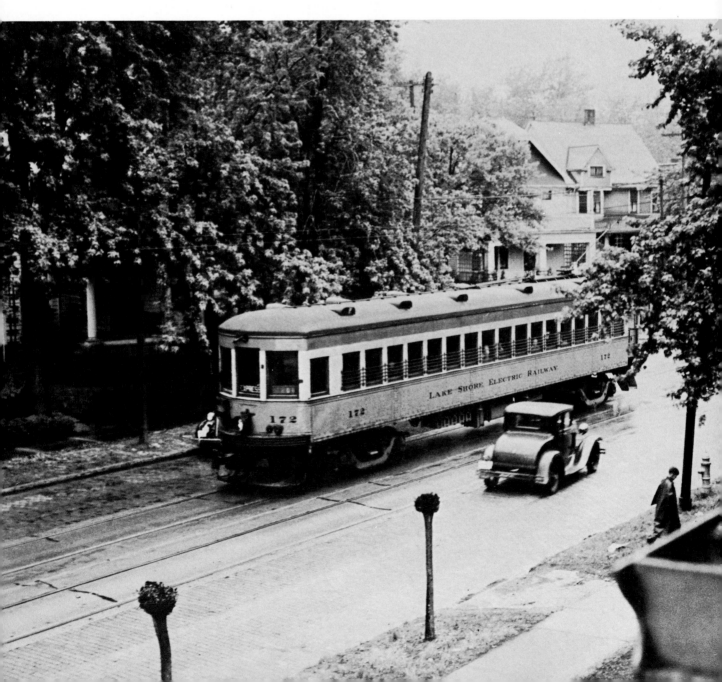

Despite phenomenal depression deficits the Lake Shore
Electric Railway, one of the most important Ohio interurbans, managed to keep going until 1938, when this
big Jewett interurban rumbled through the streets of
Lakewood to Cleveland on the last day of operation. In
more prosperous days LSE did a big excursion business
to the numerous Lake Erie resorts along its route from
Cleveland to Toledo, and through cars transported long-
distance passengers all the way to Lima and Detroit over
connecting electric lines. G. R. BOEDDENER.

The trainshed in this 1926 scene is at
the Northern Ohio's then new Akron
terminal. The motor bus connection
operated a direct service to Youngstown, which could be reached from
Akron only by roundabout interurban travel. DUDLEY S. WEAVER
COLLECTION.

143

Aside from the Ohio Electric system, Ohio's largest interurban was the Cleveland, Southwestern & Columbus Railway, which operated a total of 217 miles of track emanating from Cleveland to Wooster, Bucyrus, and Norwalk. The "Green Line" operated its route to Norwalk in spirited competition with the Lake Shore Electric Railway, which also reached the city from Cleveland. The rivalry led to a remarkable race between the two interurbans on December 11, 1903, when a Norwalk group chartered two electric cars, one from each line, for an excursion to Cleveland. Each of the lines made elaborate preparations for the race, and the chartered cars were given right of way over all other movements. The Southwestern car reached Cleveland first, requiring only an hour and a half for the 58-mile trip, 45 minutes faster than regular limited schedules. Delayed by a broken wire, the LSE car lost the race, although its actual running time excluding the delay was 10 minutes better. Ultimately, the Lake Shore's faster line won out over the Southwestern, and the "Green Line" cut its route back to Oberlin in 1924. This wrote finis to a traction version of the *Broadway* vs. *Century* races.

Among the few steel cars operated by the Southwestern were a half dozen of these heavy 37-ton, 62-foot cars of a design peculiar to the G. C. Kuhlman Car Company of Cleveland, which manufactured them in 1919 for service on the company's Southern Division. Freshly rebuilt as a parlor car and finished in new orange, blue, and ivory colors, No. 205 operated in limited train service from Cleveland to Mansfield and Galion. O. F. LEE COLLECTION.

In an early scene at Seville Junction on the Southwestern's Southern Division, a limited car is en route to Cleveland from Bucyrus, where the company made a connection for Columbus. MAX E. WILCOX COLLECTION.

Ohio's only third-rail electric line, the Scioto Valley Traction Company, operated interurban routes constructed to exceptionally high standards from Columbus to Lancaster and Chillicothe. Original equipment for the "Valley Route," such as 1903 American Car & Foundry coach 104, was of remarkably simple lines for a time when interurban car design tended to the ornate. The 60-foot wooden coach seated 71 on plain cane-upholstered seats. Later on, Scioto Valley Traction bought heavy steel cars and during the last few years of passenger operation provided several parlor car limited schedules on both of its lines. O. F. LEE COLLECTION.

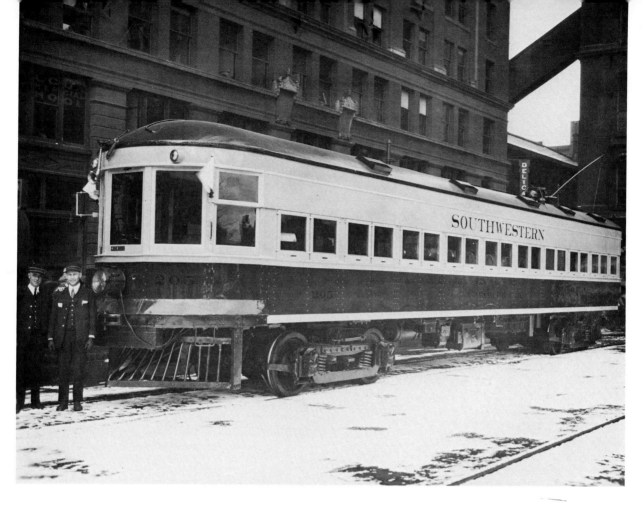

Operating over one of the few stretches of electric railway actually constructed by the company, a southbound Ohio Electric Toledo-Lima local loaded passengers on Keyser Avenue in Deshler, O., in 1910. JOHN A. REHOR COLLECTION.

Flanges squealed as this Ohio Electric wood combine negotiated abrupt track curvature in the streets of Zanesville, O. The car was characteristic of hundreds of its contemporaries on the interurban properties of the Midwestern states. STEPHEN D. MAGUIRE COLLECTION.

Largest of all the Ohio interurbans, for a relatively brief period at least, was the Ohio Electric Railway system organized in 1907 by the Schoepf-McGowan syndicate, which by leases and new construction assembled a network of over 600 miles extending from the Ohio River to Lake Erie, westward to Richmond and Fort Wayne, Ind., and as far east as Zanesville, O. In the years following World War I the financially distressed OE system began to fall apart, and by 1921 all of its various predecessor companies had resumed independent operation.

146

RED DEVILS IN THE BUCKEYE STATE

Beginning with the reorganization of the bankrupt Cincinnati & Dayton Traction Company as the Cincinnati, Hamilton & Dayton Railway in 1926, the principal lines of the dismembered Ohio Electric Railway system were reassembled by a group headed by Dr. Thomas Conway Jr. The CH&D was liberally rebuilt, new equipment was purchased, and a greatly expanded freight service developed. In 1930 CH&D was joined with the Indiana, Columbus & Eastern Traction Company and the Lima-Toledo Railroad, both former OE lines, to form the Cincinnati & Lake Erie Railroad, which extended from Cincinnati to Toledo, with a branch from Springfield to Columbus, and from 1931 to 1936 operated the Dayton & Western Traction Company. Twenty splendid lightweight, high-speed cars were acquired for new limited services, and such innovations as rail-highway containers were adopted for the system's important l.c.l. freight operation. Until abandonment of the Eastern Michigan-Toledo Railway in 1932, such C&LE limiteds as the *Meteor,* the *Arrowhead*, and the *Rocket* operated in through Cincinnati-Detroit service three times daily, and extensive through freight services were operated with connecting electric lines. The C&LE experiment only proved the hopelessness of the interurbans' plight; by 1932 the system was in receivership and by 1939 its interurban lines were entirely abandoned.

This most famous of all Cincinnati & Lake Erie photographs depicted high-speed interurban No. 126 during the course of a race with an airplane staged for newsreel cameras near Dayton in July 1930. The Cincinnati-built car attained a reputed speed of 97 miles per hour to outdistance the plane. This and similar publicity stunts served to introduce the new C&LE system to Ohioans in dramatic fashion. MAYFIELD PHOTOS INC.

"The comfortable car goes kiting along sounding a fish-horn blast like schooners on the Grand Banks," wrote Christopher Morley of a trip over the "Red Electric." A "Red Devil" sped southbound on a Cincinnati Limited schedule in 1937. ALFRED SEIBEL, FROM JEFFREY K. WINSLOW COLLECTION.

The most important of the several connecting lines between the electric systems of Ohio and Indiana was the Dayton & Western Traction Company, a link in a direct route between Dayton and Indianapolis. During the company's existence it was variously under control of the Ohio Electric Railway, the Cincinnati & Lake Erie, and finally the Indiana Railroad, with a few periods of independent operation. This freshly overhauled train was some of the equipment employed in the company's through Buckeye Special and Hoosier Special service between Dayton and Indianapolis, operated jointly with the connecting Terre Haute, Indianapolis & Eastern. O. F. LEE COLLECTION.

Among the more obscure Ohio interurbans was the Hocking-Sunday Creek Traction Company, operating a 15-mile line between Athens and Nelsonville in the coal country of southeastern Ohio. A planned extension to a junction with the Scioto Valley Traction Company at Lancaster never materialized, and the little line remained isolated from the remainder of the state's electric railway network. Unlike the majority of Midwestern interurbans, the company employed equipment of the street railway type. No. 14, on a trestle midway between the two terminals, was typical. CHARLES GOETHE COLLECTION.

Toledo, with no less than 10 interurban lines radiating in every direction, was among the leading Midwestern interurban centers. Longest lived of the Toledo lines, and indeed, one of the most enduring of all Ohio interurbans, was Toledo, Port Clinton & Lakeside Railway. TPC&L extended eastward on the Marblehead peninsula to Marblehead and Bay Point, where a connection was made with Lake Erie steamers operating to the Cedar Point resort and Sandusky. Remnants of the system survived until 1958 as the freight-only Toledo & Eastern Railroad. When Niles coach No. 6 was photographed at Port Clinton in the late '30's, the company was known as the Ohio Public Service Company. HAYDEN ALFORD COLLECTION.

151

The exquisitely furnished and detailed Martha, Union *Traction's official car, was employed only for the most important of occasions.* O. F. Lee Collection.

Rarely was interurban equipment more magnificent than that of Union Traction's Hoosierland *of 1925, headed by the new steel combine* Fort Wayne, *finished in a deep red.*
O. F. Lee Collection.

Stately Cars in Hoosierland

The first — and the largest — of the great Indiana interurban systems was that of the Union Traction Company, which operated over 400 miles of line in central Indiana radiating northeast and north from Indianapolis. The Union Traction system was initially conceived by Charles L. Henry of Anderson, the "father of the interurban," who developed plans for an interurban linking Anderson with Muncie, Marion, and Indianapolis in 1892. The panic of 1893 prevented the immediate start of construction, and it was not until 1898 that the first car operated over 11 miles of track between Anderson and Alexandria. The initial cars developed by Union Traction largely established the arrangement that was to become typical of Midwestern interurban equipment, and the company was among the first (in 1913) to acquire all-steel equipment. The company's powerhouse at Anderson was the first to employ a three-phase distribution system. Power was generated and distributed from Anderson at 15,000 volts to substations about 12 miles apart, where transformers and rotary converters changed it to 600-volt D.C. for the trolley wire, an arrangement that was to become virtually standard for interurban operation. Parlor-buffet cars were provided on a few of the chief Union Traction routes, and the company's timecard listed such memorable interurban name trains as the *Marion Flyer,* the *Kokomo Traveler,* and the *Muncie Meteor.*

152

The Indianapolis & Louisville Traction Company, which formed the Seymour-Sellersburg (Ind.) link in the route between the two cities, was the first interurban to actually begin operation with the newly developed 1200-volt D.C. electrification system. Since equipment of the other two lines in the route was capable of operation on 600-volt current only, Indianapolis & Louisville Traction cars were used exclusively for the celebrated Dixie Flyer *and* Hoosier Flyer *through limited schedules installed in 1908. Niles interurbans provided the initial service.* GENERAL ELECTRIC COMPANY.

Late in 1907, with the completion of the Indianapolis & Louisville Traction Company, a through interurban routing over the rails of three independent electric lines became available between the two cities. The southernmost portion of the route represented one of utilities baron Samuel Insull's first ventures into electric railways, and by 1912 Insull had acquired control of the entire route, which then became known as the Interstate Public Service Company.

In Dixie Flyer *service, this Interstate train included a Cincinnati combine and the parlor-buffet car* Jeffersonville. O. F. LEE COLLECTION.

During the '20's the Insull management initiated an equipment program for the Interstate that included thorough rebuilding of many existing cars and acquisition of some of the finest examples of heavy steel interurban car construction ever produced. Among them were a half dozen parlor-buffet cars which operated five daily round trips on the Dixie and Hoosier Flyers, and three sleepers for an overnight service between Indianapolis and Louisville. Since it was hardly possible to spend the entire night on the 117-mile journey, the sleepers were placed in sidings along the route during the night and brought into the terminals on the first train in the morning. A new steel combine, a rebuilt coach, a sleeper, and a parlor-buffet car respectively were included in the line-up for this publicity photograph. O. F. Lee Collection.

In 1925 the large traction holdings of the Insull interests in northern and central Indiana were further expanded with the purchase of the Indiana Service Corporation. In common with other Insull interurban acquisitions, ISC received extensive improvements, including heavy steel cars to re-equip principal schedules. Among them were the magnificent cars in this 1926 photograph. Both the combine and the parlor-buffet car Little Turtle, newly delivered by the St. Louis Car Company, were employed in the Wabash Valley Flyer service operated between Fort Wayne and Indianapolis via Peru in conjunction with the Union Traction Company. UT provided equivalent equipment for the similar jointly operated Hoosierland service via Bluffton. These and other imperious ISC "flyer" schedules deigned to stop only at county seats and points of similar importance. George Krambles Collection.

The oldest portion of the Indianapolis-Louisville route was the Indianapolis, Columbus & Southern Traction Company, which on the first day of the new century had operated the first interurban car ever to reach Indianapolis. The triumphal arrival was not without difficulty, for the big interurban proved to be too wide to clear the overhead poles located in the center of the street. In order to squeeze the car by, workmen had to remove its handrails, and passengers were obliged to shift to the far side of the car. Further complications arose when the interurban reached the Belt Railroad. The car was forced to jump the rails, since the crossing had not yet been installed. The company's No. 21, a handsome Pullman green coach, is shown in Indianapolis streets. WILLIAM D. MIDDLETON COLLECTION.

Less altered than most cars under the THI&E modernization program was No. 29, the Hendricks, seen taking the curve at Market and Capitol in Indianapolis. Despite scuffs and abrasions of long years of service, the car still bore an air of dignity lent by the classic Gothic lines of its Cincinnati builders.
JEFFREY K. WINSLOW COLLECTION.

Most interurbans were constructed for motives of profit to their stockholders, but the Winona Interurban Railway, which operated between Goshen and Peru, Ind., was devoted to more lofty objectives. The railway was constructed by the Winona Assembly and Summer School Session, and its profits went to the operation of a trade school for the education of underprivileged children. During the company's early years its hidebound directors refused to operate on Sundays, and not until bond-

holders brought suit, alleging that the policy had caused the road to fail to meet interest payments, did they relent. To operate a new Goshen-Indianapolis through service with the Union Traction Company in 1910, the Winona acquired a pair of named wooden Jewett interurbans of the parabolic-nosed "windsplitter" design. The Warsaw is shown here stuck tight in drifts not far from its namesake city during the big snow of 1918. VAN DUSEN COLLECTION.

Among Indiana interurbans the Terre Haute, Indianapolis & Eastern Traction Company was second in size only to Union Traction. Formation of THI&E was begun in 1907, and by the time the system was completed in 1912, its lines extended from Paris, Ill., across central Indiana almost to the Ohio border. The Terre Haute-Paris branch fell only 20 miles short of a connection with William B. McKinley's Illinois Traction System, which would have permitted continuous electric travel all the way to St. Louis and Peoria, but the break was never closed. A plan for a more direct connecting line from Crawfordsville to Danville, Ill., also was unfulfilled, although the idea was kept alive until as late as 1928. Never a particularly profitable in-

terurban, THI&E was unable to follow the example of the other major Indiana electrics, which invested in heavy steel rolling stock for their principal schedules during the '20's. Instead, the company began a sweeping modernization program for its heterogeneous roster of elderly wooden rolling stock for service on such celebrated THI&E limiteds as the *Highlander,* the *Tecumseh Arrow,* and the *Ben-Hur Special,* the last named for the protagonist of the famous novel written by Gen. Lew Wallace of Crawfordsville. A splashy chrome yellow and black color scheme was applied and the cars were given names selected to honor the territory served, its institutions, distinguished historical figures, and occasionally a deceased company executive.

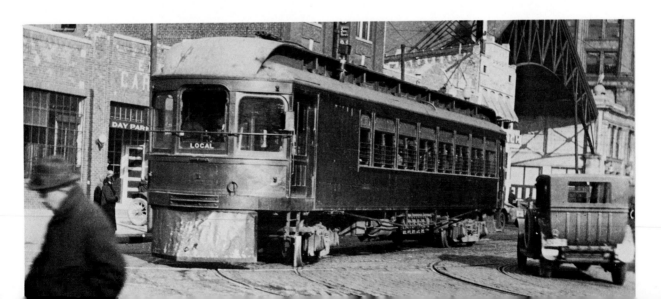

high-speed cars went into service on the principal Indianapolis-Louisville and Indianapolis-Fort Wayne lines. Another half million was spent for power supply and track improvements on the same lines. Freight traffic was aggressively solicited, and in 1933 drastic passenger fare reductions were made. In 1936 older steel equipment was refurbished and converted to one-man operation.

But modernization of the Indiana system started too late. Even as the system was being formed the nation was plunging into a deepening depression. The Insull utilities empire collapsed in 1932, before the needed Indiana Railroad improvements had barely been started. By 1933 the IRR was in receivership, and only once in its existence — in 1936 — did the system show a profit. From a brief peak of over 800 miles of track Indiana Railroad mileage rapidly declined as line after line was given up, and after barely a decade of operation the last IRR passenger service was ended in 1941, on the eve of World War II.

The abrupt decline of the Indiana interurbans during the latter part of the '20's presented Samuel Insull's Midland United Corporation with an opportunity to carry forward a grand plan for a unified Indiana interurban network. The earliest Insull interest in Hoosier traction properties dated to 1903, but not until the mid-'20's were his Indiana holdings greatly expanded. Union Traction went into receivership in 1925, and after acquiring the system for a bargain price in 1930, Midland United was able to use it as the heart of a consolidation of the Insull lines into the remarkable Indiana Railroad system. The lines of the Indiana Service Corporation and the Northern Indiana Power Company extended IRR domination throughout much of north central Indiana and to points north of Fort Wayne, and the Indianapolis-Louisville line of the Interstate carried the new system to the Ohio River. The Fort Wayne-Lima Railroad was operated under IRR supervision, but remained independent. The purchase of the bankrupt THI&E in 1931 added trackage extending across the breadth of central Indiana, and for a few years after 1936 the lease of the Dayton & Western carried IRR into Ohio.

An ambitious program was evolved for modernization of the Indiana system. Weak and clearly hopeless lines were abandoned forthwith, while major improvements were planned for those which were thought to have a future. New equipment, track and power improvements, belt lines and reroutings, and reduction of excessive curves and grades were all part of the contemplated program. An ultimate aim of IRR management was to straighten and improve the system's major trunk routes to permit the operation of standard steam railroad freight equipment. The most immediate IRR improvements were new schedules that were better co-ordinated than those of the previously independent companies, and by the summer of 1931 a million-dollar investment in 35 magnificent lightweight,

Southbound to Louisville as the Dixie Flyer, *Indiana Railroad lightweight No. 68 took a sharp curve at Sellersburg, a few miles north of the Ohio River.* BARNEY NEUBERGER COLLECTION.

In 1935 IRR secured two Railway Post Office contracts, between Fort Wayne-New Castle and Indianapolis-Peru, given up by the Nickel Plate Railroad. To operate the service four former Indiana Service Corporation combines were rebuilt with RPO compartments. A fan excursion brought the 376 to the White River bridge near Anderson. The Union Traction name was still visible on the bridge.

The company's glittering parlor car 7500, available for official duties or charter service, was fitted with deep solarium windows at the front end and this elegant observation platform at the rear. GEORGE KRAMBLES COLLECTION.

Detroit United's finest line was the Detroit, Monroe & Toledo Short Line, built with a maximum grade of 1 per cent and standards of curvature which obviated speed restrictions. The line was well graded and track was laid with 70-pound rail and rock ballast. About half of the route was double tracked, and grade crossings with other railways were avoided. Beginning in 1911 frequent through limited service was operated between Detroit and Cleveland over the connecting Lake Shore Electric Railway, and for a few years after 1930 through Detroit-Cincinnati cars were operated with the new C&LE. Rebuilt Kuhlman steel car 8003 was operated in a de luxe, reserved-seat chair-car service between Detroit and Toledo installed during the mid-'20's. GEORGE KRAMBLES COLLECTION.

The large interurban system of the Detroit United Railways, which was assembled in 1901 by the Everett-Moore syndicate from a wide variety of predecessor companies, radiated from the city in all directions and even had a Canadian affiliate, the Sandwich, Windsor & Amherstburg Railway, which operated along the Ontario shore of the Detroit River. Detroit was one of the earliest traction centers, and almost all of its interurban lines were built in the '90's or the first few years of the new century. Detroit also, of course, became one of the early automobile centers, and its interurbans turned out to be some of the first casualties among major Midwestern systems.

Detroit United car 7794 made a special trip over branch-line trackage which was an extreme example of the meandering, hill-and-dale, roadside variety of interurban construction. BARNEY NEUBERGER COLLECTION.

161

In the areas west and north of the territory served by the Detroit United system, extensive interurban operations were conducted by the Michigan Railways system, whose main routes north from Flint and Jackson, and west from Jackson, served as extensions of the Detroit system. The company, whose corporate structure and history were among the most involved in Midwestern traction, was distinguished by a large mileage of third-rail track and by some notable — though generally unsuccessful — experiments in high voltage, direct current systems. Several of the Michigan Railways' main routes were constructed to some of the highest standards in the industry, and the company was among the earliest to make wide use of steel equipment. At one time the Michigan Railways entertained ambitions of an electric line across the state connecting Kalamazoo with a Lake Michigan port or, even better, with Chicago. For this purpose the company in 1911 leased a steam railroad, the Kalamazoo, Lake Shore & Chicago, which reached South Haven on Lake Michigan and connected with the Benton Harbor-St. Joe interurban at Paw Paw Lake Junction. Plans to electrify the line were never carried out, and after five years of operation with steam equipment, the lease was given up.

These splendid Niles interurbans were operated by Michigan Railways in through Bay City-Detroit service. From Bay City to Flint the journey was made over the company's Northeastern Division, which employed both overhead trolley and third-rail power distribution, while the remainder of the trip was made over Detroit United rails. GEORGE KRAMBLES COLLECTION.

One of the most magnificently engineered lines of the interurban era was the Michigan Railways' Western Division, which opened a 50-mile main line between Kalamazoo and Grand Rapids in 1915. Track was built on a 100-foot-wide private right of way and laid with 80-pound rail, with a maximum curvature of 3 degrees and maximum grades of 1 per cent. Rural portions of the line were provided with a unique 2400-volt D.C. third-rail system. So extreme was the resulting safety hazard that passengers at way stations were loaded from enclosed floor level "safety platforms" which have been described as reminiscent of cattle pens. Conductors unlocked a switch lock to drop the front side of the enclosure, which formed a bridge between the platform and the car floor for boarding passengers. Even more serious were the frequent cases of an arc striking from the third rail to journal boxes.

This burned away the box and then the end of the axle. To extinguish the arc motormen laid a metal bar between the third rail and a running rail, which short-circuited the power feed and tripped the substation breakers, killing the power supply on the line. After a year of such difficulties, the line was converted to 1200-volt power. A 44-mile branch between Allegan and Battle Creek, purchased from the Michigan Central, was similarly electrified. The Kalamazoo-Grand Rapids main line was designed for maximum speeds of 90 miles per hour, and even though actual maximum speeds were lower than this figure, the line was one of the fastest of all interurbans. "Flyer" schedules between the two cities covered the 50-mile route in 1 hour 10 minutes, and for several years during the '20's the company was among the top five in the U.S. in the annual *Electric Traction* speed trophy competition.

On display in Grand Rapids for a 1922 convention is one of the seven huge coach-parlor-observation cars delivered in 1914-1915 by the St. Louis Car Company for limited service over the Western Division. Weighing 70 tons, and over 67 feet in length, they were the heaviest interurban cars ever built. Although of all-steel construction, they were provided with scribed sides to simulate wood siding. GEORGE KRAMBLES COLLECTION.

162

The only connection between Michigan and the traction network of Indiana was provided by the Southern Michigan Railway, which operated from South Bend to St. Joseph, Mich. In 1914 the company was among those that joined in the operation of the new Cannonball Express, an overnight interurban fast freight which operated between Indianapolis and Benton Harbor, where a connection was made with Chicago steamships. Brand new from the St. Louis Car Company, interurban No. 304 passed through Niles, Mich., in 1906 on one of the first through trips over the newly completed line between South Bend and St. Joseph. GEORGE KRAMBLES COLLECTION.

The Rock Island Southern Railway, whose main line between Rock Island and Monmouth, Ill., opened in 1910, employed steam power for freight trains, but the Westinghouse single-phase alternating current system was installed for passenger trains. RIS was the last interurban to begin operation with an alternating current power system, which by this time had proven considerably less satisfactory than the direct current systems then available. Six big Niles "Electric Pullmans," acquired secondhand from Washington, Baltimore & Annapolis, operated the infrequent passenger schedules. Here, one of them crosses the Pope Creek trestle. The electrification was junked in 1926, but steam freight operation continued for another quarter century. WILLIAM D. MIDDLETON COLLECTION.

To Green and Rural Places

Among the finest of Midwest traction properties was the elaborate system of The Milwaukee Electric Railway & Light Company, which between 1896 and 1909 constructed some 200 miles of high-speed interurban routes running from Milwaukee to Kenosha, Burlington, East Troy, and Watertown, Wis. The Milwaukee Northern Railway, which completed a line north along Lake Michigan to Sheboygan in 1908, was merged with TMER&L in 1928.

Projected Milwaukee Electric extensions to Chicago, Lake Geneva, Beloit, Madison, and Fond du Lac were never built; instead, most were eventually reached with joint rail-bus services. In 1922 the company began a massive improvement program for its interurban lines, expending in the vicinity of 6 million dollars before the depression finally halted work. A superb new rapid-transit right of way was built for the interurban routes from the west, bringing them within a few blocks of the company's downtown Milwaukee terminal. To the south a new

166

The Milwaukee Northern's Lake Shore Limited was one of several extra-fare, parlor car limited schedules installed by the company in a 1923 burst of competitive spirit. Close connections were made at Milwaukee with the North Shore Line's parlor and dining car limited trains to Chicago. With but one scheduled stop en route, the MN limiteds covered the 57 miles to Sheboygan in only 1 hour 39 minutes, despite extended street running in Milwaukee. STATE HISTORICAL SOCIETY OF WISCONSIN.

Deck-roofed TMER&L interurban No. 1101 is seen operating on the line to Oconomowoc and Watertown shortly after the line's conversion in 1910 to the 1200-volt D.C. system from the unsatisfactory 3300-volt single-phase A.C. power supply originally provided. During the company's great improvement program of the '20's, cars of this type were rebuilt into the handsome cars of entirely dissimilar appearance shown on the next few pages. GENERAL ELECTRIC COMPANY.

10½-mile belt line around South Milwaukee and Cudahy cut 30 minutes from timings on the route to Racine and Kenosha. A similar project on the Sheboygan line and a half-mile subway into the terminal from the western route were both started in 1930 but were never completed. Elsewhere on the system the original interurban lines were reconstructed with heavier rail and new ballast. Block signals were installed and the system's power supply improved. Forty-one interurban passenger cars were completely rebuilt in company shops, receiving new motors, trucks, and controls. Exterior appearance of the cars was completely altered, and interiors were refinished and fitted with new leather bucket seats. Eight secondhand steel cars were rebuilt into 84-passenger articulated units, and a few new steel cars were purchased or manufactured in company shops, including a pair of articulated coach-diner units for through limited service between Kenosha, Racine, Milwaukee, and Watertown, where a Madison bus connection was provided.

Work was still under way on the Milwaukee Electric's new rapid-transit route to West Junction when this rebuilt motor car and trailer came out of the shops for a 1926 inspection trip. Car 1111 was soon nicknamed the Four Aces by crews.
STATE HISTORICAL SOCIETY OF WISCONSIN.

West of the city proper, Milwaukee Electric interurbans shared their superb rapid-transit right of way with the company's massive high-tension towers, resulting in some impressive scenes of heavy-duty electric railroading. The single car in this scene, 1119, was eastbound at 40th Street in 1948.
WILLIAM D. MIDDLETON.

169

One of the articulated "duplex" units rebuilt by TMER&L shops from conventional equipment in 1929 crossed the substantial steel structure that carried the rapid-transit route over the Menomonee River and the Milwaukee Road main line. WILLIAM D. MIDDLETON.

Among the extensively rebuilt Milwaukee Electric interurbans of the '20's were four of these parlor-observation cars for limited train service on the Racine-Kenosha and Watertown lines. The Mendota was rebuilt in 1924 from a coach almost identical in appearance to that shown on page 167. In 1941 the Mendota was sold to the London & Port Stanley in Ontario, but is now back in home territory in the ownership of a Chicago historical group. To accommodate extremes in Great Lakes weather, TM cars were fitted with removable screens and storm windows. GEORGE KRAMBLES COLLECTION.

Inbound from Hales Corners in 1949, a Milwaukee Electric interurban crossed over the Chicago & North Western at West Junction on a bridge that was clearly constructed to accommodate future multiple track. The structure was part of a mile-long cutoff completed in 1927 which afforded Burlington and East Troy interurbans access to the new rapid-transit entry to Milwaukee, cutting 23 minutes from previous running times via city streets. WILLIAM D. MIDDLETON.

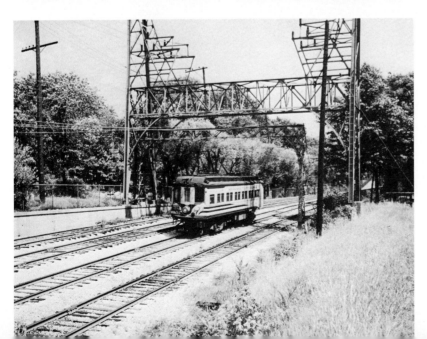

The two near tracks west of Soldiers Home carried interurban traffic, while the remainder accommodated West Allis local cars. The Waukesha-bound car appeared in the Milwaukee Electric's bright yellow and green postwar color scheme, which replaced the more dignified Pullman green with yellow trim of earlier years. WILLIAM D. MIDDLETON.

171

Southbound from Port Washington on the last day of operation of former Milwaukee Northern trackage in 1948, a Milwaukee Electric interurban rumbled across the Milwaukee River bridge near Grafton, providing the scene for what is among the finest of all Milwaukee Electric photographs. These through truss spans were nearly 100 years old. They were built in the 1850's for the Michigan Central Railroad and were purchased secondhand for $5722 by the MN in 1906. GEORGE KRAMBLES.

Following World War II, TMER&L's Waukesha and Hales Corners routes, all that remained of the original Watertown, East Troy, and Burlington lines, were operated briefly by two bus companies before becoming the Milwaukee Rapid Transit & Speedrail Company in 1949. The Speedrail effort to rebuild the property into a profitable concern ended ignominiously with a disastrous wreck in 1950, bankruptcy, and final abandonment in 1951. Lightweight cars operated most of the schedules under Speedrail management. This Cincinnati car departing from the Milwaukee terminal, interestingly enough, had replaced heavy steel cars on the Indianapolis & Southeastern in 1929, which were then rebuilt into articulated units by Milwaukee Electric. After passing through the hands of two Ohio companies in the intervening 20 years, the lightweights turned up in Milwaukee in 1949 to again displace the same heavyweight equipment. WILLIAM D. MIDDLETON.

173

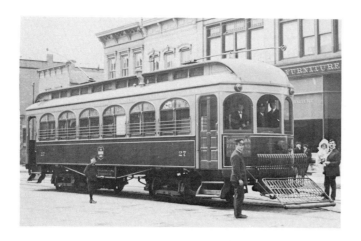

This particularly attractive interurban, built by Cincinnati in 1908, operated over the Sheboygan Light, Power & Railway Company's interurban line to Plymouth and Elkhart Lake, the northernmost point from Chicago that could be reached by continuous electric travel. The photograph was taken at the Sheboygan depot. FRANK E. BUTTS COLLECTION.

In addition to purely streetcar services in Minnesota's twin cities of Minneapolis and St. Paul, the Twin City Rapid Transit Company operated interurban routes to White Bear Lake, Stillwater, and Lake Minnetonka, where the cars connected with the company's express steamer service to points on the lake. Interurban cars built for the lines in the company's Snelling shops were identical in appearance to its city cars, but interurban trucks and motors enabled them to attain mile-a-minute speeds with ease. In 1906 a Twin City interurban, shown at Excelsior on the Lake Minnetonka line, was rebuilt as a double-deck car, rare in North American electric railway practice. The experiment met with only indifferent success and the second story was removed about 1909. BROMLEY COLLECTION, MINNEAPOLIS PUBLIC LIBRARY.

TRACTION ON THE IRON RANGE

One of Greyhound's earliest victims was the little-known Mesaba Electric Railway, which opened a 35-mile line across the Missabe Range of northern Minnesota in 1913. The well-constructed line between Hibbing and Gilbert employed 70-pound rail and gravel ballast, and cars were provided with a cab signal system. In deference to the Minnesota winters, the composite wood and steel cars delivered by Niles were built with double side walls and fitted with storm sash. Unfortunately, the small livery service that was the earliest forerunner of the Greyhound Lines bus system got its start in Hibbing only a year after the Mesaba Railway opened and no doubt was a factor in the interurban's early demise in 1927. FRANKLIN A. KING COLLECTION.

Twin City Rapid Transit's half dozen express steamers, like almost all of its passenger cars, were built in the Snelling shops. As can be seen in this photograph of the Hopkins, cabin design on the steamers bore a family resemblance to that of the company's electric cars. STEPHEN D. MAGUIRE COLLECTION.

In an earlier, more prosperous time passengers on the predecessor lines of the Clinton, Davenport & Muscatine rode in big wooden cars of traditional pattern, and such attractions as joint interurban-Mississippi River steamer excursions, with an observation car trip through Davenport, Moline, and Rock Island thrown in, drew a big business. Long before this car was photographed in 1938 climbing out of the Mississippi Valley westbound from Davenport to Muscatine, declining traffic had forced the CD&M to adopt the economies of lightweight, one-man cars, which were no more than old Davenport city cars, rebuilt and souped up for interurban service. PAUL STRINGHAM.

Unique among Midwestern electric railways were the Iowa interurbans. Some had originally been steam short lines and others developed as connections too, complementing the steam railroad net more than they competed with it. The steam line-interurban relationship was usually, therefore, a more cordial one than elsewhere in the Midwest, and carload freight traffic, freely interchanged with the trunk lines, was substantial from the very beginnings of the Iowa interurbans, a major factor in their remarkable longevity. Almost half of them continued to operate passenger service until well after World War II, and a majority remained active as freight-only short lines in 1961.

Bearing green flags for a following second section, this Cedar Rapids & Iowa City interurban, bright in canary yellow with brown and red trim, raced south to Iowa City in 1950 beside a row of overhead poles that extended to the horizon of the rolling rural landscape. WILLIAM D. MIDDLETON.

Roaring downgrade to the Iowa River bridge, a Crandic "Comet," as the one-time C&LE "Red Devils" became informally known in their new corn belt home, headed northward to Cedar Rapids in 1949. WILLIAM D. MIDDLETON.

One of the most prosperous of all the Iowa lines was the Cedar Rapids & Iowa City Railway, known widely by the "Crandic" abbreviation of its corporate title. At one time the company's ambitions extended well beyond the two cities named in its title. A projected eastern extension to Davenport never got beyond Lisbon, 17 miles out of Cedar Rapids, but the interurban's bus subsidiary, Crandic Stages, ranged from Chicago to Denver with a fleet of some 60 buses before it was sold to another bus operator. Crandic passenger service achieved its greatest distinction after 1939, when the company acquired a half dozen of the Cincinnati & Lake Erie's notable lightweight, high-speed cars, later augmented by a similar Indiana Railroad unit. During World War II the high-speed cars, aided by older wooden equipment, transported the greatest passenger traffic in the Cedar Rapids & Iowa City's history, reaching a peak of more than 573,000 in 1945.

Before the arrival of its secondhand lightweight equipment, Crandic passenger service was maintained by rebuilt wooden cars. Soon after this photograph was taken on the Iowa River bridge during a 1941 excursion, car No. 109, a former Southern New York Railway car built by Cincinnati in 1908, was leased to the hard-pressed Des Moines & Central Iowa Railroad for wartime service. CHARLES A. BROWN.

During the '40's the CR&IC acquired a variety of used freight equipment to accommodate a rapidly growing traffic. Seventy-ton locomotive No. 73, southbound from Cedar Rapids in 1950, was one of two purchased in 1948 from the Union Electric Railway, which in turn had obtained them from the Oklahoma Railway. After CR&IC converted to diesel power in 1953, the two much-traveled locomotives moved on to the Chicago Aurora & Elgin. WILLIAM D. MIDDLETON.

The CR&IC's lone former Indiana Railroad lightweight, No. 120, took siding at Oakdale for a northbound ex-C&LE car in 1950. Such meets were facilitated by a unique trolley wire switch — developed by Crandic master mechanic John Munson — which automatically moved with the track switch, eliminating the need for resetting the trolley pole when entering or leaving a siding. WILLIAM D. MIDDLETON.

178

Rebuilt into a solarium-observation coach during the '20's, car 100 (at Cedar Rapids station) was the only member of WCF&N's trio of de luxe cars to survive a 1954 roundhouse fire that wiped out the road's shops in Waterloo. The 100 continued to operate in interurban passenger service until 1956. The unused semaphore alongside the station dated from the days when trains continued into downtown Cedar Rapids over city streets. WILLIAM D. MIDDLETON.

A McGuire-Cummings steeple-cab locomotive headed this 1954 WCF&N freight train which was southbound near Waterloo on the Elk Run bridge, one of two substantial concrete arch crossings of the Cedar River that characterized the high-class construction of the company's southern extension. The Cedar Valley Road was among the earliest interurbans to pursue a volume carload freight business, and its efforts met with extraordinary success. In relatively recent years WCF&N freight revenues have been in the vicinity of 2 million dollars annually. Of particular value in the development of freight traffic was the company's industrial belt line around Waterloo which provided exclusive service to several industries. WILLIAM D. MIDDLETON.

Since its donation to the Iowa Railway Historical Museum in 1956, No. 100 has operated on occasional excursion trips over the Southern Iowa Railway at Centerville. This was a 1957 fall foliage outing. WILLIAM D. MIDDLETON.

A line-up of equipment was photographed just outside Hutchinson, Kans., on the opening day of through service to Wichita by the Arkansas Valley Interurban Railway in 1915. The complete absence of ballast was a condition that, unfortunately, remained permanent on much of the AVI. Car No. 6, in the foreground, expired in spectacular fashion in 1928 when it was wrecked and burned in a high-speed head-on collision with a freight train. WILLIAM J. CLOUSER COLLECTION.

Center-door steel cars of substantial appearance operated on Missouri's largest interurban system, the 79-mile Kansas City, Clay County & St. Joseph Railway, which opened a pair of high-class 1200-volt lines from Kansas City to Excelsior Springs and St. Joseph in 1913. Cathedral glass panels in the upper window sash provided just the right touch of elegance. To accommodate special parties the rear of the cars was designed for conversion to an observation compartment. Regular seats were removed and carpeting and mahogany lounge chairs installed. STEPHEN D. MAGUIRE COLLECTION.

An obscure Midwestern interurban was the Burlington's 5-mile electrification of a portion of the 3-foot-gauge Deadwood Central Railroad between Lead, Pluma, and Deadwood in the Black Hills of South Dakota. Passenger car 12150, a little interurban with a big number, was one of five cars operated over the line. Here it is at the three-level crossing with the North Western and a mine railroad in Lead about 1906. STEPHEN D. MAGUIRE COLLECTION.

Electric cars of the Union Electric Railway wandered over a devious 77-mile route from Nowata, Okla., to Parsons, Kans. The entire trip, which few attempted, required about 4 hours. Hard pressed to make ends meet throughout much of its existence, the company economized by purchasing lightweight, one-man cars from the American Car Company in 1925. One of them waited for the passage of a Frisco freight at Cherryvale, Kans., in 1946. GORDON E. LLOYD.

The McKinley Lines
Illinois Traction System

Headlight aglow, an Illinois Terminal interurban waited at the joint IT-Wabash depot in Champaign during a 1955 snowfall. WILLIAM D. MIDDLETON.

The McKinley Lines

Illinois Traction System

DURING the first decade of the new century, as a great interurban network spread across Mid-America, the Illinois Traction System assembled by Illinois congressman and utilities tycoon William B. McKinley clearly emerged as the giant of Midwest traction.

Only seven years after he opened his first electric line in 1901—a 6-mile stretch between Danville and Westville, Ill.—McKinley had pushed the main lines of his traction empire to their full geographical extent. From Granite City, across the Mississippi from St. Louis, the McKinley lines extended 167 miles northward to Springfield and Peoria; 125 miles eastward from Springfield to Decatur, Champaign, and Danville, on the Indiana border; and from Decatur to Peoria via Bloomington. In 1910 a great new Mississippi River bridge was opened and Illinois Traction trains rolled across to a new St. Louis terminal. That same year a sleeping car service was inaugurated — the only one of its kind on any interurban — with specially designed cars that outdid even Pullman, and a year later a fleet of luxurious parlor-observation cars appeared on limited trains operating over the main lines from St. Louis to Springfield, Peoria, and Danville. Small wonder that they were calling Illinois Traction the "greatest interurban system in the world."

Only a few years later McKinley acquired the Illinois Valley lines of the Chicago, Ottawa & Peoria, which reached neither Chicago nor Peoria but had connections at Joliet with the Chicago & Joliet and plans for extensions from Streator to Peoria and Mackinaw Junction on the main IT system. It was considered only a matter of time before the missing links would be filled in and through service over an uninterrupted Chicago-St. Louis electric route would become a reality. As early as 1906 ITS had purchased three special *Corn Belt Limited* cars that were to enter a through St. Louis-Indianapolis service just as soon as the 20-mile gap was closed between the McKinley Lines at Ridge

Farm, Ill., and the Terre Haute, Indianapolis & Eastern at Paris, Ill.

Illinois Traction or its subsidiary companies operated local streetcar lines in 19 Illinois cities, and fully half of the electric railway mileage in the state was under McKinley control. By 1916 McKinley owned some 40 railway, light and power companies in Illinois, Kansas, Missouri, Iowa, Nebraska, and Wisconsin, and an estimated 800 miles of electric railway track was under ITS supervision.

Expansion of the system continued even in later years, although the Chicago and Indianapolis connections were never realized. In 1928 Illinois Traction was merged with the prosperous and strategic Illinois Terminal Company, a steam-operated terminal line in the Alton-East St. Louis area. Two years later still more electric mileage was added to what was now known as the Illinois Terminal Railroad System when the St. Louis & Alton Railway was leased.

The greatest single undertaking of the McKinley Lines, and indeed the greatest engineering work ever attempted by any interurban, was the mighty bridge McKinley flung across the Mississippi to gain access to St. Louis for his traction empire. Finding the lack of a direct entry to the city a hindrance to the development of his company, and barred from the only available bridge to downtown St. Louis by a monopoly of his steam road competitors, the undaunted McKinley undertook the 4.5-million-dollar project in 1906. The structure, at the time the largest and strongest Mississippi crossing ever built, took four years to build, and its completion was observed on November 10, 1910, with appropriate ceremony. Special trains bearing Governors Hadley of Missouri and Deneen of Illinois met at the center of the flag-bedecked span; the two men "clasped hands, each congratulating the other on this newest bond between Missouri and Illinois"; and Congressman McKinley's niece raised the U. S.

192

Running in place of the streamliner Mound City, Illinois Terminal *interurban car No. 283, trailed by the parlor-buffet-observation car* Cerro Gordo, *headed south from Mackinaw Junction in 1950 on a fast Peoria-St. Louis schedule.* WILLIAM D. MIDDLETON.

flag to the peak of the bridge as a band played the national anthem. That evening, while the Illinois Traction System entertained 700 prominent guests at a banquet in St. Louis' Planter's Hotel, thousands watched a fireworks display on the bridge.

McKinley Bridge, the only exclusive river cross-

ing to St. Louis owned by any railroad, greatly strengthened the competitive position of Illinois Traction's far-flung interurban passenger service, and by gaining direct access to St. Louis industry, greatly accelerated the growth of an ITS freight business that was already assuming major propor-

A typical Peoria-St. Louis limited train of 1925, made up of a handsome arch-roofed coach and match-ing parlor-buffet car with open observation platform, rolled across the jackknife draw span of Illinois Traction's substantial Illinois River bridge at Peoria. This structure became insignificant only in comparison with the company's Mississippi span at St. Louis. WILLIAM J. CLOUSER COLLECTION.

tions. A new suburban service between St. Louis and Granite City, inaugurated with the opening of the bridge, proved to be a lucrative by-product. Only a few months after the line was opened, ITS was able to report an average of 10,000 passengers a day, a figure that tripled on Sundays when thirsty St. Louis citizens fled their dry-on-Sunday city for the saloons of nearby Illinois.

Far earlier than most of its contemporaries, Illinois Traction recognized the value and importance of a carload freight traffic interchange with steam railroads. Like most interurbans, ITS usually traversed the streets of intermediate cities and towns, where sharp curves or legal limitations frequently precluded the operation of long freight trains, and as early as 1906 the system began the construction of belt lines around its principal cities, a move that ultimately was to prove the means for survival of

the Midwest's largest interurban. Early attention was also given to the improvement of the system's power supply, to satisfy the demands of heavy freight locomotives.

William B. McKinley built his Illinois Traction System into the Midwest's greatest interurban railway. His distinguished career in business and public life was climaxed with a term in the U. S. Senate. ILLINOIS STATE HISTORICAL LIBRARY.

194

Workhorse combine 283, seen in the gloom of the St. Louis terminal in 1955, bore the unmistakable imprint of Illinois Traction electric car architecture, despite the blocked-off side window arches of a '30's rebuilding. Operation from the left-hand side was an unusual IT feature. The rectangular insert of safety glass in the motorman's window was a modern-day innovation. WILLIAM D. MIDDLETON.

The crew of this Illinois Traction interurban viewed the roadbed from behind a truly generous expanse of plate glass. An early arrival in ITS ranks (American Car Company, 1904), car 252 predated the distinctive car design that soon became a virtual company trademark. WILLIAM D. MIDDLETON COLLECTION.

Splendid in tangerine, a special train, including the parlor-observation car Lincoln, headed south across the Sangamon River bridge near Springfield, Ill., in 1938. PAUL STRINGHAM.

196

With controller wide open, a St. Louis-Peoria local skimmed downhill into a little valley not far from Edwardsville, Ill., in 1955. By this time the bright orange of earlier years had been replaced by less flamboyant blue and silver colors. WILLIAM D. MIDDLETON.

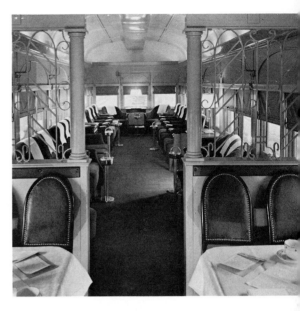

Trolley Car Luxury

Finished in Honduras mahogany, heavily carpeted, and richly furnished, Illinois Traction's parlor-buffet-observation cars provided all of the appropriate comforts and a suitably dignified atmosphere for extra-fare travelers on the company's crack Peoria-St. Louis limited trains. In later years observation platforms were enclosed, and such up-to-the-minute features as air conditioning and indirect lighting were provided, along with a less somber décor. GEORGE KRAMBLES COLLECTION (ABOVE LEFT, CENTER); HERBERT GEORG STUDIO, SPRINGFIELD (ABOVE RIGHT); WILLIAM D. MIDDLETON COLLECTION (BELOW).

The interurban sleeping cars introduced by Illinois Traction in 1910 featured such advantages as upper-berth windows, extra-long berths, and individual safety deposit boxes. The Edwardsville *was built by the St. Louis Car Company in 1913.* WILLIAM J. CLOUSER COLLECTION.

Extensive through rates and divisions were established with connecting steam railroads. Illinois Traction freight service was even extended to Chicago in 1910 by means of specially equipped cars for less-than-carload-lot package freight shipments, which were interchanged with the Chicago & Eastern Illinois at Glover, Ill. A similar service was offered via Peoria, where l.c.l. freight was transferred to the Rock Island.

Under the skilled direction of Master Mechanic J. M. Bosenbury, Illinois Traction early evolved a passenger car design of altogether distinctive appearance; and the high arched "crown" roof and a front end with three graceful arched windows became a virtual company trademark. Until three new streamliners arrived in 1948-1949, IT's newest mainline passenger car dated to 1918, and most of its rolling stock was considerably older than that. In the interim the company's Decatur shops assumed the substantial task of rebuilding and modernizing the elderly equipment in order to maintain a competitive position in the passenger trade. Through the years many of the venerable interurbans received such improvements as reclining seats, air condition-

Illinois Traction brass and distinguished visitors rode in baronial elegance aboard private car 233. Originally constructed in 1906 as the Missouri *for the projected St. Louis-Indianapolis* Corn Belt Limited *service, No. 233 was rebuilt and sumptuously furnished for its official duties by the St. Charles (Mo.) shop of American Car & Foundry in 1910.* GEORGE KRAMBLES COLLECTION (UPPER); WILLIAM J. CLOUSER COLLECTION (LOWER).

Shortly after World War II Illinois Terminal made an ill-advised million-dollar bid to stay in the passenger business with three streamlined blue and aluminum interurban trains. The City of Decatur, *the* Fort Crevecoeur, *and the* Mound City *were delivered by the St. Louis Car Company in 1948-1949. Provided with every comfort of comparable steam railroad equipment, the trains were costly proof that interurban passenger traffic was irrevocably lost, and were withdrawn from service by 1956. Hoof-nosed streamliner No. 300 headed a two-car St. Louis limited train at the East Peoria station in 1955.* WILLIAM D. MIDDLETON.

ing, and other interior refinements. Illinois Terminal was, incidentally, the first electric line to operate air-conditioned equipment, beginning in 1935 when a car was equipped for a new high-speed Peoria-St. Louis service.

Illinois Terminal continued to develop its passenger service long after most interurbans. In the early 1930's, while much of the nation's electric railway mileage was being abandoned, IT completed

After 1917 the mainstay of the high-speed Alton service was a group of high-wheeled, center-door cars, some of which were capable of speeds in excess of 85 miles per hour. Two of the breed entered St. Louis over the elevated line from McKinley Bridge in 1948. Motorman W. "Dutch" Horrman (far right), who began operating cars over the line in 1903, was at the controls of an Alton Limited in 1941. WILLIAM J. CLOUSER (RIGHT); LINN H. WESTCOTT (FAR RIGHT).

An early version of the Alton-St. Louis Limited waited at the end of historic Eads Bridge in 1916. The Alton line, then operated by the East St. Lou- is & Suburban, *later became part of Illinois Terminal.* WILLIAM T. DIESING, FROM WILLIAM J. CLOUSER COLLECTION.

In the final years of its St. Louis-Granite City suburban service, Illinois Terminal provided streamlined PCC trolleys, modified for multiple-unit, double-end operation. A pair of them descended the St. Louis approach to McKinley Bridge in 1955. The Granite City cars, Illinois Terminal's last passenger operation, continued to run until 1958. WILLIAM D. MIDDLETON.

a new elevated structure that brought its passenger trains from McKinley Bridge close to the heart of St. Louis, and a short subway that took them the rest of the way to a basement terminal in the company's huge new Central Terminal Building. New passenger stations were constructed at such important points as Peoria, Springfield, and Decatur, and passenger train schedules were accelerated by routing the cars around traffic-congested streets on IT's freight belt lines at a number of cities. ⅃

HOME-BUILT FOR TONNAGE

These photographs record the evolution of the distinctive motive power constructed in Illinois Terminal's Decatur shops over a 32-year period. Earliest of the home-built products were 18 of these 60-ton Class B box-cab locomotives built between 1910 and 1918. Class B No. 1566 entered East Peoria, Ill., in 1950 with interchange from the Peoria & Pekin Union. WILLIAM D. MIDDLETON.

After World War I a steadily increasing freight traffic made the small two-truck Class B locomotives inadequate for mainline tonnage, and 20 of these four-truck articulated Class C machines rolled out of the shops between 1924 and 1930. Weighing 80 tons, they were powered with eight motors salvaged from scrapped passenger cars. No. 1597 was photographed near Allentown, Ill., in 1941 with a northbound extra. PAUL STRINGHAM.

Largest of the Decatur-built locomotives were five streamlined Class D units built in 1940-1942. Weighing 108 tons and developing 1800 horsepower with eight traction motors, they required double trolley poles to draw sufficient current. Virtually identical carbodies gave all three classes of IT freight power a strong family resemblance. The five Class D's, as a matter of fact, utilized frames and carbodies from scrapped Class C units. With blowers whining, a Class D rolled into Springfield from St. Louis in 1950. DAVID A. STRASSMAN.

Insull's Interurbans

The Great Chicago Systems

Lengthened and rebuilt with "picture windows," air conditioning, and foam rubber seats, the big steel interurbans which were constructed during the South Shore Line's overhaul by Insull management in the '20's still provide the last word in passenger comforts. Two of them operated a South Bend-Chicago schedule near Gary in 1953. LINN H. WESTCOTT.

Insull's Interurbans

The Great Chicago Systems

AMONG the men who achieved prominence during the interurban era, one of the greatest traction tycoons of them all was Chicago's Samuel Insull, whose Midwestern power, gas, and traction empire was truly one of the wonders of the '20's. The phenomenal business career of the London-born magnate began in 1881 when, at the age of 21, he became private secretary to Thomas Edison. Insull stayed with Edison long enough to assist in the organization of the General Electric Company, then moved west to begin a conquest of Chicago's public utilities. By 1907 the city's entire electric power business was under the control of Insull's Commonwealth Edison Company, and only three years later an Insull "superpower" system, destined to embrace the entire state of Illinois and much of the Midwest as well, began branching out from Chicago. Within 20 years Insull's Middle West Utilities empire had assets in excess of 2 billion dollars, produced a tenth of the nation's electricity, and served over 1,800,000 customers in some 3500 communities in 39 states.

If only a minor part of his incredibly complicated holdings, Insull's traction network was nonetheless impressive. Convinced that electric transportation would ultimately supplant all other mass transportation media, Insull acquired control of Chicago's surface and elevated railways, and provided ample cash to place them in top condition. His interurban interests, usually interlocked with associated power companies, included a network that covered much of Indiana, and eventually every line of consequence that radiated from Chicago.

Pre-eminent among the Insull traction holdings were the three superb interurbans which extended north, west, and southeast from Chicago. Each already enjoyed a measure of distinction when Insull acquired control in the decade following 1916, but Insull provided the management and hard cash to transform these railways into some of the most re-

markable properties of the entire interurban era.

The oldest of the three, Chicago North Shore & Milwaukee, began operation in typically modest interurban fashion in 1894 as the Bluff City Electric Street Railway at Waukegan, Ill. Reorganized a few years later as the Chicago & Milwaukee Electric Railway, the line was reorganized twice again before receivers finally managed to complete in 1909 a main line which extended from Evanston to Milwaukee. Hindered by the lack of an entrance to the heart of Chicago, the line was only a modest success until a 1916 reorganization under Insull control created the Chicago North Shore & Milwaukee Railroad, and the new management invested 5.5 million dollars in an extensive development program. By 1919 North Shore trains were running to the Chicago Loop over elevated tracks, and a few years later passengers were being transported between Chicago and Milwaukee aboard such luxurious limited trains as the *Eastern Limited*, the *Badger*, and the *Interstate*, which numbered parlor-observation cars and diners among their features and offered close Chicago connections with the *20th Century Limited* and the *Broadway Limited*. Powerful new steel cars sped between the two cities over newly rebuilt roadbeds in as little as 2 hours 10 minutes, and North Shore billboards challenged, "Did you ever travel 80 miles an hour?" Between 1916 and 1922 the number of daily trains increased from 192 to 295, and the North Shore enjoyed a 350 per cent increase in gross operating revenues.

Chicago's interurban to the western suburbs was several cuts above ordinary interurbans right from its opening day in 1902. Conceived as a "super interurban," the Aurora, Elgin & Chicago Railroad employed the third-rail system then highly regarded for heavy-duty, high-speed lines and was engineered to the extremely high standards required for a contemplated 70-mile-per-hour continuous maximum speed. A ruling grade of 1 per cent and a maximum

Near Four Mile Road, north of Racine, Wis., on an August morning in 1955 a four-car North Shore Line Milwaukee Limited thundered across the Root River which meanders on through lush farmlands to Racine and Lake Michigan. WILLIAM D. MIDDLETON.

Utilities magnate Samuel Insull built his three big Chicago electric lines into the wonders of the interurban era. CHICAGO HISTORICAL SOCIETY.

209

A splendid double-track roadbed between Chicago and Milwaukee enabled the North Shore to gain international recognition for its speed achievements and permanent possession of the Electric Traction *interurban speed trophy in 1933. Freshly ballasted in crushed stone and straight as a rifle bore, this stretch of track near Racine was typical. A Milwaukee Limited traveled it in 1956 at a speed considerably in excess of a mile a minute.* WILLIAM D. MIDDLETON.

Southbound on its last trip of the day, an Electroliner *paused briefly at North Chicago on its flight between Milwaukee and Chicago.* WILLIAM D. MIDDLETON.

curvature of 3 degrees were maintained, and the line employed 80-pound rail, rock ballast, and sturdy bridges of concrete and steel construction. Unlike other Chicago interurbans, the AE&C enjoyed the advantages of a direct entrance to the Loop early in its history, inaugurating through service over the tracks of the Metropolitan West Side Elevated Company in 1905. The superior transportation represented by the AE&C encouraged rapid development of the western suburbs, and within a very few years after the line's opening the number of intermediate stations, originally planned at 3-mile intervals, had increased to 27 in the 25 miles between Chicago and Wheaton.

Reorganized as the Chicago Aurora & Elgin in 1922 by Dr. Thomas Conway Jr., later to earn further distinction as the organizer of the Cincinnati & Lake Erie system and the rebuilder of the Philadelphia & Western, the line received the benefit of bet-

ter than a million dollars in improvements, including stone reballasting between Chicago and Wheaton, power system and shop improvements, and 20 heavy Pullman-built steel passenger cars.

Employing a 6600-volt, single-phase power system, the Chicago, Lake Shore & South Bend Railway, opened in 1908, achieved early prominence as one of the most important alternating current interurbans. Constructed to high standards, and equipped with unusually large and handsome Niles wooden interurbans, the Lake Shore line did a substantial business between the communities at the foot of Lake Michigan and South Bend. The necessity for a transfer to the Illinois Central at Kensington, however, had a discouraging effect on the interurban's business into Chicago, until an agreement was negotiated with the steam road in 1913 whereby through trailer cars from seven Gary-Chicago limiteds daily were attached to IC steam locomotives,

211

The North Shore by Night

In this series of nighttime camera studies, the North Shore is depicted as it went about "business as usual" after a January 1958 blizzard. This snowfall, of the prodigious proportions common to the shores of the Great Lakes, had raged across Chicago's North Shore suburbs, thoroughly disrupting road traffic and other activities similarly less reliable than the electric cars. The white stuff was still drifting down as a Skokie Valley local stopped at the Libertyville (Ill.) station. WILLIAM D. MIDDLETON.

Surrounded by darkened interurbans awaiting the morning rush back to the city, a late evening local was about to depart from Mundelein for Chicago. WILLIAM D. MIDDLETON.

While compressors hammered air into the train line, a trio of GE steeple-cab locomotives waited at Pettibone Yard in North Chicago with 29 cars for the Elgin, Joliet & Eastern at Rondout and the Soo at Mundelein. WILLIAM D. MIDDLETON.

213

After 1926 interurbans of Sam Insull's South Shore Line operated straight through to the Chicago Loop from Kensington over the rails of the Illinois Central's superbly engineered suburban electrification. In 1956 a four-car Chicago Express, operating over the outer "special" track reserved for nonstop trains, was about to overtake an IC local on six-track right of way not far from the Loop. WILLIAM D. MIDDLETON.

A Pullman-built North Shore coach, trimmed in the Silverliner colors of recent years, got a new set of wheels in the company shops at Highwood, Ill., in 1955. WILLIAM D. MIDDLETON.

passengers from Chicago's Loop to Mundelein and back, and another 60,000 were transported between the Chicago & North Western station at Lake Bluff and Mundelein. Six-car trains of borrowed Chicago Rapid Transit equipment left the Loop every 2 minutes beginning at daybreak, and 13 eight-car trains shuttled steadily between Lake Bluff and Mundelein to carry the record crowd.

Working through his Midland Utilities Company, Insull next acquired the Chicago, Lake Shore & South Bend at a foreclosure sale in 1925, reorganized it as the Chicago South Shore & South Bend, and during the next three years gave it a 6.5-million-dollar transfusion of Insull capital for rehabilitation and new equipment. At the peak of its overhaul program the South Shore had 900 men at work laying rail, reballasting, and building new

structures and line relocations. The Illinois Central had just completed the 1500-volt D.C. electrification of its suburban system, so the South Shore scrapped its A.C. equipment, rebuilt its electrical system to conform with the IC's, and negotiated a new trackage rights agreement that permitted South Shore electrics to operate through to Randolph Street station, cutting some 12 minutes from previous running times behind IC steam power. Pullman and other builders turned out 49 new steel cars for the system, among them 15 handsome parlor-observation and dining cars. When South Shore began operation of limited name trains with the new de luxe equipment, the trade periodical *Electric Railway Journal* termed it a "smashing blow to competition." The newly overhauled South Shore did well indeed, for in only one year — between 1926 and 1927 — gross passen-

Eastbound with afternoon commuters in 1955, a Michigan City train pounded past Burnham Yard near Hammond, Ind., where one of the South Shore's three 273-ton "Little Joe" locomotives made up an eastbound freight. WILLIAM D. MIDDLETON.

Late on a rainy evening a train of heavy Pullman interurbans rolled through the streets of East Chicago, Ind. By the mid-'50's South Shore was running its trains around the city on a new bypass route built to trunk line standards. H. A. LIST.

In pre-Insull days the South Shore Line operated its passenger service with unusually large and heavy wooden interurbans constructed by the Niles Car & Manufacturing Company. Three of them headed an eastbound special, which included a Chicago & Alton diner, in a scene at the Michigan City (Ind.) shops. CHICAGO SOUTH SHORE & SOUTH BEND RAILROAD.

221

BEFORE AND AFTER INSULL

Geared for pulling power, a Niles combine of Chicago, Lake Shore & South Bend days, photographed in 1926 at Lake Park siding, was able to make good time with a six-car special of borrowed Illinois Central coaches of the familiar arch-roofed Harriman lines pattern. VAN-ZILLMER COLLECTION.

A quarter of a century later a 24-wheeled "Little Joe," developing better than 5000 horsepower, made even easier work of a 10-car Illinois Central picnic special made up of the selfsame Harriman coaches. The train is seen eastbound at the Pennsylvania overpass east of Gary. VAN-ZILLMER COLLECTION.

Carefully arranged for a 1927 publicity photograph, a Chicago Aurora & Elgin train, made up of four handsome

Pullman steel interurbans and a buffet-parlor car, presented a fine sight. CHARLES A. BROWN COLLECTION.

the point-to-point bookings are probably without rival, and the timings of the hourly trains between leaving the Milwaukee suburban area and entering that of Chicago make the whole service the fastest of its kind in the world."

Such high speed dominance among electric railways has continued even into recent years, when the North Shore has regularly scheduled nearly 2000 miles daily of mile-a-minute or better timings.

Samuel Insull's great public utilities complex weathered the stock market crash of 1929, but financial reverses of the next few years forced the utilities mogul into an increasingly difficult position

From a tower overlooking the junction of CA&E's Aurora and Elgin branches at Wheaton, the line's dispatcher ran his busy railroad. WILLIAM D. MIDDLETON.

Drab platforms were transformed by wet, sticky snow at the CA&E National Street station in Elgin as this cold passenger contemplated the joys of electric heat aboard the coming train. DALE BUFKIN.

and finally, in 1932, the Insull empire collapsed. Thousands of small investors found their savings wiped out and Insull, harassed by intense public feeling, fled to Europe to escape prosecution. Seized aboard a Greek vessel at Istanbul in 1934, Insull was returned to the U. S. for trial on charges of mail fraud, violation of federal bankruptcy laws, and embezzlement, from all of which he eventually won acquittal.

It is interesting to speculate on what might have been had the Insull empire survived the depression. As early as 1925, when Insull's Midland Utilities acquired the bankrupt Chicago, Lake Shore & South Bend, the electric railway trade press gave serious attention to rumors that formation of a single giant Insull interurban extending all the way from Milwaukee to Louisville was in the making. The affairs of the three big Chicago interurbans were closely interlocked following acquisition of control by Midland Utilities. The three lines engaged in joint traffic promotion, and two of them, the North Shore and the South Shore, were headed by the same president, Britton I. Budd. The purchase by the South Shore in 1930 of two new locomotives, designed for either 1500- or 600-volt operation and trolley, pantograph, or third-rail current collection to permit their use on any of the three Chicago lines, hinted at an even closer relationship to come. The extensive Indiana properties of another Insull holding company, Midland United, were actually consolidated in 1930 into the statewide Indiana Railroad System, but no effort was ever made to join it with the Chicago lines. Some initial improvements were made to the Indiana system, but by this time the kind of capital needed to rebuild the lines after the pattern of the Chicago super interurbans was no longer available and the network vanished scarcely 10 years later. I

An Insull interurban that never made the grade was the Chicago & Interurban Traction Company, which got as far as Kankakee with a line that was projected to reach Lafayette, Ind. Ill equipped to compete with the neighboring Illinois Central for through business, and paralleled by Illinois's first paved highway in 1921, the line suffered from a chronic shortage of passengers and fre- *quent financial crises. Electrification of Illinois Central suburban service in 1926, which absorbed most of the company's suburban business, was the last straw, and C&IT promptly folded. Soon after delivery from St. Louis in 1907, car No. 202 of C&IT-predecessor Chicago & Southern Traction stepped out on a special excursion. WILLIAM D. MIDDLETON COLLECTION.*

Way Down South
The South Central States

These Cincinnati interurbans operated on Galveston-Houston Electric Railway's midafternoon Galveston Flyer of the '20's. The cars were blue and white, trimmed in red and gold. Some were provided with extra-fare observation compartments, individual parlor chairs, and heavy carpeting. GEORGE KRAMBLES COLLECTION.

Way Down South

The South Central States

As in the states of the Confederacy along the Atlantic coast, interurban development in the central states of the Deep South was rare. In the entire region, plus the border state of Kentucky, there were to be found barely a half dozen important interurban systems. Farther west, in Oklahoma and Texas, electric line development was more frequent, and the two states boasted several of the most distinguished — and financially successful — properties of the interurban era. Almost every important population center in the two states had at least one interurban; and Dallas, the leading traction center of the entire South Central region, had no less than six radiating routes, operated by three different interurban systems. Interurban development in the two states began relatively late, and continued well after the beginning of the decline and disintegration of traction systems elsewhere in North America. The Northeast Oklahoma Railway, for example, did not electrify its original line until 1921, and continued the construction of new lines until 1923. The ill-considered Texas Interurban Railway, which operated 62 miles of track from Dallas to Terrell and Denton, was not completed until 1924, although total abandonment came only eight years later. The very last interurban to begin operation in North America was the Missouri Pacific's Houston North Shore Railway, which opened in 1927.

The most successful of the two interurbans operating from Nashville, Tenn., was the Nashville Interurban Railway, later the Nashville-Franklin Railway. These two photographs showing a freight train and one of the company's original passenger cars were taken shortly after the line began operation in 1909, and track ballast was still conspicuously absent. Both Photos: Mack Craig Collection.

During the '30's the N-F acquired a few secondhand Cincinnati lightweights such as this one at the Tennessee Central crossing in Nashville in 1940, the last year of passenger operation. Nashville's other interurban, the Nashville-Gallatin Interurban Railway, opened a 24-mile high-speed, 1200-volt route to Gallatin in 1913. The company proposed ultimately to extend its system clear across the state of Kentucky through Bowling Green to Louisville, where a direct connection was to be made with the great traction networks of Ohio, Indiana, and Illinois. Nothing, of course, ever came of the scheme, and the company quietly folded after 19 years of operation. STEPHEN D. MAGUIRE.

The first interurban to adopt the Cincinnati curved-side lightweight car was the Kentucky Traction & Terminal Company, which bought 10 of them in 1922 for service on its four interurban routes radiating from Lexington. The phenomenal success of the lightweights in achieving economies and increasing patronage led to their wide adoption on Midwestern interurbans. One of the original KT&T lightweights, No. 311, was photographed at Frankfort en route to Lexington in 1932. Abandonment came two years later. HOWARD E. JOHNSTON COLLECTION.

Although brightly painted cars such as the Piankasha *provided frequent passenger service to points in the mining district in the Oklahoma-Missouri-Kansas corner, the Northeast Oklahoma Railroad's principal business was the transportation of ore from the lead and zinc mines to the smelters of owner Eagle-Picher Mining & Smelting Company. The last passenger cars quit running in 1940, but freight traffic continues behind diesel power.* GEORGE KRAMBLES COLLECTION.

The 24-mile Pittsburg County Railway began operation between McAlester and Hartshorne, Okla., in 1903. Although frequent passenger service continued almost to the time of abandonment in 1947, carload coal traffic from the mines of eastern Oklahoma brought in most of the company's revenue. Box motor 52 switched a strip mine near Alderson in 1946. PRESTON GEORGE.

The Pittsburg County, in operation for four years when Oklahoma became a state, originally was called the Indian Territory Traction Company. In 1946 car 35 zipped along the highway between Bache and Dow. After 1924, three of these Cincinnati cars operated all passenger schedules. PRESTON GEORGE.

The Sand Springs Line began the replacement of its original heavy wooden equipment with secondhand lightweight cars during the '30's. Here, at Lake Station in 1946, are former Oklahoma Union Railway lightweight No. 69, en route from Tulsa to Sand Springs, and Tulsa-bound No. 62, one of the five lightweights acquired from the Cincinnati, Lawrenceburg & Aurora in 1934. Built by the Cincinnati Car Company in 1918, the CL&A cars were among the first lightweight cars built. GORDON LLOYD.

Former Union Electric Railway No. 75 arrived at Tulsa in 1954 on double track which paralleled the Frisco's Tulsa-Oklahoma City main line. WILLIAM D. MIDDLETON.

236

To augment the motive power available for its growing freight traffic, the Sand Springs purchased two 43-ton locomotives from the Niagara Junction Railway of New York in 1946. One of the radio-equipped steeple-cabs, No. 1006, pulled a cut of tankers from the Sinclair plant at Sand Springs in 1954. WILLIAM D. MIDDLETON.

CHARITY'S INTERURBAN

In 1908 Oklahoma oilman, industrialist, and philanthropist Charles Page began construction of his Sand Springs Home for orphans and widows on 160 acres of onetime camping ground in the former Osage Indian Nation a few miles west of Tulsa. Displeased with the undependable flagstop transportation service afforded by a nearby Katy br. ch line, Page decided to build his own railroad to the Home. Completed in 1911, the Sand Springs Railway was initially operated with McKeen gasoline cars, but was soon electrified. To assure a permanent income for the Home, Page established the City of Sand Springs as a model industrial center and liberally endowed the Home with tracts of industrial land and a multitude of business enterprises, chief among them the Sand Springs Railway itself. A highly successful electric railway, the Sand Springs Line continued passenger operation until 1955, when lack of profits, not a shortage of passengers, brought its abandonment. Diesel freight operation continues.

The Oklahoma Railway's steel combine Lindbergh *was built for the company in 1917 by the St. Louis Car Company. Scrollwork painting and the glass in the lower panels of the baggage door augmented the "de luxe" appearance lent by white tires.* O. F. Lee Collection.

Oklahoma's largest traction system was that of the Oklahoma Railway, which operated interurban routes from Oklahoma City to Guthrie, El Reno, and Norman, as well as street railway lines within the capital city. The company's interurban routes survived through World War II, when they were subjected to a tremendous traffic growth resulting from defense plant activity and installation of a huge Naval Training Station at Norman. The company, which had purchased a considerable number of relatively modern interurbans on the secondhand market during the '30's, sought still more, and old passenger cars which had been converted for freight service were re-equipped for passenger operation.

Arriving at Oklahoma City from Guthrie in 1946 was a former Rockford (Ill.) Public Service Company interurban obtained in 1937. PRESTON GEORGE.

One of the different car types acquired by the Oklahoma Railway from abandoned Midwestern properties during the '30's was this former Fort Wayne-Lima Railroad lightweight shown at the Norman depot in 1938. PRESTON GEORGE.

239

These interurban terminal facilities in Dallas were provided by the local city system. At the terminal in 1948 were red and cream TE RPO car No. 350 and coach No. 326, one of the few all-steel cars operated by the company. GEORGE A. ROUSH.

Shortly before abandonment in 1948 of the largest interurban of the entire South Central region, this Texas Electric interurban traveled to Waco on a special run with a party of railroad enthusiasts. W. P. DONALSON JR.

After Northern Texas Traction was abandoned in 1934, Texas Electric acquired a few of NTT's distinguished arch-roofed wooden cars. Two of them met at George siding between Dallas and Denison in 1940. C. D. SAVAGE.

242

AMERICA'S FASTEST INTERURBAN

Throughout the age of electric traction there were few interurbans that equaled the magnificent Galveston-Houston Electric Railway, which was completed between the two cities in 1911 by the Stone & Webster Engineering Company. Built with what the railway's house organ termed "utter disregard for expense," the line observed exceptionally high standards of engineering and construction. For 34 of its 50 route miles the railway's track was laid on a perfect tangent, and altogether there were only six curves on the entire interurban section, none of them exceeding 2½ degrees. The maximum grade on the entire line was only 0.5 per cent, with the single exception of the approaches to a crossing over the Santa Fe. Private right of way was a full 100 feet wide. Eighty-pound rail, founded in shell ballast, was employed throughout the length of the line. Catenary construction was employed for the overhead system, and power was generated in the company's own modern steam turbine plant. Galveston-Houston traffic proved highly profitable from the start. During the '20's some of the company's splendid standard interurbans were provided with parlor sections, and accelerated schedules were installed. Beginning in 1924 the parlor car limiteds *Galveston Flyer* and *Houston Rocket* were scheduled twice daily between the two cities on 75-minute timings, requiring an average speed of over 40 miles per hour between downtown terminals. It was the fastest electric railway service in America, and for two consecutive years the Galveston-Houston line was awarded the *Electric Traction* interurban speed trophy. During the summer months Houston pleasure seekers rode down to the Gulf on equally rapid schedules aboard the weekday *Pleasure Limited* and the Sun-

day-only *55 Limiteds,* which operated directly to the beach in Galveston. Late in the evening the northbound *Moonbeam* was scheduled for the return home. Special excursion fares were offered, among them such combination tickets as the *Pleasure Limited* round trip which included admission to a bathhouse and the Tokio dance hall, and a tourist outing which included a sight-seeing tour of either Houston or Galveston. For the convenience of dance hall patrons, the last train north in the evening, the *Nighthawk* local, was routed by the Tokio at 12:05 a.m.

This gay drawing appeared in local newspapers at the time of the Galveston-Houston's opening in 1911. HERB WOODS COLLECTION.

A concrete causeway, over 2 miles in length, afforded the interurban, five railroads, and a highway access to Galveston Island. The electric line contributed a quarter of the 2-million-dollar construction cost. During the great hurricane of 1915 portions of both approaches to the causeway were wrecked, stranding a passenger train and a work train as winds approaching 100 miles per hour *swept sheets of water across the structure. The passenger-train conductor and a number of passengers who took refuge in the nearby Causeway Inn lost their lives when the building was swept away at the height of the storm. Two passenger cars and an electric locomotive were eventually recovered from the bay, but a tower car was swept away and never found.* HERB WOODS COLLECTION.

Two four-car special trains loaded a crowd of Galveston-bound pleasure seekers on Texas Avenue in Houston about 1927. The two wooden trailer cars in the foreground had come to the railway second-hand from Pennsylvania's Laurel Line. HERB WOODS COLLECTION.

To Far and Lonely Places
The Mountain States

Against a stern Wasatch Range backdrop, a sleek Bamberger Railroad Bullet raced southward to Salt Lake City in 1950 across the vast and open spaces that characterized the Utah interurban. WILLIAM D. MIDDLETON.

To Far and Lonely Places

The Mountain States

WEST of the Great Plains, in the forbidding reaches of the Rockies and lesser ranges, the electric cars became only an infrequent sight. The transportation needs of the thinly populated Mountain states were already amply accommodated by the great transcontinentals, and the gold and silver diggings of the Colorado Rockies had been thoroughly covered by the narrow gauge frenzy of a few decades earlier. Only in the fertile lowlands of Mormon Utah, where a chain of interurbans extended nearly 200 miles southward from the Idaho border through the Great Salt Lake basin, did traction development approach that of the Midwestern states.

The operations of the omnipresent Anaconda Copper Mining Company of Anaconda, Mont., extended even to a Street Railway Department, whose interurban trains ran to the company's nearby smelter and the town of Opportunity. Almost in the shadow of the great smelter stack, a St. Louis motor car struggled into Anaconda with four trailers of homeward-bound workers in 1950. JOHN STERN.

Aside from portions of major lines of Utah and Washington which extended into the state, Idaho's few miles of electric railway were concentrated in the Boise region. Largest of several Idaho interurbans was the Boise Valley Traction Company that operated westward from Boise to Caldwell over two alternate routes. The company's combine No. 7, shown at the Ballantine way station in 1919, was built by American Car Company in 1911. Smokers were expected to ride in the baggage compartment, which was fitted with folding wooden seats. ALLAN H. BERNER COLLECTION.

Between Denver and D&I Junction, a distance of some 16 miles, Colorado &
Southern deemed it advisable to construct a new and separate line for its electric
subsidiary, but the remainder of the distance to Boulder was operated over either
of two C&S steam lines which had been electrified for the interurban service.
This activity at Louisville about 1910 indicates the close integration of D&I

*schedules with those of the parent C&S. The two interurban cars, en route to
and from Denver, are meeting the C&S's Lafayette Stub local, powered by
4-4-0 No. 303. The dual-gauge track was employed for mixed-gauge freights transporting ore concentrates from the Denver, Boulder & Western interchange at
Boulder to the smelter in Denver.* BOULDER HISTORICAL SOCIETY.

An interurban with an ambitious past was the Denver & Intermountain, which extended west from Denver to Leyden and Golden. Originally built by David Moffat as the narrow-gauge Denver & Northwestern, the line was once possessed of plans to cross the Continental Divide to Grand Lake, a popular resort near what is now the Rocky Mountain National Park. Instead, Moffat built his Denver & Salt Lake line through Corona Pass and Denver & Northwestern became an interurban affiliate of the Denver Tramways. Later on, a second, more direct route to Golden was provided when the Tramways took over and electrified a standard-gauge steam line. Between Arvada and the Leyden Mine the company operated a rare stretch of dual-gauge electric track.

This D&IM narrow-gauge interurban, a converted city car, was running at a respectable 30 miles per hour near Arvada, Colo., in 1948 on dual-gauge track of the old Denver & Northwestern, which was parallel to the rails of D&RGW's Moffat-built transcontinental. A onetime funeral car which transported mourners while the coffin rode in a four-wheel trailer behind, car .03 retained its black leather upholstery to the end. For reasons now obscure, Denver & Intermountain applied decimal numbers to its narrow-gauge interurbans. ROSS B. GRENARD JR.

Lava-capped North Table Mountain provided a scenic background as a standard-gauge D&IM interurban rolled eastward out of Golden, Colo., in 1949, a year before abandonment. JOHN STERN.

Trailing a former Colorado & Southern combine which served as a caboose, a pair of D&IM narrow-gauge steeple-cab locomotives ran M.U. near Leyden in 1950. The unusual engines were leased from Denver Tramways. Freight equipment was painted a simple black, but passenger cars were the same golden yellow as DT streetcars. ROSS B. GRENARD JR.

Arriving from Colorado Springs, a deck-roofed Colorado Springs & Interurban car headed through the streets of Manitou Springs, past the terminal where passengers transferred to the cog railroad that scaled nearby Pikes Peak. Rambling resort hotels, such as the one seen in the background, accommodated passengers who came to partake of the health-giving benefits of the mineral springs. FROM RAILROAD MAGAZINE.

256

The Highest Interurban

The gold mining camps of the mountainous Cripple Creek district, the scene of Colorado's last great mining boom, were linked by the rails of an early U. S. interurban, the Cripple Creek District Railway, that began service between Cripple Creek and nearby Victor early in 1898. This original "High Line" between the two points traversed an extremely mountainous area, affording what was perhaps the most spectacular interurban ride available in North America. The electric cars negotiated severe grades, which reached a maximum of 7.5 per cent up Poverty Gulch, and climbed to an elevation of near-ly 2 miles above sea level at Midway, making the line easily the highest electric railway in all of North America. A year after its opening the electric line was purchased by the new Colorado Springs & Cripple Creek District Railway and the latter constructed a second, shorter "Low Line" between Cripple Creek and Victor in 1901. During the Cripple Creek boom times the interurban transported such later distinguished personages as Bernard Baruch, Jack Dempsey, Tom Mix, and "Texas" Guinan; and the famous vaudeville team of Gallagher and Shean first tried out their routines for passengers on the mountain interurban, on which they worked as motorman and conductor.

About 1900, Cripple Creek District Railway's car No. 1, the Evelyn, *a Barney & Smith motor car, stopped at Midway en route from Cripple Creek to Victor. Barely visible to the south are the peaks of the Sangre de Cristo range.* EDDIE WIWATOWSKI COLLECTION.

The interurban's route and the irregular topography of the Cripple Creek District are shown in some-what exaggerated fashion in this early promoter's view. TRAINS COLLECTION.

Controlled by the Carlton interests, the Grand River Valley Railroad, which extended 16 miles from Grand Junction, Colo., to Fruita, was once scheduled to become a part of the Colorado Midland's projected western extension to Salt Lake City. Instead, following World War I, *the Midland earned the unfortunate distinction of being the largest single abandonment in railroad history, and the "Fruit Belt Route" continued to the end of its existence in relative obscurity. Combine No. 51 is seen in Grand Junction.* FRED FELLOW COLLECTION.

South from Salt Lake City into the Utah Valley, during the final years of the great electric railway boom, Boston mining and railroad tycoon Walter C. Orem pushed the rails of his high grade Salt Lake & Utah Railroad. Among the contractors who built the "Orem Road" was Mrs. W. M. Smith, a rather remarkable lady who was claimed to be the only woman railroad contractor in the world. Reputed to be worth a half million dollars, Mrs. Smith had built branches for Union Pacific and Southern Pacific and a portion of the Western Pacific main line before taking the Salt Lake & Utah job. Working with Mrs. Smith on the interurban was her daughter Irene, who was learning the business. Said Mrs. Smith, who bossed her own track gangs, "There is good money in the contracting business and I don't see why a woman shouldn't succeed in it as well as a man. Certainly I can look along a rail and see if it is laid straight. If it isn't I make the men take it up and fix it."

In company with their steam railroad contemporaries, interurban proprietors considered the monumental passenger terminal, befitting the importance and substantial character of their lines, a necessary adjunct to the passenger business. Among the most imposing of such structures was the great terminal erected in 1923 on Salt Lake City's Temple Square by Utah interurban tycoons Simon Bamberger and W. C. Orem for the joint use of their Bamberger Railroad and Salt Lake & Utah electric cars. FRED FELLOW COLLECTION.

In common with most western interurbans, Salt Lake & Utah operated an extensive freight business, interchanging traffic with its interurban and steam railroad connections alike. Steeple-cab locomotive No. 52, shown with a tonnage train of coal from the line's Utah Railway connection at Provo, was a 1922 product of the company shops at Payson. Rebuilt from the remains of an earlier locomotive demolished in a head-on collision with a steam locomotive, No. 52 met a similar fate 20 years later when it was completely wrecked in another "cornfield meet," an event that occurred altogether too frequently in SL&U history. FRED FELLOW COLLECTION.

Marble and tile finishes were lavishly employed in the public rooms of the Salt Lake terminal, which cost $300,000. Space was provided for a restaurant, stores, and other facilities befitting an important passenger terminal, as well as office spaces for both companies. A Salt Lake & Utah train unloaded at the platforms in the rear of the terminal. FRED FELLOW COLLECTION.

SALT LAKE & UTAH

752

THROUGH DAILY
PACKAGE CAR SERV
FROM ALL
EASTERN POIN

Only two years after completion of the Orem Road, these SL&U trains met on multiple track not far from Salt Lake City. FRED FELLOW COLLECTION.

265

In the Far West
The Pacific States

Luxurious Oregon Electric rolling stock such as that shown in this verdant Willamette Valley scene, combined with lower fares and superior schedules, diverted large numbers of passengers from rival Southern Pacific's steam trains. For only 35 cents extra passengers could ride in the opulent parlor-buffet-observation car Sacajawea, or the identical Champoeg, delivered in 1910 by the Niles Car works. Light lunches and spirituous refreshments were dispensed from the car's miniature buffet. UNIVERSITY OF OREGON LIBRARY.

In the Far West

The Pacific States

IN the states of the Pacific Coast grew some of the finest traction properties of the interurban era. Except in the matter of their motive power, the traction systems of the Far West frequently resembled steam railroads more than they did their electric contemporaries of the Midwest and East. Construction standards were usually high, steam railroad operating rules were frequently observed, and many of the Western electrics engaged in heavy freight business from their very beginning, often functioning essentially as short line feeders to the steam systems. Such attributes served them well, for long after the decline of interurban passenger business and electric traction many of the Far West interurbans continued to perform a useful service as freight-only carriers.

19 ORDERS AND MOTORNEERS

A dominant force in electric interurban development in the Puget Sound region was Boston's Stone & Webster Engineering Company. The earliest of the Stone & Webster interurbans was the splendidly engineered third-rail Puget Sound Electric Railway opened in 1902 between Seattle and Tacoma. By 1907, when Stone & Webster's Seattle-Everett Traction Company was reaching northward from Seattle and construction forces were ready to move south

from Bellingham, company executive C. D. Wyman was able to speak confidently of plans for a Stone & Webster traction empire that would soon stretch from the International Boundary south to Olympia and Chehalis, and perhaps eventually to the Grays Harbor country and Portland. By 1913 Stone & Webster's Pacific Northwest Traction Company was operating two separate divisions, between Seattle and Everett and between Mount Vernon and Bellingham, with construction of the 30-mile missing link scheduled for the "near future." To the north the British Columbia Electric Railway was ready with plans for a new line into Bellingham that would have completed an unbroken interurban route between Seattle and Vancouver. Temporarily postponed during World War I, neither project ever materialized, and interurban construction south of Tacoma never amounted to more than a few short branches to nearby towns.

With trolley rope bowed in the breeze, a Puget Sound Electric Railway Seattle-Tacoma local raced along near Fife on a stretch of track where the transition from overhead to third-rail power collection was made. GENERAL RAILWAY SIGNAL COMPANY.

274

Led by a combine laden with an impressive variety of front-end accessories, a three-car Puget Sound Electric Seattle Limited paused near Kent in 1915. Operating in strict accordance with steam railroad rules, PSE crews picked up "19" orders and clearances on the fly with traditional order hoops, and the motorman went by the hybrid title of "motorneer." A never fully explained PSE phenomenon was the tendency of its third rail to travel — one stretch of third rail moved over 60 feet in the space of only a few years — and PSE maintenance crews were forever removing or adding pieces of third rail. H. A. HILL COLLECTION.

Street traffic magically melted in the path of PSE's formidable interurbans. This Tacoma Limited was all set to rumble off from Seattle in 1924. WASHINGTON STATE HISTORICAL SOCIETY, FROM ROBERT S. WILSON.

Virtual twins of the handsome cars that plied Stone & Webster's Texas interurban properties, a half dozen wooden Niles interurbans were standard equipment for Pacific Northwest Traction's Seattle-Everett Southern Division from 1910 until abandonment nearly 30 years later. No. 54 was fresh from the Ohio builder's plant when this view was recorded. WASHINGTON STATE HISTORICAL SOCIETY, FROM ROBERT S. WILSON.

Grown shabby in their last years in the damp coastal air, these two North Coast Lines interurbans met at Ronald siding on the Seattle-Everett line shortly before abandonment in 1939. STUART B. HERTZ.

Operating eastward to Coeur d'Alene, Ida., and south to Colfax, Wash., and Moscow, Ida., the interurbans of the Inland Empire System traversed the rich agricultural and forest lands of the Columbia Plateau. In the early years the electric cars did a brisk picnic business out of Spokane to nearby lakes in Washington and Idaho, and during the summers a special "Campers' Limited Train" operated between Spokane and Hayden Lake. This holiday crowd jammed a Coeur d'Alene train at the big Spokane terminal not too many years after the line's 1903 opening. LeRoy O. KING JR. COLLECTION.

Inland Empire luxury travel was provided by two Brill parlor-observation cars. The Shoshone, shown here, operated over the Coeur d'Alene line, while the Kootenai handled extra-fare trade on the Moscow line. The company's crack Shoshone Flyer covered the 32 miles to Coeur d'Alene in an even hour, making connections with the Coeur d'Alene Lake steamers of the Red Collar Steamboat Company for widespread western Idaho points. LeRoy O. King Jr. Collection.

Brill-built combine 8 and trailers 61 and 62 rested at Coeur d'Alene in 1908. The trailers had observation platforms, and trolleys for standby lighting. LeRoy O. King Jr. Collection.

Four cars of excursionists prepared to venture down the Liberty Lake branch, while a Coeur d'Alene local paused on freshly ballasted mainline double track at Liberty Lake Junction. After an involved series of changes in organization and corporate title, the Inland Empire System became a Great Northern subsidiary in 1927, and was eventually merged with the steam road. GN freights still traverse the one-time interurban main lines, but the electric cars are long gone. LeRoy O. King Jr. Collection.

In true Western railroad fashion, white flags and an "X-6" train indicator designated an extra train of Brill cars bound out of Spokane on Washington Water Power Company's 17-mile line to Medical Lake. Short lived (1906-1921) because of poor patronage, this route and a branch to Cheney were nevertheless distinguished for their open-platform observation cars and an interesting automatic block system with train stop. Mechanically linked to upper quadrant semaphores, an arm extending from the mast in the stop position would break a glass tube on the car roof, exhausting the brake line and applying the brakes. O. F. LEE COLLECTION.

A lonely survivor of Washington's interurban era is the Yakima Valley Transportation Company, which still does a modest freight business. Steeple-cab locomotive No. 298 headed for the Union Pacific interchange in 1958 with a single reefer from a packing shed near Yakima. In passenger-carrying days the company's two short lines out of Yakima were serviced by two wooden Niles interurbans that, although compact in their dimensions, were constructed to the classic pattern. FRED MATTHEWS.

On rails which once led all the way to Estacada, a Portland Traction utilitarian-pattern wooden interurban, constructed by the company shops in 1910, rolled through a forested countryside near Gresham about 1952. AL HAIJ.

In its declining years Portland Traction operated a collection of secondhand rolling stock of widespread origins. Lightweight car 4007, shown on the Bellrose line in 1952, had previously operated on New York's Albany Southern and Fonda, Johnstown & Gloversville lines. WILLIAM C. DOWNEY JR.

To Forest and River

Generally regarded as the first true interurban line, the Portland Traction Company's Oregon City line very nearly survived long enough to become the last as well. In their earlier years the Portland electric cars did a lively excursion business. Picnickers rode the cars to Canemah Park above the falls of the Willamette, south of Oregon City, and the unhurried among them took advantage of round trip tickets offered jointly by the interurban and the steamship company that provided a rival service on the Willamette River. Long trains of open trailers pulled by electric locomotives operated between Portland and the big Oaks amusement park, and those who wanted to really get away from the uproar of the city rode all the way to Estacada, far up the Clackamas River on the interurban's Springwater Division, where the company provided a park and a hotel in a tranquil setting.

Portland Traction No. 4001 — photographed in 1957 on the Clackamas River bridge not far from the onetime grounds of the Gladstone Chautauqua, a source of considerable traffic for the electric cars in earlier years — originally plied Indiana Railroad rails. EDWARD S. MILLER.

Bursting forth from the east portal of SN's tunnel, a Comet *headed by Holman-built combine 1006 gathered speed for the downhill ride to tidewater.* ARTHUR R. ALTER.

Long after first-class schedules disappeared from the Sacramento Northern time-card, freight tonnage continued to roll through the canyons. In 1951 this eight-car freight crept up the hill from Oakland, propelled by a big Baldwin-Westinghouse steeple-cab, with an identical machine shoving mightily behind the caboose. Even though they represented Sacramento Northern's heaviest electric motive power, these 68-ton locomotives were rated at only 400 tons on the formidable track through the canyon. WILLIAM D. MIDDLETON.

To Sea by Interurban

The waters of Suisun Bay presented a natural obstacle in the path of Oakland, Antioch & Eastern's "short line" to Sacramento. To cross it company engineers planned a 10,000-foot bridge, 70 feet above high water at the navigable part of the stream, estimated to cost 1.5 million dollars. Preliminary work was actually under way when the project was postponed due to unsettled business conditions resulting from the outbreak of World War I, and the car ferry that was to have been only a temporary expedient became a permanent feature of the line. The delay occasioned by ferrying trains across the Bay was not serious during the early days of OA&E passenger operation, for the company's chief competitor for San Francisco-Sacramento traffic—Southern Pacific — likewise was forced to ferry its trains across the Bay. But in 1930 Southern Pacific completed its great Martinez-Benicia bridge, and Sacramento Northern was thereafter placed at a severe disadvantage.

In 1951 one of SN's black and orange striped motors eased out toward the apron at Mallard, pushing a cut of cars onto the ferry Ramon. WILLIAM D. MIDDLETON.

From 1914, a year after the Suisun Bay car ferry crossing was opened, until its abandonment in 1954, SN trains were shuttled across the half mile of open water and tricky currents by the ferry Ramon, *a steel-hulled vessel powered by a remarkable 50-ton, 600-horsepower distillate-fueled engine which represented the largest electric-ignition, internal-combustion engine ever constructed.* ARTHUR R. ALTER.

With the train safely stowed, the Ramon *headed across the Sacramento River. In the days of passenger service, coffee and doughnuts were served during the voyage in a small lunchroom on the vessel.* WILLIAM D. MIDDLETON.

The flatland running that carried Sacramento Northern trains from the Suisun Bay ferry to Sacramento was broken by the 2-mile Lisbon trestle which crossed the Yolo Basin. Such was the quality

of this 1500-volt, catenary-equipped speedway that the Comet *was able to cover 47 miles from the ferry to Sacramento Union Station at an average speed of 50 miles per hour.* FRED FELLOW.

One leg of the SN turning wye in Woodland was under the station arches. Train 47 was heading for a connection with the westbound Comet. B. H. WARD.

294

Sacramento Northern passengers to Woodland enjoyed the facilities of a mission-style structure that was without question one of the handsomest of all interurban stations. The 18-mile Sacramento-Woodland branch was as far as predecessor Northern Electric ever got with plans for its own route to San Francisco, conceived at a time when Oakland, Antioch & Eastern, later to become part of the same Sacramento Northern, was a fierce rival. WESTERN PACIFIC RAILROAD.

This solid-tired, chain-driven "auto bus" transported passengers between the third-rail Northern Electric's East Gridley station and nearby Gridley. At the time of its completion in 1913 NE had the longest third-rail interurban line in the United States. The earliest portions of the line were constructed with overhead trolley wire, but so successful was the later adoption of the third-rail system that the trolley wire was replaced, resulting, in one case, in the resignation en masse of the section gang along the affected stretch of track. WESTERN PACIFIC RAILROAD.

Early in 1939 Sacramento Northern trains, which had previously terminated on the Key Route ferry pier out in the Bay, began operating across the new Bay Bridge into East Bay Terminal in downtown San Francisco. The expected traffic boom failed to materialize and within two and a half years SN ended its interurban passenger business. Few were on hand in August 1940 when train No. 10 departed from East Bay Terminal on the last through trip to Sacramento. ARTHUR R. ALTER, AL HAIJ COLLECTION.

Between runs at the Northbrae terminal of the "F" line, this Key unit waited on track which was until 1941 a part of Southern Pacific's rival East Bay electrification. After SP abandoned its operation, Key System trains began service over several stretches of former SP track. DONALD SIMS.

During earlier years the Key Route offered high-class electric traction service to San Francisco's East Bay cities with commodious wooden cars of typical interurban pattern, one of which won a first prize at the 1904 Louisiana Purchase Exposition, and thereafter displayed a bronze plaque to that effect. Chefs on the big orange Key ferries that plied between the company's Oakland Pier terminal and San Francisco served up such specialties as "Key Route Corned Beef Hash," and stringed orchestras provided Sunday entertainment. Altogether it was a most satisfactory method of commutation. In preparation for through service to San Francisco over the new Bay Bridge which replaced the ferries in 1939, the Key System designed an unusual type of articulated unit. In this 1951 photograph an inbound Bethlehem-built unit from the Berkeley "F" line headed for the Bay Bridge, dipping under the Southern Pacific main line and a highway approach to the bridge in a three-level montage of electric, steam, and internal combustion transport. WILLIAM D. MIDDLETON.

A Key System predecessor, California Railway, bought masterfully painted car 11 from Carter Brothers of Newark, Calif., in 1896. Its proportions and massive clerestory indicate a greater familiarity with steam car construction than with electric car building on the part of the local builder. INDUSTRIAL PHOTO SERVICE.

297

In 1939 NWP's car from Manor waited at San Anselmo station for the connecting train from San Rafael. The owl-faced cars ran south to the ferry terminal at Sausalito on this former narrow-gauge trackage. ARTHUR R. ALTER, AL HAIJ COLLECTION.

NORTH FROM THE GOLDEN GATE

From 1903 until 1941, commuters from the Marin peninsula north of San Francisco rode down to the ferries at Sausalito on the first third-rail electric line in California. Originally narrow gauge and operated with steam motive power, the North Pacific Railroad was renamed North Shore Railroad when it was electrified in 1903. The Northwestern Pacific Railroad took over operations in 1907. Some of the first cars built for the railroad in 1902 — open platform wooden coaches — were outfitted with electrical equipment and operated right to the end of service as rush hour extras. Soon after Southern Pacific took control of the NWP in 1929, 19 steel and aluminum interurbans were put into service. Almost identical in dimensions and appearance to cars built before World War I for SP's East Bay electrification, the 55-ton cars incorporated many other improvements in addition to the use of aluminum in the bodies. Completion of the Golden Gate Bridge and through bus service to San Francisco doomed interurban service, but the big orange cars went south to the Pacific Electric where many of them operated in Long Beach service until early 1961. ⏚

Northbound at Alto, five big orange cars of the NWP's extra "school train" carried Tamalpais High School students home to Ross Valley suburban towns. These 72-foot cars, built in 1929 and 1930 by St. Louis Car Company, had no doors on their semi-enclosed platforms. Sliding screen gates closed the double-width vestibule steps. STEPHEN D. MAGUIRE.

The longevity of the electric car was ably demonstrated by the vehicles which inaugurated service on the United Railroads of San Francisco's San Mateo interurban line in 1904 and were still around for last-day festivities in 1949. One of them raced southward down the peninsula at Lomita Park in 1947, by which time the line had long since become part of the San Francisco Municipal Railways. ARTHUR R. ALTER, AL HAIJ COLLECTION.

These steel passenger cars of the San Francisco & Napa Valley Railroad borrowed gas-electric body styling, and were noteworthy as the last interurbans constructed (in 1933) before depression and the decline of the electric railways almost entirely wiped out the carbuilding industry. A serious equipment shortage resulting from a carbarn fire, rather than any sudden increase in traffic, necessitated the purchase of these cars. Only five years later the company's Napa Valley passenger service between Calistoga and Vallejo was ended. GEORGE KRAMBLES COLLECTION.

The Central California Traction Company, which began operation between Stockton and Lodi in 1907, was an early user of the 1200-volt D.C. power system and was the first electric line to employ 1200-volt third-rail power distribution. These two wooden cars were part of a six-car order constructed by the Holman Car Company of San Francisco in 1910 to operate passenger schedules over the company's newly completed extension to Sacramento. Ready to roll northward on the 53-mile trip to the state capital, they were near the docks in Stockton, where a connection was made with overnight San Joaquin River steamers from San Francisco. GEORGE KRAMBLES COLLECTION.

302

Red Cars in the Southland
Pacific Electric Railway

Six cars of pleasure-bent Southern Californians raced southward over the four-track main line of Pacific Electric's Southern District, bound for the docks at Wilmington and the connecting steamer to Avalon in the carefree days before World War II. The 1200-class steel interurbans were PE's fastest and finest cars. DONALD DUKE COLLECTION.

Red Cars in the Southland

Pacific Electric Railway

GREAT RED TRAINS of heavy steel interurbans, their air whistles shrieking hoarsely for road crossings, hurtled at mile-a-minute speeds down the inner rails of the Pacific Electric's four-track steel boulevards, overtaking mundane locals that skipped from stop to stop on the outer tracks. Multiple-unit trains of suburban electric cars worried their way through the congested boulevards of Hollywood and then, like big red snakes, darted into the subway that sped their way to downtown Los Angeles. Polished parlor-observation cars with guide-lecturers transported breathless tourists over the length and breadth of a trolley empire of over a thousand miles that ranged from the snow-capped peaks of the San Gabriel Mountains to citrus groves, vineyards, and endless Pacific beaches. Sumptuously furnished private cars glided along the rails bearing high officials on their errands of importance. In a time before Southern California became the world's most automobile-oriented society almost everyone rode Pacific Electric's "big red cars" to the beaches, mountains, race tracks, and other pleasure spots of the Southland, as well as to and from their daily work.

Pacific Electric freight trains rumbled in every direction across the red car network behind electric, steam, and later, diesel motive power, and a comprehensive box motor service delivered package freight, express, and mail to every extremity of the system. Full-fledged Railway Post Office cars raced imperiously along the more important routes.

"The World's Greatest Interurban Railway" was what they labeled this Los Angeles-centered traction colossus assembled under Southern Pacific control in the Great Merger of 1911. And even in a region prone to generous superlatives and overstatement, the title was one that could hardly be disputed, for the Pacific Electric Railway simply encompassed more miles of track, operated more cars, and hauled more passengers and freight than any other interurban. It has been estimated that nearly 10 per cent of the U. S. interurban investment was represented by this one system.

In the geographic extent of its interurban services Los Angeles was eclipsed by Indianapolis, but in sheer numbers of passengers PE easily made Los Angeles America's leading interurban center. In 1914, for example, a total of 1626 trains, made up of 3262 cars, entered or left Los Angeles daily over PE's three operating districts.

Pacific Electric was largely the creation of Henry E. Huntington, wealthy heir and nephew of Collis P. Huntington, one of the Southern Pacific's "Big Four." Arriving on the Southern California scene in 1898 with a broad background of experience on Southern Pacific and other family railroad properties, Huntington purchased a pioneer Los Angeles-Pasadena interurban and within 10 years parlayed it into a traction giant that reached out from Los Angeles to San Pedro, Long Beach, Newport Beach, Santa Ana, Glendora, and Glendale.

Huntington's electric railway activities were closely allied with his extensive real estate interests, and the advance of the red cars into new territory was carefully co-ordinated with the operations of his Pacific Electric Land Company. Southern California was then enjoying a period of unparalleled growth and prosperity, and Huntington profited handsomely from his dual interests.

Retiring from active management of his electric railway interests in 1910, Huntington sold out to Southern Pacific which a year later merged PE with other Southern California traction properties into the greatest electric railway system in history. New construction continued until 1914 when the last major Pacific Electric line, a high-speed route to San Bernardino, was opened.

Had the favorable climate for interurban development lasted a few years longer than it did, Pacific Electric might have grown to even greater dimensions. As early as 1906 the "Huntington syndicate"

The first interurban route of what was to become the world's greatest traction system was created when Gen. Moses H. Sherman and Eli P. Clark connected two local lines with this bridge across the Arroyo Seco and inaugurated electric car service between Los Angeles and Pasadena in 1895. This is the first car. HISTORICAL COLLECTIONS, SECURITY FIRST NATIONAL BANK, LOS ANGELES.

After retirement from business affairs Henry E. Huntington, who made a fortune from his Southern California real estate and electric railway activities, devoted his last years and his fortune to the distinguished library and art gallery at San Marino which bears his name. HENRY E. HUNTINGTON LIBRARY AND ART GALLERY.

Both the Sixth and Main Street terminal building and the San Pedro interurban line were new when this photograph was taken about 1906. No. 279, scraping the pavement as it heeled into the terminal, was one of 130 semi-open cars delivered by the St. Louis Car Company between 1902 and 1906. The sidewalk semaphores and track switches were operated from the raised bay-window office to expedite heavy two-way movements in this then stub terminal, and to protect narrow-gauge city cars which also used Main Street's three-rail trackage. AL HAIJ COLLECTION.

All dressed up for a day's outing, a crowd of excursionists unloaded from a Pasadena & Pacific train at Santa Monica around the turn of the century. The P&P was constructed with such rapidity by promoters Gen. Moses H. Sherman and Eli P. Clark that some called it another "Sherman's March to the Sea." Later known as the Los Angeles Pacific, the company came under Southern Pacific control in 1906 and became part of Pacific Electric in the 1911 merger. HISTORICAL COLLECTIONS, SECURITY FIRST NATIONAL BANK, LOS ANGELES.

was believed to be backing a group which proposed to build a Los Angeles-San Diego electric line along the coast, and Huntington's name was associated with grandiose plans for a high-speed electric line through the San Joaquin Valley which would extend all the way to San Francisco. Still other proposals envisioned lines to Santa Barbara via San Fernando, and from Santa Monica to Ventura.

Then as now, Southern California was a favored vacation spot, and Pacific Electric developed the tourist excursion business into a fine art. The most popular of PE's inexpensive electric tours of the Southland was the "Balloon Route Trolley Trip" originated by Los Angeles Pacific and continued by PE after the 1911 merger. Tourists flocked aboard the "palatial observation cars" of the Balloon Route specials by the thousands. On one record day 18 carloads of excursionists were transported on the tour, and in 1909 an average of 10,000 monthly rode the trip during the tourist season. First stop on the "101 miles for 100 cents" tour was the Hollywood Boulevard home and gallery of renowned French floral artist Paul de Longpré, where this tour party posed self-consciously early in the century. HISTORICAL COLLECTIONS, SECURITY FIRST NATIONAL BANK, LOS ANGELES.

Midway through the Balloon Route all-day outing, the excursion cars stopped at the Playa del Rey Pavilion, where a fish dinner was served. Boat rides on the lagoon and skating on a rink were also possible during the stopover. Freshly rebuilt for regular service on the Balloon Route trip, Los Angeles Pacific cars 900 and 901 were photographed at Playa del Rey with a group about 1910. AL HAIJ COLLECTION.

307

De luxe excursion car 023 transported Southland tourists on the "Old Mission Trolley Trip" to San Gabriel Mission, Pasadena, Bush Gardens, and the Cawston Ostrich Farm, all for a dollar. AL HAIJ COLLECTION.

THE GREATEST MOUNTAIN TROLLEY TRIP

Among the greatest of Southern California's tourist attractions of the early 20th century was Pacific Electric's amazing trolley ride up the slopes of the Sierra Madre to Mount Lowe, named for Prof. Thaddeus S. C. Lowe, who built the railway in 1893. In this rare photograph Professor Lowe (with field glasses) and two ladies are studiously ignoring construction progress in the vicinity of the Cape of Good Hope on the Alpine Division. CHARLES S. LAWRENCE.

Throughout most of its existence as a passenger interurban PE was subdivided into three major districts, each virtually a complete interurban system in itself. Largest of them was the Northern District, operating north and east from Los Angeles, which included no less than 400 miles of track and 33 separate routes. Main artery of the PE north was a great four-track right of way along Huntington Drive that carried trains to Pasadena and other San Gabriel Valley points, and within the district's jurisdiction were such diverse operations as the Great Cable Incline and narrow-gauge Alpine Division that elevated excursionists to the scenic heights of Mount Lowe, and the 48-mile, 1200-volt San Bernardino route that was PE's longest and fastest line.

At the top of the standard-gauge Mount Lowe interurban line, the Great Cable Incline (designed by Andrew S. Hallidie, who engineered San Francisco's early cable railways) carried passengers up to the Alpine Division's narrow-gauge trolleys. At this level were a hotel and dance pavilion; at the top of the incline stood Echo Mountain House, an observatory, and a 3-million-candlepower searchlight said to be visible from 150 miles at sea. HISTORICAL COLLECTIONS, SECURITY FIRST NATIONAL BANK, LOS ANGELES.

Above Echo Mountain, the Alpine Division wound through 127 curves and crossed 18 trestles to reach Mount Lowe Springs, just 1100 feet below the summit. This is Circular Bridge, with a fearless group posing in skeletal car 9. In the background is the trolley line down to the summit of the incline. ELDON M. NEFF.

The Western District, made up largely of the lines of the premerger Los Angeles Pacific Company, operated 260 miles of track and 12 lines which served a vast area to the west of Los Angeles, and included among its destinations Hollywood, Beverly Hills, Glendale, Burbank, the San Fernando Valley, and the beaches at Santa Monica, Venice, and Redondo.

The Southern District, with 400 miles of track and 17 lines under its supervision, reached south from Los Angeles to the busy harbors of Long Beach and San Pedro, southeast along Pacific beaches to the Newport and Balboa resorts and through the orange groves to Santa Ana, and southwest to the El Segundo oil fields and Redondo Beach.

The Alpine Division was carved out of solid granite for its entire 4-mile length, and its grade sometimes exceeded 7 per cent. A dusting of snow was not entirely unusual at this 5000-foot altitude, making a unique ride even more spectacular for Southern California tourists. PE purchased the line in 1902, and double-truck car 123 replaced the original Mount Lowe cars in 1906. CHARLES S. LAWRENCE.

In vivid contrast to the snow scene on page 310 is this view of PE interurban No. 1044 tarrying along the beach south of Long Beach on the way to the seaside resorts of Newport and Balboa. Such diverse scenes were only a few hours apart on the "big red cars." DONALD DUKE COLLECTION.

311

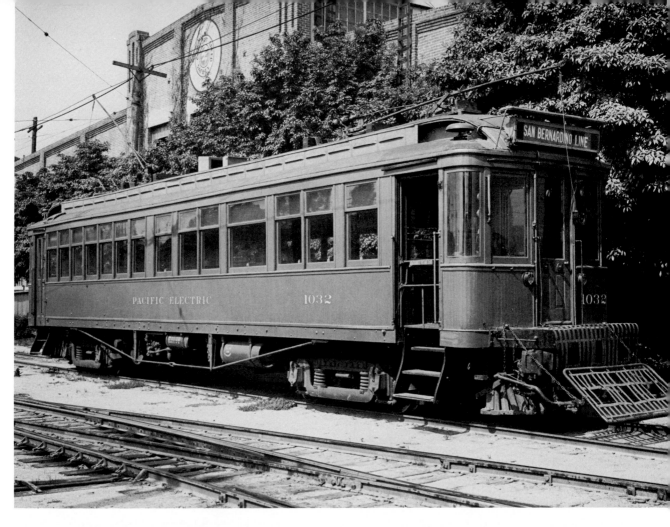

An almost universal feature of the hundreds of wooden interurban cars operated by Pacific Electric was a generous expanse of front-end glass, which extended clear around the corners in an early version of the "wraparound" windshield. Exceptional among these spacious wooden chariots were the cars of PE's 1000 class, which arrived from the Newark (O.) works of the Jewett Car Company on their own wheels in 1913. A year later they were featured participants in the gala celebration and parade attended by 20,000 which marked the opening of PE's celebrated San Bernardino line. WILLIAM D. MIDDLETON COLLECTION.

Slated with other PE wooden cars for scrapping on the eve of World War II, the 1000's were reprieved to meet the severe test of record PE passenger loads. These five jam-packed 1000's hurtled down multiple track to Long Beach in 1942. The Long Beach line, the last PE interurban line to operate, was abandoned April 1, 1961. H. L. KELSO.

In 1929, when PE converted six cars purchased from the SP Oregon lines into reserved-seat parlor cars, extra-fare passengers on boat trains to Los Angeles Harbor enjoyed the questionable privilege of viewing each other's knees, rather than the scenery. The service didn't last long, thanks to the depression. IRA L. SWETT — MAGNA COLLECTION.

During the final years of its passenger operation PE acquired from abandoned interurban properties in the San Francisco Bay Area a fleet of owl-faced electric cars of prodigious dimensions. Over 72 feet in length, and weighing up to 61 tons, the big cars provided seats for 80 passengers after remodeling and refurbishing by the company's Torrance shops in 1947. Led by combine No. 498, a four-car special train of former Southern Pacific Oakland-Berkeley-Alameda suburban cars rolled northward to Los Angeles off the San Pedro line at Dominguez Junction. DONALD DUKE.

The great length of these massive cars is evidenced in this broadside view of No. 312 — an aluminum-bodied car that once rolled down to the Golden Gate on Marin County rails of the Northwestern Pacific — entering the Los Angeles elevated terminal. WILLIAM D. MIDDLETON.

For services more suburban than interurban in character, Pacific Electric had 160 cars of the "Hollywood" type, so called for their long association with the lines to the film capital. In 1950 No. 752 burst from the gloom of the mile-long subway into bright Southern California sunshine on the long journey to the San Fernando Valley. These low-floor, center-door cars, built between 1922 and 1928, were unusually successful. WILLIAM D. MIDDLETON.

*Deadheading into Subway Terminal for rush-hour service on the Glendale-Bur-
bank line, a two-car train of Hollywoods snaked its way out of Toluca Yard in
1954. Some of these cars now operate in Argentina (see page 367).*
WILLIAM D. MIDDLETON.

318

Shortly before World War II Pullman-Standard delivered 30 PCC-type streamliners, modified for double-end, multiple-unit operation, for service on PE's Glendale-Burbank route, which was thereupon restored to all-rail operation after a highly unsatisfactory experiment with joint bus-rail service. In 1950, 5026 crossed the high Fletcher Drive trestle on the climb over Elysian Hills on the way from Glendale to Los Angeles. WILLIAM D. MIDDLETON.

An outbound Edendale-Atwater local dropped downgrade from the hills into the Los Angeles River valley at Montesano in 1954. In 1959 the 30 PCC's joined two previous PE car types on Argentina's Ferrocarril Nacional General Urquiza at Buenos Aires. WILLIAM D. MIDDLETON.

PE trains to San Pedro mingled intimately with harbor traffic. Momentarily seen from the bridge of a tanker tied up in the San Pedro Harbor's West Basin, an interurban train from Los Angeles was about to cross the huge SP bascule bridge that separated the basin from the remainder of the harbor. H. L. KELSO.

320

The intense activity characteristic of Pacific Electric's four-track steel boulevard leading south from Los Angeles is evident in this scene near Watts. At left, a freight train had just entered the line from Graham Freight Yard. On the right, a northbound drag of oil tankers struggling upgrade was being passed by a fast-moving passenger train inbound from San Pedro. WILLIAM K. BARHAM.

In downtown Los Angeles, Pacific Electric operated two major passenger terminals, and it had both an elevated and a subway line. In 1905 Henry E. Huntington opened the 2-million-dollar nine-story terminal building at Sixth and Main streets which was Los Angeles' first "skyscraper" and, at the time, its largest building. Hundreds of daily train movements caused intolerable congestion in surrounding streets, and in 1916 an elevated approach was constructed, which thereafter accommodated a majority of train movements. In 1925 PE opened a 4-million-dollar subway and terminal that took at least some Western District trains off the downtown streets.

Merchandise and small freight shipments of every description were loaded aboard box motors at Pacific Electric's Eighth Street Yard. Car 1459, in the foreground, came from SP's Portland (Ore.) interurban lines. PACIFIC ELECTRIC RAILWAY.

In earlier years, PE-predecessor Los Angeles Pacific had formulated plans for a far more ambitious subway than the mile-long tube finally opened in 1925. In 1906, only months after the Southern Pacific's E. H. Harriman had purchased control of LAP, plans were announced for a four-track subway and private-right-of-way route from Vineyard to downtown Los Angeles, along with new connecting cutoff routes, which would have created the greatest rapid transit system west of Chicago. But Harriman's plans were "temporarily postponed" during the panic of 1907, and LAP's great subway was never built. 1

Mail and express activity was concentrated around PE's Sixth and Main Street terminal and the Los Angeles Union Passenger Terminal. It was handled by box motors such as 1415, a standard type constructed in large numbers by PE. The extra train approached Slauson Junction inbound from the Whittier line in 1950. WILLIAM D. MIDDLETON.

The scattered industry of the Southland was well served by Pacific Electric, and the greatest of all interurbans became California's third-ranking freight railroad. Electric freight activity centered around compact Butte Street Yard, where traffic was interchanged with the major transcontinental systems. Steeple-cab locomotive No. 1610 worked the south end of the yard. PACIFIC ELECTRIC RAILWAY.

Moving behind one of the standard Baldwin-Westinghouse steeple-cab designs that served PE in large numbers, a solid block of refrigerator cars hurried along the Santa Monica Air Line near Palms. DONALD DUKE.

The extraordinary freight traffic of World War II was responsible for such dramatic activ-
ity as this combination of Mogul and steeple-cab working an eastbound extra freight
through the vineyards near Etiwanda on the San Bernardino line. Overburdened with

wartime traffic on its main line east of Los Angeles, Southern Pacific diverted much tonnage to the line of its parallel subsidiary. Confronted with a resulting motive power shortage, Pacific Electric borrowed SP steam to help out. F. J. PETERSON.

Sunset on the Fraser River . . . and this British Columbia Electric 1200-class car tripped lightly over the trestle from Lulu Island, bound for Marpole and Vancouver. Symbolic of the Pacific Northwest are a sawmill burner and fishing boat masts in the dusky background. STAN F. STYLES.

Maple Leaf Traction

Canada's Interurbans

Maple Leaf Traction

Canada's Interurbans

NORTH of U. S. borders the interurban was less frequently seen, and nowhere were to be found the interconnecting electric networks common to New England or the Midwestern states. Over half of the Canadian mileage was located in the Province of Ontario and virtually all of this was concentrated in the southern part of the province bordering Lakes Erie and Ontario, where industrial development and population were greatest. Elsewhere the vast distances and sparse population of the Dominion offered scant inducement to interurban promoters, and few lines were built except those which ventured out from the largest metropolitan centers.

The two great Canadian transcontinentals occasionally took an interest in the interurbans. Canadian National acquired several important properties from predecessor companies upon its formation after World War I, and added another to its holdings as recently as 1951. Canadian Pacific's electric line activities were confined to an important pair of interconnected lines in Ontario, the Hull Electric Railway in Quebec, and the Aroostook Valley Railway in Maine. Government ownership of electric railways, a practice which was virtually unknown in the United States, was much more frequent in the Dominion.

On a quiet Sunday evening in 1958 a Quebec Railway, Light & Power Company interurban waited at Montmorency Falls, Que., for a late evening local run into Quebec City. WILLIAM D. MIDDLETON.

328

CHEMIN DE FER DE LA BONNE SAINTE ANNE

Aside from returns on traffic of a suburban nature, passenger revenues on the Quebec Railway, Light & Power Company's interurban were derived in large measure from the movement of summer visitors to one of North America's most celebrated Roman Catholic shrines at Ste. Anne de Beaupre. Such was the identification of the railway with the shrine that among French-Canadians the former was widely known as the "Chemin de Fer de la Bonne Sainte Anne." Long after its disappearance elsewhere the trolley excursion continued on the Quebec interurban, and the "Special Tourist Electric Train Service" remained on summer timecards until the end of passenger operation. Excursion car 455, whose crew included a bilingual guide-lecturer, waited for the return trip in a siding at Ste. Anne during the last summer of passenger operation in 1958. WILLIAM D. MIDDLETON.

For peak movements to the shrine the railway retained a fleet of incredibly antique rolling stock, much of it constructed during the 19th century for QRL&P's steam road forerunner. This string of 1889 Jackson & Sharp coaches rolled down the north bank of the St. Lawrence to Ste. Anne behind a steeple-cab passenger locomotive on the occasion of the annual feast day of Ste. Anne in 1958, the tercentenary of the shrine. WILLIAM D. MIDDLETON.

Over 100 feet higher than Niagara, Montmorency Falls, not far from Quebec, constituted a major attraction for trolley excursionists. In earlier years the interurban operated a park and menagerie at the base of the falls, and an incline railway carried tourists to a hotel at the top of the cliff. A short pause on the electric line's bridge below the falls was always scheduled for the enjoyment of passengers on "tourist specials." After completing a local run from the city, this interurban turned on the wye beside the falls in 1952. Wooden car No. 401, built in 1902 by Ottawa Car, remained in operation until abandonment of the electrification in March 1959, by which time the car had long since assumed the title of North America's oldest interurban car still operating in revenue service. ROBERT J. SANDUSKY.

Until Canadian National acquired the line in 1951, the 25-mile QRL&P interurban was the only link between the transcontinental and its isolated Murray Bay Subdivision. To power CNR passenger trains moving over the electric line, QRL&P provided a pair of big steeple-cab locomotives. After CNR purchased the line steam and diesel power operated straight through, but the passenger electrics were retained for special movements, such as this train of Canadian Pacific equipment leaving Quebec in 1958 with 275 nuns from Montreal on a pilgrimage to the shrine. WILLIAM D. MIDDLETON.

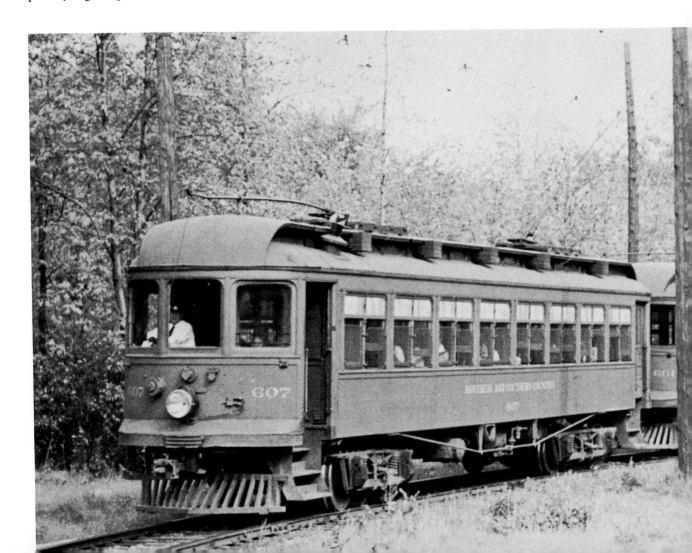

Among the assets acquired by Canadian National from its predecessor Grand Trunk Railway was the Montreal & Southern Counties Railway, an interurban which represented, in part, electrification of former steam lines of the Grand Trunk's subsidiary Central Vermont. An eventual long-distance electrification of CV lines was contemplated, but the trolley wire never extended beyond Granby, some 47 miles east of Montreal, which was reached in 1916. Much of the company's traffic was of a commuter nature to suburban communities across the St. Lawrence from Montreal. In 1953 this wooden car waited at the McGill Street terminal in Montreal for a run to suburban Mackayville. PHILIP R. HASTINGS.

At the conclusion of its electric passenger operation in 1956, M&SC still used much of the same equipment acquired to inaugurate service nearly a half century before. This train of wooden coaches, approaching Canadian National's Victoria Jubilee Bridge from St. Lambert in 1949, was typical. Trailer car 201, at the rear of the train, had been on hand at the opening of initial Montreal-St. Lambert service in 1909. WILLIAM D. MIDDLETON.

This M&SC "mixed train," made up of a pair of l.c.l box cars and a like number of passenger coaches, was photographed at St. Lambert in 1949. CHARLES A. BROWN.

Following discontinuance of passenger service to Granby in 1951, M&SC electric cars terminated their runs at Marieville, backing around this wye to reverse direction. ROBERT J. SANDUSKY.

Waving the motorman back on dead slow, an M&SC conductor at Marieville ponders the difference in drawbar levels as he makes up his train. He's going to have to get in between there, against the rules, and armstrong 601's coupler up about 5 inches. PHILIP R. HASTINGS.

North from Lake Erie

An important figure in Ontario traction was Sir Adam Beck, founder of the Hydro-Electric Power Commission of Ontario. In 1912 he advanced an ambitious scheme for a system of "radial railways" (as interurbans were commonly known in Ontario) which, together with already existing lines, would link the Toronto area, the Niagara peninsula, and the cities north of Lake Erie with an integrated network of high grade electric railways. Sir Adam, whose power commission represented the first major successful public power project in North America, envisioned that the Commission would construct, equip, and operate the radials for the benefit and at the expense of the municipalities concerned, with the initial financing to come from bond issues which would be guaranteed by the provincial government. The Hydro proposal was delayed during a decade of political bickering and cessation of construction during World War I, perhaps fortunately, as the ultimate collapse of interurban railways was to prove. Eventually government skepticism about the ability of the lines to become self-supporting and the all-too-evident growth of highway travel killed the plan.

Electrification of the London & Port Stanley Railway, a former steam railroad, in 1915 afforded a prototype of the sort of electric railways contemplated by the Hydro Commission. Originally constructed in 1856 by London business interests to obtain lower freight rates than those charged by the Great Western (now CNR), the municipally owned L&PS was rebuilt and electrified under the direction of Sir Adam Beck and the Hydro Commission. A 1500-volt D.C. system was employed and the new all-steel cars for the service were built to specifications of the Commission. Beck himself invited guests to the line's June 30, 1915, opening celebration, where the project was described as the first step in a 1500-volt D.C. electrification of Ontario municipal railways which would ultimately extend through central Ontario from Lake Erie to Georgian Bay. So successful was the London & Port Stanley electrification that within three years of its opening the parallel London & Lake Erie electric line had been forced into bankruptcy and abandonment.

Heading southward to Lake Erie in 1952, a two-car L&PS train sped under the catenary just south of the Thames River bridge at London. A motorless control trailer of wooden construction preceded the steel motor car. ROBERT J. SANDUSKY.

The steel Jewett coach that headed this northbound L&PS train at St. Thomas in 1949 had an all-steel roof of unique contour. Constructed for the original electrification in 1915, the car was considered a prototype for electric cars that radial railway proponents believed would soon traverse much of central Ontario. To combat the rigors of the Canadian winter, the cars came equipped with storm sash, a not infrequent feature on Dominion interurbans. WILLIAM D. MIDDLETON.

With some 100 railroad enthusiast passengers aboard, a three-car London & Port Stanley train raced southward across the substantial Kettle Creek viaduct just north of St. Thomas in 1952. The train was made up of cars acquired in 1941 from the Milwaukee Electric Lines, on which they had been the de luxe parlor cars Mendota, Waubasee, and Menominee. JOHN A. MYERS.

L&PS trains provided Londoners convenient connections with Michigan Central (NYC) trains at St. Thomas, where this train waited at the steam line's depot in July of 1956. The diesel in the foreground headed a westbound freight. HERBERT H. HARWOOD JR.

Three of these GE box-cab locomotives powered L&PS freight trains from the time of the 1915 electrification until dieselization in 1957. This one switched at the London yard in 1949. A. C. KALMBACH.

The combined trackage of the Lake Erie & Northern Railway and the Grand River Railway, closely associated under Canadian Pacific ownership, extended southward from the CPR main line at Galt to Port Dover on Lake Erie, affording the transcontinental system a strategic connection to the cities of the Grand River valley. Like some of the other important Ontario lines, LE&N-GRRy operated at right angles to the east-west trunk lines of the major steam railroads. This is the bridge which carried the electrics over the Michigan Central and Toronto, Hamilton & Buffalo lines at Waterford. The car was northbound on the last day of passenger operation in 1955. ROBERT J. SANDUSKY.

Southbound to Port Dover, an LE&N car rolled into Simcoe over a well-maintained roadbed in 1950. During the latter years of passenger service the Canadian Pacific electrics experimented with various front end color schemes, designed to improve visibility of the oncoming cars for motorists. A yellow checkerboard effect had been applied to this wine red coach. WILLIAM D. MIDDLETON.

Though elsewhere on the system freight traffic predominated, the Grand River Railway's short Preston-Hespeler branch did a lively passenger business, and even after World War II some 35 daily round trips were offered. The sturdy wooden car arriving at Preston was a 1915 product of the home-town Preston Car & Coach Company. DAVID H. COPE.

Just arrived from Brantford behind a pair of Baldwin-Westinghouse steeple-cabs one leaden winter day in 1956, an LE&N freight pulled into the Canadian Pacific interchange at Galt, where a Mikado freight engine of the parent road waited for a westbound trip. Electric freight operation on the combined LE&N-GRRy continued into 1961. WILLIAM D. MIDDLETON.

Prominent in Ontario traction development were Sir William MacKenzie and Donald Mann, who had been contractors in the construction of the Canadian Pacific, and later began construction of their rival Canadian Northern in 1896. The most important of the four interurbans developed by the MacKenzie, Mann & Company partnership was the Niagara, St. Catharines & Toronto Railway, which operated across the Niagara peninsula between Lakes Erie and Ontario, and into Niagara Falls. Ultimately, the NStC&T, along with other Canadian Northern electric properties, became part of the Canadian National system.

Before the decline of electric railway travel NStC&T formed a link in leisurely travel between Buffalo and Toronto. From a Niagara Falls (N.Y.) connection with the International Railway's Buffalo-Niagara Falls High Speed Line, cars of the Canadian line operated over the old Rainbow Bridge and across the peninsula to Port Dalhousie East, where a shipside connection with Toronto-bound Lake Ontario steamers was made. Such traffic still moved in profitable volume in the '20's, as evidenced by this train of elegant wooden cars, representing a 1914 Preston Car & Coach order in its entirety. WILLIAM S. FLATT COLLECTION.

In the final years of its electric operation NStC&T used a group of widely traveled cars on its remaining passenger line between Thorold and Port Colborne. Built by the Ottawa Car Company in 1930 for an ill-advised modernization of the Windsor, Essex & Lake Shore Railway under Hydro Commission management, the original group of five medium-weight interurbans spent but two years on the "Sunshine County Route" before its abandon-ment. The cars then moved to Canadian National's Montreal & Southern Counties, where they operated until 1955, when one went to a Maine museum and the remainder were transferred to NStC&T. No. 620 was ascending the steep grade between Merritton and Thorold early on a Sunday morning in 1956 en route from the carbarn at St. Catharines to begin the day's operation. WILLIAM D. MIDDLETON.

At speed near Port Colborne on a bleak March day, 620 typified the exciting, exhilarating operation of a cross-country interurban paralleling a highway. Unfortunately, no passengers were aboard to enjoy the sensation. WILLIAM D. MIDDLETON.

343

Except for two Ft. William (Ont.) city cars, Canada's only curved-side Cincinnati lightweights. were operated by the Niagara line in local service on the St. Catharines-Port Dalhousie route. CHARLES A. BROWN.

Motors and gears groaned as NStC&T's little steeple-cab locomotive No. 19 slowed almost to a walk and then settled into a steady stride that finally gained her the summit of the steep Merritton hill with seven cars of freight for the Welland Subdivision in 1956. WILLIAM D. MIDDLETON.

344

In all the vast reaches of the Canadian prairie there was but one interurban, the Winnipeg, Selkirk & Lake Winnipeg Railway, which radiated from the Manitoba capital to Selkirk and Stonewall. Against a frosty backdrop near Stony Mountain, one of the line's big wooden combines headed south to Winnipeg on a midafternoon run in the early '30's. STAN F. STYLES.

The winter of 1928-1929 and its aftermath proved difficult for the Winnipeg interurban. Motorman Ray Styles and two sectionmen posed atop a snowbank on the Stonewall line after the railway's rotary plow had cleared up the results of a February blizzard. STAN F. STYLES.

In April of 1929, the winter's snow melted and produced a severe spring flood, causing this two-car train on the Stonewall line to make its way cautiously through water that lapped at the rails. STAN F. STYLES.

Bound for a Fraser Valley excursion on the Chilliwack line, a train of commodious BCER interurbans paused at New Westminster in 1914, four years after the line was opened. Outings to the valley by interurban were long popular.

As late as 1940 BCER operated special "bicycle trains" into the country for a Vancouver club. A baggage car was provided for the transportation of members' bicycles. ERNIE PLANT COLLECTION.

INTERURBAN TRAMS TO CHILLIWACK

Canada's largest interurban system was that of the British Columbia Electric Railway, which operated an extensive suburban service around Vancouver, a long and scenic route through the Fraser River Valley to Chilliwack, and a disconnected, short-lived line north from Victoria on Vancouver Island. Vancouver is more British in character than much of Canada, and it was not uncommon to hear local people speak of the "interurban trams." British capital, as a matter of fact, built BCER, and this may have accounted for the presence of several British-built Dick Kerr electric locomotives among the company's roster of otherwise conventional equipment of North American manufacture. ⊥

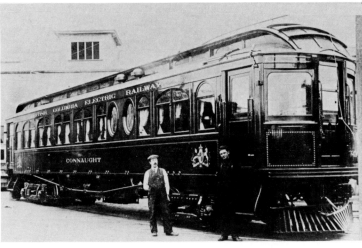

In 1912, *upon the occasion of a visit to western Canada by the Duke of Connaught, interurban car No. 1304 was repainted, fitted with drapes and a red carpet, and the Connaught crest applied to each corner in preparation for service on a special train transporting the Duke over the Chilliwack line. Following completion of the trip No. 1304 was shorn of its special furnishings and operated in more mundane passenger service until the mid-'50's. It is now owned by an Oregon historical group.* ERNIE PLANT COLLECTION.

349

Against a backdrop of threatening skies, this Fraser Valley train waited on the loop at Chilliwack before beginning the 76-mile return trip to Vancouver. DAVID A. STRASSMAN.

While one of the company's PCC streetcars discharged passengers in the street, a pair of BCER interurbans waited to depart from the Carrall Street depot in Vancouver on their respective late evening journeys to Burnaby Lake and New Westminster. STAN F. STYLES.

Highlighted by the morning sun, three cars full of BCER commuters hurried across Gladstone Trestle on a 12-mile run from New Westminster to Vancouver over the Central Park line. STAN F. STYLES.

Two steam railroads shared the Fraser River bridge at New Westminster with interurbans of British Columbia Electric's Chilliwack line. In 1948 the two-car interurban train was about to follow the center track to Chilliwack. The track to the right carried Canadian National transcontinental traffic, while that to the left handled international traffic on Great Northern's line to Seattle. ERNIE PLANT.

Behind a former Oregon Electric steeple-cab locomotive, freight extra 961 West waited in a forested siding at Bradner, on the Chilliwack line, to permit the passage of a Vancouver passenger train headed by baggage motor No. 1700. STAN F. STYLES.

Traction in the Tropics

Hershey Cuban passengers begin their journey from Havana aboard 5-cent motor launches, which cross the harbor between the old colonial section of Havana and the interurban terminal at Casablanca. Just beyond the noisy waterfront dive that houses the ticket office, a three-car train waited for the run to Matanzas in 1957. The big maroon cars were little changed from the day they rolled out of the J. G. Brill plant 40 years before. WILLIAM D. MIDDLETON.

Traction in the Tropics

SOUTH of U. S. borders the interurban was almost nonexistent. Street railways were a common means of mass transportation in the larger cities of Central and South America, and remain so today in many cases. But only occasionally, in such cities as Mexico City and Buenos Aires, did electric railways venture into the suburban countryside on lines with interurban characteristics.

Both severe topography and an almost continual state of revolution that discouraged investment capital during much of the interurban era combined to deter the development of true interurbans in Mexico. The Mexican Tramways Company in 1927 advanced an interesting proposal to construct a 130-mile electric interurban from Mexico City to Pueblo, and another, 60 miles in length, to Pachuca, but nothing ever came of it.

A notable exception to the dearth of interurbans in Latin America was Cuba's Hershey Cuban Railway, which survives into 1961 as the last example in all North America of the typical heavy electric interurban railway.* The Hershey Cuban's principal reason for existence was the development by the parent Hershey Chocolate Corporation of its own Cuban sugar enterprise at the end of World War I. A vast acreage of sugar plantations and several mills, for conversion of the cane to raw brown sugar, were centered around the company's prin-

cipal mill, a refinery, and power plant at Central Hershey, east of Havana. A network of rail lines was constructed to gather the cane from the surrounding plantations, and a main line was installed to transport the refined sugar down to Havana harbor. Developing its railroad on the principle that it should be a self-supporting enterprise rather than just an accessory to sugar manufacture, Hershey extended the main line to Matanzas, 56 miles east of Havana, in order to establish a year-around common carrier freight and passenger business.

Crews of Jamaican laborers completed the first section of line, between Havana and Central Hershey, in 1918, and it was immediately placed in operation with steam power to haul construction materials for the refinery and power plant. The entire railway, comprising some 100 track miles under a 1200-volt D.C. catenary system, and several times that amount of steam-operated sugar cane trackage, was officially opened four years later.

The J. G. Brill Company delivered a fleet of heavy maroon-clad wood and steel multiple-unit interurbans. Interiors were plainly finished in mahogany and were fitted with durable rattan-upholstered walkover seats. Splendidly maintained by the railway's thoroughly equipped shops, these cars remain today in virtually "as built" condition. A group of lighter single-unit cars, designed for branch-line service, came a few years later from the Cincinnati Car Company. ⊥

---

*Late in 1960 the Hershey Cuban was nationalized by decree of the Castro government.

Late one June afternoon in 1957 train No. 33, westbound from Central Hershey to Casablanca, backed into the siding at Justiz for a cruzando (meet) with eastbound Matanzas train No. 8. Headed by a big wood-bodied mail-baggage car, the three-car train came swaying through the tropical undergrowth at a respectable 30 miles per hour. Train crews shouted cheerful Spanish greetings, the conductor threw the switch to let No. 33 back on the main line, and the journey to Casablanca was once more in progress. WILLIAM D. MIDDLETON.

357

Central Hershey is a handsome "company town" with elegant residences for company executives and such attractions as a golf course, tropical gardens, and a comfortable small hotel. Tours of the refinery have long been popular, and in earlier years the railway offered a handy "package tour" from Havana which included interurban transportation, a conducted tour of the sugar mill, lunch at the Hershey Hotel, and an automobile tour through the scenic byways of the surrounding countryside. Four times daily the Hershey Cuban's mainline passenger trains are scheduled to meet at Central Hershey. During the 3-minute stop of a pair of Casablanca-Matanzas trains one hot June morning, the quiet station became the scene of frantic

activity. The brown-uniformed train crews gathered on the platform to exchange small talk, while crowds of passengers boarded and left the interurbans. The camarero (baggageman) unloaded a few pieces of express. Friends and idlers chatted through open windows, and a boy passed from window to window hawking candies held up on a stick for the passengers' inspection. Then the motoristas returned to their controllers, and the conductors signaled departure time with a blast from their whistles. The big red cars went rumbling out of town, the crowd thinned, dogs went back to sleep in the shade, and Central Hershey station grew quiet again. ALL PHOTOS, WILLIAM D. MIDDLETON.

Clattering along an irregular roadbed, the ponderous interurbans nosed gently from side to side as they followed the rails through a verdant trough in vegetation that frequently stands as high as a man. Windows were thrown wide open to the warmth of the Cuban summer. WILLIAM D. MIDDLETON.

Awaiting the end of the day shift, a Cincinnati-built interurban stood in the street outside the main gate of the Central Hershey sugar mill and refinery. Soon the train would be off with homeward-bound workers to Santa Cruz del Norte, on the edge of the Atlantic. The June afternoon was hot and humid, and an ice cream salesman was doing business in the shade of a nearby tree. WILLIAM D. MIDDLETON.

Approaching Matanzas the Hershey Cuban traverses some of central Cuba's finest scenery. Having just completed its circuit of the spectacular Yumuri Valley, an eastbound train came rolling between the rock cliffs of the gap which carries the Yumuri River, a country road, and the interurban from the valley to the Bay of Matanzas. WILLIAM D. MIDDLETON.

361

Interurban No. 213 had just completed its daily afternoon run from Central Hershey to Bainoa. While the crew stepped into the weathered masonry depot shared with the Occidentales de Cuba to call the dispatcher for return trip orders, a small boy clambered about the fascinating electric car. WILLIAM D. MIDDLETON.

Returning to Central Hershey from an afternoon trip down the Bainoa branch, Cincinnati interurban 213 rejoined the Hershey Cuban main line at San Mateo Junction. WILLIAM D. MIDDLETON.

Powered by a bright silver and red diesel, Hershey's weekly mixed train departed from Central San Antonio for the return trip over nonelectrified branch-line trackage to Central Hershey. With eight tank cars of molasses, a box car of miscellaneous freight, and a Brill interurban trailer, the little diesel had all it could do to get the train under way. WILLIAM D. MIDDLETON.

Time freight No. 53, westbound from Matanzas to Havana harbor behind a pair of GE steeple-cab locomotives, headed out of the siding at Canasi as an eastbound passenger train cleared the main line. WILLIAM D. MIDDLETON.

Almost hidden by trackside growth, eastbound Havana-Matanzas time freight 52 came grinding up the long grade into Central Hershey. The steeple-cabs' pantographs reached high for the 1200-volt catenary. WILLIAM D. MIDDLETON.

A trim little GE locomotive switched Ferrocarriles Occidentales de Cuba passenger cars at Havana's Central Station in 1957. The Occidentales, formerly the Havana Central, once operated interurban passenger equipment in an extensive suburban service, and is still possessed of a generous amount of 600-volt overhead in the Havana area. WILLIAM D. MIDDLETON.

As the electric street and interurban railways declined in North America, a considerable amount of their still-serviceable rolling stock found its way to the electric lines of Central and South America. In 1952 a train of former Pacific Electric Hollywood suburban cars, still attired in PE red and orange colors, operated left-handed on the Federico Lacroze line of the Ferrocarril Nacional General Urquiza at Buenos Aires. WILLIAM D. MIDDLETON COLLECTION.

Wrecks and Other Mishaps

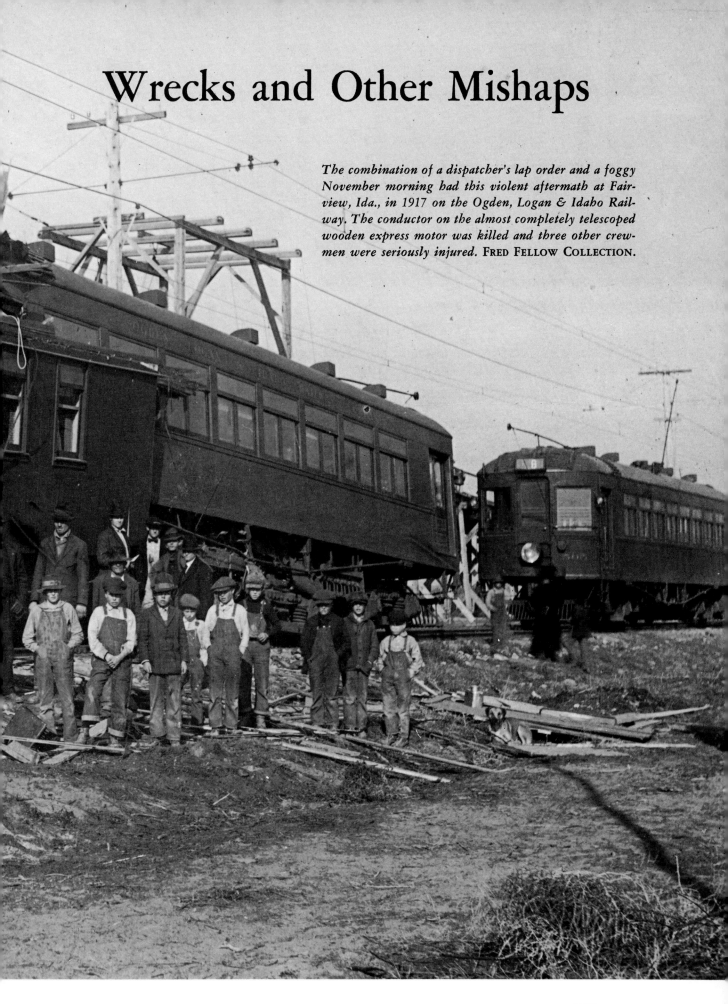

The combination of a dispatcher's lap order and a foggy November morning had this violent aftermath at Fairview, Ida., in 1917 on the Ogden, Logan & Idaho Railway. The conductor on the almost completely telescoped wooden express motor was killed and three other crewmen were seriously injured. FRED FELLOW COLLECTION.

Wrecks and Other Mishaps

DISASTER AND DEATH along the rails were sometimes a part of the interurban era. Most interurbans were single tracked and rarely were equipped with such safety refinements as block signals. The tragedy of a high-speed collision resulting from an overlooked meeting point or a forgotten special train, combined, perhaps, with the restricted visibility of hills and curves or a foggy night, is a recurring theme in interurban history.

The first interurban, Portland's East Side Railway, was only a few months old when the car *Inez*, inbound from Oregon City one misty November morning, slid on frosty rail and plunged through the open Madison Street drawbridge in Portland. Most of the passengers saved themselves by jumping as the interurban hung in the air momentarily, but 7 were killed when the car plummeted into 35 feet of water.

The worst interurban accident of all occurred at Kingsland, Ind., on September 21, 1910, when an extra car on the Fort Wayne & Wabash Valley Traction Company overran a meeting point and collided head-on at high speed with a northbound local. The crowded local was completely telescoped, and 41 lost their lives in the splintered wreckage of the wooden car.

The old adage that "bad accidents come in threes" seemed to hold some truth, for during the same week that the Kingsland disaster occurred, 5 were killed in a collision on the neighboring Indiana Union Traction Company, and less than two weeks later 36 met death in a head-on Illinois Traction System crash, which took place under similar circumstances of an overlooked meet.

The public outcry following the Kingsland and other accidents was predictable. The Indiana Railroad Commission demanded the installation of block signals on all interurbans in the state. Illinois Traction voluntarily began the costly installation of sig-

nals on all of its major lines and by 1915 had 150 miles of track under continuous block signals. Adept at making the best of a bad thing, ITS extracted maximum publicity benefits from its new signals. Full-size models of the signals were displayed on street corners in principal cities, and the workings of their mechanism explained to the curious. "Travel is perfection under IT block protection," proclaimed the company's advertising, and nervous passengers were assured "they never sleep."

Sometimes the lessons taught by disaster are forgotten, and in 1950, 40 years after the Kingsland wreck, the last big accident of the interurban era occurred under almost identical circumstances, when two Milwaukee interurban excursion trains collided head-on with a loss of 10 lives. A misunderstanding of orders sent the two trains racing toward each other on single track, and just as at Kingsland, an overgrowth of trackside brush at a curve obscured visibility for the motormen until too late.

More often though, interurban mishaps were not so deadly. One of the most bizarre and spectacular interurban accidents, which happened on the Indiana Service Corporation at Lafayette, Ind., in 1930, took place with the almost miraculous absence of serious injury or death. Approaching Lafayette from Fort Wayne, motorman Frank Simons, after apparently suffering an attack of dizziness or a fainting spell, toppled through the open door of his interurban car. Running wild with the power still on, the big wooden car reached an estimated speed of 45 miles per hour before leaving the rails on a curve in the streets of Lafayette and plunging into a grocery store, tearing out the entire front of the building and finally coming to rest within the store in a mass of tumbled merchandise and debris. The interurban's passengers escaped with bruises and were severely shaken up. The narrowest escape of all was experienced by little Jimmy Moore, who was in the

Forty-one persons died when these two interurbans slammed together with brutal force at Kingsland, Ind., in 1910. It was the worst crash of the interurban era. STEPHEN D. MAGUIRE COLLECTION.

store directly in the path of the runaway car. Buried in the wreckage, the 7-year-old emerged with only minor cuts. An estimated 10,000 people visited the scene of the crash and watched efforts to free the interurban from the wreckage.

An Illinois line, the Rockford & Interurban, seemed to have recurrent trouble with dairy cattle. On one occasion, not far from Rockford, one of the line's cars struck a cow, which became wedged under the car, threw it off the track, and left it at right angles to the rails. On another occasion a car ran

into a whole herd of cows which had lain down on the rails at night. Twenty cattle were killed before the car finally derailed and very nearly plunged into the Pecatonica River.

A somewhat similar mishap occurred in Ohio in 1907, after a bull escaped from a slaughterhouse at Jimtown, near Wapakoneta. After chasing residents, the bull wandered onto the nearby tracks of the Western Ohio Railway where it charged head-on into an interurban car. The contest was a draw, for the bull was killed and the interurban derailed.

Little more than twisted steel remained of these Waterloo, Cedar Falls & Northern interurbans in 1954 after a nocturnal fire wiped out the Waterloo roundhouse. The lone interurban that escaped the blaze managed to provide all of the company's passenger service until its discontinuance in 1956. WILLIAM S. KUBA JR.

Fire, as a matter of fact, was a constant threat to the interurbans, particularly during the earlier years, when wooden cars and inflammable carbarns were common and electrical apparatus was often erratic. A few years after the Vanderbilt party mishap another fire had more serious consequences and the glittering *Josephine* was completely destroyed. Similar spectacular conflagrations were recorded in the history of almost every interurban road with usually little more remaining than a few smoldering embers and a tangle of heat-twisted metal parts. Another all too common occurrence was the midnight carbarn fire, which more than once left a line with hardly a single car available at the start of business the following morning.

The heyday of the train robber was fairly well over by the time the interurban arrived on the American scene, but there were a few more or less amateurish attempts to knock off an interurban car in the grand manner of the Old West. One of the first trolley car holdup attempts occurred on the St. Paul-Minneapolis Inter-Urban Electric in 1893. Five toughs boarded the midnight car from St. Paul, and when it had reached a deserted spot along the line, one of them pulled down the trolley pole while the others set upon the conductor, one of them inflicting a 2-inch stab wound. The intrepid motorman came to the rescue with his brass lever and, according to a contemporary account, "the way he cranked it was a caution to evil-doers, and caused a general stampede." The conductor replaced the trolley pole and the car escaped amidst a shower of stones that smashed all its windows and caused other damage, but no money was lost to the thugs.

What newspapers described as the most sensational street accident in Vancouver (B. C.) history occurred in 1947 when a British Columbia Electric interurban train (left) ran amuck. As the train left the interurban depot, motorman James Dinsmore was knocked unconscious when a 500-volt short circuit passed through the controls of his two-car train. Hurtling out of control into the street, the interurban sent a taxi flying, derailed two streetcars, and crushed an automobile in the wreckage. A hundred persons were shaken up by the crash but miraculously there were no fatalities. ERNIE PLANT.

As automobiles became commonplace, the grade-crossing accident became a distressingly frequent occurrence. The interurban, like this Pacific Electric car, usually won out over the early flivvers. IRA L. SWETT COLLECTION.

Dewirement was a frequent minor mishap on trolley lines. After the 620's trolley left the wire in a high cross wind and slammed against the cross-arms, the Niagara, St. Catharines & Toronto crew struggled to replace the wrecked pole with the spare carried for just such emergencies. WILLIAM D. MIDDLETON.

A pair of bandits who attempted to stick up a Seattle-Tacoma car on the Puget Sound Electric Railway in 1914 fared even worse. Once their intentions were made known, the pair were overpowered and beaten into insensibility by passengers, and a news account of the affair held little hope for their recovery.

Two masked bandits who held up a British Columbia Electric interurban train on the Marpole line in 1913 were more successful, managing to make their escape into a nearby wood after extracting approximately $100 from the train crew and passengers.

Another pair of masked bandits, who knocked off a Terre Haute, Indianapolis & Eastern car at Maywood, Ind., in 1923, were better compensated for their efforts. After stopping the car on signal, the two climbed aboard, firing into and through the car. The passengers and crew were forced outside, lined up along the track, and relieved of better than $1000 in cash and valuables.

What was probably the most lucrative heist of the traction era took place on Pennsylvania's Laurel Line interurban in 1923. Bearing $70,126 among them, the paymaster of the West End Colliery of Mocanaqua, an assistant paymaster, and two armed guards boarded a morning limited at Scranton. Taking the group by surprise, five roughly dressed armed bandits opened fire within the car near Moosic station, successfully relieved the men of the payroll, and made good their escape from the interurban. During the melee one passenger was killed, and the motorman and two other passengers wounded. Eventually the entire band was apprehended and brought to justice.

Two Fonda, Johnstown & Gloversville cars suffered embarrassment after unsuccessfully contesting track space in the Gloversville (N.Y.) yard. WILLIAM R. GORDON COLLECTION.

Weather sometimes got the best of the electric cars. Floodwater stranded an International Railway Niagara Falls interurban at Tonawanda, N. Y., in 1918. WILLIAM R. GORDON COLLECTION, FROM STEPHEN D. MAGUIRE.

Sometimes individuals of a larcenous bent applied more subtle methods against the traction companies. In 1930 a crew engaged in an electrolysis survey on the lines of the Milwaukee Electric was sent out to take ground current flow readings during the early morning hours when no cars were operating. The men were puzzled to find that large amounts of current were flowing through the rails despite the absence of interurban cars. Investigation revealed that a Cudahy garage owner had rigged a bare copper wire across a street above the trolley wire. At night, when no one was looking, the wire was lowered onto the trolley wires and free electricity was drawn for battery charging and other operations.

Trespassers on private right of way were found to be a problem by many interurbans. In 1910 one line tried the experiment of providing its motormen with circular letters of warning which could be thrown to trespassers. No one, it was discovered, took much notice of the circulars, and the practice was discontinued.

Collapse of the bridge over the Miami River at Dayton, O., under a two-car freight train in 1932 was the last straw for the bankrupt Dayton & Troy Electric Railway. With no money in the till to repair the damage, the company abandoned its entire line a week after the mishap. O. F. LEE COLLECTION.

A trainload of steel proved too heavy for the Sacramento Northern's long Lisbon trestle in 1951, and the structure went down like a row of dominoes. Getting the train out proved to be a major task. FRED H. MATTHEWS JR.

Obstreperous passengers sometimes made life difficult for the interurban trainmen. Consider this accident report filed by a conductor on the Grays Harbor Railway & Light Company (Washington) in 1914: "A man at Hoquiam came on the car at 7 p.m. He spit and expectorated all over the car and when I asked him to quit he swore strong at me. Then he vomited all over a seat and on the floor. I told him to clean it up or I would have him arrested. He started to clean it up, and then he went to the door, jumped from the car, and ran down E Street to the river and jumped in. I stopped the car, ran after the man, jumped in the river, dragged him out, and had him arrested for spitting on the floor of the car."

Another interurban rescue, under more heroic circumstances, brought Lake Shore Electric motorman William Lang national recognition in the form of a Carnegie Medal and an I.C.C. medal approved by President Roosevelt. Rounding a curve at 55 miles per hour Lang spotted a child playing on the tracks and slammed on the brakes of his Toledo limited car. Realizing that the wheels were sliding and the car could not be stopped in time, Lang climbed out on the car fender and snatched 2-year-old Lelia Smith to safety.

Life was seldom dull for the men who ran the cars. ⊥

The electric-powered rotary plow that kept the line clear on the Oneonta & Mohawk Valley, in upstate New York's snow belt, obviously had its work cut out for it. In addition to snow removal problems, winter weather provided a few difficulties peculiar to interurban operation. Sleet frequently disrupted current collection from both third-rail and overhead, and the trolley wire sometimes snapped under the contraction caused by extreme cold. STEPHEN D. MAGUIRE COLLECTION.

Where they traversed city streets, interurban and street railways usually took care of snow removal with electrically powered rotary sweepers. The McGuire-Cummings standard four-wheel sweeper was common anywhere snow fell, and its big rattan brushes sent up a barrage of ice chips that had the hardiest of pedestrians ducking for cover. This sweeper cleared track in Winnipeg after a Manitoba blizzard in 1949. STAN F. STYLES.

The Philadelphia & West Chester's rotary No. 1, shown on the West Chester line around 1907, didn't have quite such arduous duties as the O&MV's plow, and the company's successor, Philadelphia Suburban, manages to get along very well without it. These plows had rotary blades at both ends, a practice more common on electric than on steam railroads. STEPHEN D. MAGUIRE COLLECTION.

Trolley Freight

The Inland Empire System, whose electric lines centered about Spokane, Wash., was typical of the western interurbans on which carload freight traffic was a major revenue source from their very beginning. These Baldwin-Westinghouse box-cab locomotives were on the company's Moscow (Ida.) line, which was electrified with a 25-cycle, 6600-volt single-phase system. Wheat was the principal commodity carried on Inland Empire freights. LeRoy O. King Jr. Collection.

Trolley Freight

IN a few cases the interurban railways were former steam-powered short lines, already doing a substantial freight business, and in many still developing areas of the West, where only limited steam railroad service was available, electric lines were often built to serve as both passenger and freight carriers. Indeed, many of the Western interurbans were built as feeder lines to the large steam railroads, or were later acquired by them for that purpose. But the majority of interurban roads were conceived principally as passenger carriers, and generally little attention was given in their design and construction to the requirements of freight train operation.

Even those lines originally built exclusively for passenger transportation soon found that light freight and express traffic could be a profitable sideline. The very nature of interurban service, with cars operating on fast, frequent schedules, made it possible to provide a service far superior to that of the steam railroads. Such traffic as newspapers, milk and cream, fruit, produce, and small merchandise shipments could be loaded aboard the baggage compartments of the regular cars, and even lines without cars so arranged found they could develop worth-while extra revenues by transporting small parcel shipments on the front platform with the motorman at nominal charges of 25 cents or 50 cents per parcel.

Once the possibilities of the trolley freight business became apparent, interurbans began to intensively promote its development. Even before World War I, when a few lines were starting to lose passengers to automobiles, interurbans began to regard freight traffic as a good area to recover the lost revenues.

The handling of perishables between farm and market, with their requirement for fast service, was a particularly lucrative traffic. To help develop such business the New England Investment & Securities

Company, a New Haven Railroad subsidiary which controlled a group of electric lines in central Massachusetts, sponsored in 1910 a four-car "Trolley Farming Special," which toured 300 miles of trolley line in the Springfield-Worcester area with agricultural and forestry exhibits. In 1915 Fort Wayne & Northern Indiana operated a similar two-car agricultural exhibit and lecture train over electric lines in Indiana. The Portland Railway, Light & Power Company organized an agricultural department to furnish farmers with information on the growing of feed for hog and cattle raising, and the Bangor Railway & Electric Company operated a 40-acre demonstration farm — staffed with a University of Maine agriculturalist — to promote better farming practices in its territory. In 1914 the Lehigh Valley Transit Company and the Philadelphia & Western Railway joined in establishing a "farmers' market" at 69th and Market streets in Philadelphia for the sale of produce brought in on the electric cars.

Efforts to develop interurban freight traffic were confronted with numerous difficulties. The physical limitations of steep grades, light construction, and sharp curves often precluded the operation of standard freight equipment, and made necessary the construction of special cars which were noninterchangeable with steam railroads. In some areas trolley lines were built to nonstandard track gauges, effectively preventing interline freight traffic development. Pennsylvania electric lines, for example, were generally built to a 5-foot 2½-inch "Pennsylvania broad gauge."

Often severe restrictions on freight operation through city streets proved a handicap. Many cities restricted the length and frequency of freight trains, and some confined freight operation to nighttime hours only. Such objections were not without reason. Long, lumbering trolley freight trains could be an infernal nuisance in traffic-congested streets, and there were valid objections on grounds of safety.

382

Pennsylvania's Hershey Transit Company was representative of the majority of electric lines which derived nonpassenger revenues from the box-motor carriage of express and small freight shipments. Transportation of milk to the plant of parent Hershey Chocolate Company was a major traffic for the Hershey line. FROM STEPHEN D. MAGUIRE.

Usually unable to engage in freight interchange with steam railroads, the interurbans of the Ohio-Indiana-Michigan network turned to development of their own interchange operation, employing equipment designed to negotiate restrictive interurban curves. These electric freight trailers were lined up at the Northern Ohio Traction & Light Company's Akron freighthouse in 1926. GEORGE KRAMBLES COLLECTION.

The trailers hauled by this Fort Wayne, Van Wert & Lima box motor were constructed to standards established by the Central Electric Railway Association to permit their use in the interline freight operation of the Midwestern interurbans. The Fort Wayne-Lima line was one of three connecting routes between the Ohio and Indiana systems. O. F. LEE COLLECTION.

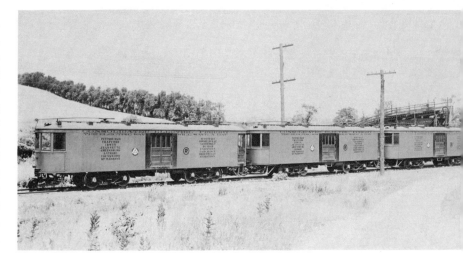

In addition to the usual problems which made freight interchange with steam lines difficult, the broad-gauge track of many Pennsylvania interurbans prevented them from handling steam road cars. The West Penn Railways and the connecting Pittsburgh Railways managed to develop their own modest l.c.l interchange business with these "Consolidated Electric Freight" box motors. CHARLES A. BROWN COLLECTION.

This was convincingly demonstrated in 1927 by the Detroit, Jackson & Chicago Railway at Ann Arbor, Mich., when four cars of sheet steel got away from a trolley freight crew on the West Huron Street hill. Failing to make the curve at Main Street, the runaway cars demolished the Farmers & Merchants Bank, doing $50,000 worth of damage.

The City of Detroit required that freight cars be similar in appearance to passenger cars, and restricted operation of the freight cars to single units only, not less than 2 hours apart in each direction. A gondola car built for coal and ash service on the Philadelphia & Easton Electric Railway in 1910 had to be disguised with a roof and gaily striped side curtains before city officials would permit it to be moved through the streets. In 1932 Milwaukee residents, complaining that the passage of heavy Milwaukee Electric freight trains was damaging their homes, obtained a court order requiring the

company to limit freight space to not more than a quarter of the total area of the car.

But in many regions the greatest obstacle to the development of widespread interurban freight traffic was the refusal of steam railroads to have anything at all to do with the electric lines. The intervention of the courts, state public utilities commissions, or the Interstate Commerce Commission was not infrequently required to compel steam railroads to interchange carload freight traffic with interurbans, and in more than one case a steam road fought its case to the U. S. Supreme Court before accepting such a ruling. The steam railroad opposition to the new electric lines sometimes reached ridiculous extremes, as in the case of the Youngstown & Southern, an Ohio interurban, which was forced to power its freight trains with steam before the steam road members of the Central Freight Association would agree to interchange traffic with it.

Despite the broad-gauge handicap, Philadelphia & West Chester Traction Company was able to do a brisk business in l.c.l. freight and milk. A box motor unloaded milk for Philadelphia about 1923 at the company's 63rd and Market freight station. PHILADELPHIA SUBURBAN TRANSPORTATION.

In addition to a carload freight business the Salt Lake & Utah offered a "Red Arrow Fast Freight" service for express and small freight shipments. Free pickup and delivery were provided for l.c.l. shipments. Unfortunately, this type of business, which constituted the majority of interurban freight traffic, proved just as vulnerable to highway competition as passenger traffic had. FRED FELLOW COLLECTION.

This scene on the Illinois Terminal at Bloomington, Ill., illustrates the difficulty encountered in handling freight around the streetcar curves found on interurban lines. HENRY J. McCORD.

Illinois Terminal developed a special double-jointed coupling for company-owned box cars in order to make the curves on its line through Bloomington. Other interurbans used radial couplers, or employed slotted coupler knuckles and intermediate drawbars. HENRY J. McCORD.

Largely unable, because of physical restrictions and steam road intransigence, to interchange freight cars with steam railroads, Midwestern interurbans developed their own standard trolley freight car designs and operated an extensive interline freight service over the interconnecting traction networks of Ohio, Michigan, and Indiana. The traction freight service was usually far superior to that of the steam roads.

A freight terminal was built in conjunction with Indianapolis' great Traction Terminal, and the interurban people boasted that they could deliver shipments within 75 miles of the city the same day the goods were ordered. Following-day deliveries

were possible almost anywhere in Indiana and Ohio.

A number of electric lines in northern Indiana and southern Michigan joined in through less-than-car-load-lot traffic arrangements with Lake Michigan steamship companies, a service that saved a day or more for shipments destined beyond Chicago. Faster electric service made it possible to get livestock to market before the usual shrinkage in weight occurred, and several of the Indiana lines developed a profitable stock business employing special trolley cattle cars. In 1922 some 8500 cars of livestock were moved into Indianapolis by interurban.

Occasionally the Midwest interurbans joined in the operation of fast through freight trains, similar

in concept to the lines' many through passenger operations. Perhaps the first such service was the *Cannonball Express,* inaugurated in 1914 as a joint operation of five electric lines and the Wells Fargo Express Company. The *Express* ran on a fast limited schedule between Indianapolis and Benton Harbor, Mich., where Chicago connections were made with the Graham & Morton Steamship Company. Such fast time freights as the overnight Indianapolis-Detroit *Aeroplane* connected many of the major cities of Ohio, Indiana, and Michigan.

Trolley freight equipment was constructed in a tremendous variety of types and sizes. For express or light freight service the "box-motor" or "express-motor" unit, more or less resembling a motorized baggage car, was widely employed. Usually equipped with more powerful motors than passenger cars, and geared for pulling power rather than speed, box motors were often capable of operating with short trains of freight trailers. Some lines built similar motors which were equipped as refrigerator or cattle cars.

For heavier freight operation, particularly when steam railroad cars were handled, small electric locomotives, usually of the B-B double-truck arrangement, were favored. Most were some variation of the "steeple-cab" type, which derived its name from the appearance suggested by low hoods at each end sloping up toward a cab in the center. Noisy equipment, such as blowers and compressors, was

The bane of freight operations on the Sacramento Northern Railroad was the route over the Oakland hills, where grades up to 4 per cent were encountered. This southbound freight had successfully made the climb and was descending into Oakland late one afternoon in 1951. Pusher engine No. 652, a standard General Electric unit, had already dropped its pantograph. WILLIAM D. MIDDLETON.

During the last years of the interurban era a lively trade in used freight locomotives developed, and some of the machines survived as many as three abandonments of electric service. The 50-ton Charles

City Western No. 303, wheeling westward across Iowa farmland to Marble Rock in 1955, had originally operated on the Texas Electric Railway, where it had been built. WILLIAM D. MIDDLETON.

Potomac Edison steeple-cab locomotive No. 10 was typical of the hundreds of double-truck units operated by interurban railways. Most of them averaged 50 to 60 tons, but weights ranged from 30 to 100 tons. The 10, at Frederick, Md., was dwarfed by an ordinary box car. H. N. PROCTOR.

usually enclosed in the hoods, and the shortened cab provided excellent visibility during switching operations. A less widely seen variation was the "box-cab" locomotive, which had a cab extending the full length of the locomotive, containing all of its electrical and mechanical equipment.

A few of the larger interurban roads found that the double-truck locomotive just wasn't big enough for their requirements, and developed 16-wheel, 4-truck locomotives which employed articulated frames to permit negotiation of tight interurban curves. The biggest interurban locomotives of all were three 24-wheel monsters acquired in 1949 by the Chicago South Shore & South Bend. Originally built for the U.S.S.R. but never delivered because of strategic export restrictions, the GE machines were among the most powerful single-cab electric locomotives ever constructed, weighed better than 270 tons, and had an hourly rating of over 5500 horsepower.

In several notable respects interurban freight operators pioneered important innovations in railroad freight equipment and service well ahead of their steam railroad competitors. Locomotive standardization, for example, was common in the traction industry years before the diesel motive power revolution brought it to the steam roads. While steam lines were still ordering custom-built motive power, such manufacturers as Baldwin-Westinghouse and General Electric were offering standard lines of electric locomotives to electric railways. And multiple-unit control made it possible for trolley roads to operate together any number of their standardized freight motors controlled from a single unit, employing the same fundamental "building block" principle now used with diesel power to assemble a motive power combination suitable for trains of any size.

At the time of its construction by Northern Electric's Chico (Calif.) shops in 1911, 82-ton No. 1010 was said to be the largest and heaviest interurban locomotive in the West. All electrical equipment was carried beneath the floor and the elongated body provided space for l.c.l. freight. In 1930 NE-successor Sacramento Northern rebuilt the big locomotive along more conventional lines. WESTERN PACIFIC RAILROAD.

Pennsylvania's Lackawanna & Wyoming Valley Railroad operated a pioneer locomotive in No. 401, seen here emerging from the Scranton tunnel in 1950. The 401 was built as an experimental combination passenger-freight locomotive by Baldwin-Westinghouse in 1895, and was acquired by the Laurel Line in 1906. After 59 years of service, 401 was retired in 1953, when the company converted to diesels. WILLIAM D. MIDDLETON.

388

Wooden-bodied 5502, built in the Piedmont & Northern Railway's Greenville (S. C.) shops, hauled new Buicks around 1916. This was one of the first interurban locomotives of the four-truck, articulated-frame pattern. PIEDMONT & NORTHERN RAILWAY.

Evolution of the four-truck wheel arrangement on P&N continued through 1941, when General Electric built the 118-ton No. 5611. GENERAL ELECTRIC COMPANY.

Last in a long line of home-built Illinois Terminal electric motive power were five of these 16-wheeled Class D locomotives upgraded by Decatur shops between 1940 and 1942. They weighed 108 tons and were equipped with eight traction motors totaling 1800 horsepower.

390

The largest of all interurban locomotives were three 5500-horsepower units which were originally destined for Soviet Russia but which went to work on the South Shore Line instead. Still very much in use in 1965, they are brothers to 12 units operated by the Milwaukee Road. WILLIAM D. MIDDLETON.

A chore peculiar to trolley freight haulage was the necessity of tending the trolley pole during switching operations. This Potomac Edison brakeman guided the pole during a backup move. H. N. PROCTOR.

Multiple-unit control enabled interurbans to assemble their freight locomotives into a motive power combination suitable for trains of varying tonnage. This "building block" principle, which later contributed greatly to the success of the diesel-electric revolution in steam railroading, is illustrated by this train about to depart from the North Shore Line's Pettibone Yard at North Chicago, Ill. WILLIAM D. MIDDLETON.

Municipal ordinances governing freight operation in city streets sometimes resulted in oddities such as this Illinois Traction box motor, which was built to resemble a passenger car in order to satisfy St. Louis authorities. STEPHEN D. MAGUIRE COLLECTION.

The Bonner "rail wagon" equipment operated by the Lake Shore Electric in 1930 employed an unusual flat car with inside-bearing trucks which was rolled under three 18-foot trailers. These were then fixed to the car with lug latches. The idea had some similarity to the "Clejan" system adopted by some steam railroads in more recent years. GEORGE KRAMBLES COLLECTION.

This unusual General Electric locomotive, operated on the Hutchinson & Northern in Kansas, was equipped with a "frameless truck." Axle bearings were placed in an extra-heavy traction motor frame, which was provided with lugs over the bearings to receive the equalizer bars. FRED FELLOW.

An Insull interurban, the North Shore Line, pioneered "piggyback" transportation of truck trailers in its present-day form in 1926 when it began hauling trailers, loaded with small freight shipments, on flat cars between Chicago and Milwaukee. A few years later, in 1932, the North Shore offered what was perhaps the first modern "common carrier" piggyback service when it began transporting trucks on flat cars for either trucking companies or shippers themselves. And as early as 1930 an Ohio interurban, the Lake Shore Electric Railway, was moving trailers between Cleveland and Toledo on Banner "rail wagon" cars which were similar to the specially designed cars developed several decades later for steam railroad piggyback services.

Interurban roads made early use of special freight containers which could be lifted from flat cars to truck beds, permitting "door to door" freight service. Many lines were thus able to extend the radius of their freight service far beyond the limits of their own lines. The Cincinnati & Lake Erie, for example, in addition to the overnight "store door" container service available between Cincinnati and Toledo on its own line, was able to offer shippers second-morning deliveries in Kentucky and Michigan cities.

Mechanical refrigerator cars, which have only recently begun to replace ice-refrigerated cars on steam railroads, were in operation on several interurban roads during the '20's. Electrically driven refrigeration equipment was used.

In 1926 an interurban, the Northern Ohio Traction & Light Company, even participated in a joint rail-air freight service. A shipment of 670 pounds of forgings was moved from Alliance, O., to the Cleveland airport in 3 hours 18 minutes by trolley freight and an airplane completed the journey to the Ford plant in Detroit in another 1 hour 45 minutes.

Freight traffic on interurban railways grew to substantial proportions. In 1902 it was estimated that interurban companies received about 2 million dollars for hauling such commodities as newspapers, mail, milk, and express. By 1925 trolley freight revenues were in the vicinity of 65 million dollars annually, and some 15 per cent of electric railway gross revenues came from freight.

Unfortunately, the light package freight and express business that generated most of the trolley freight income proved just as vulnerable to the competition of the new trucking industry as the passenger business had to the automobile, and during the '20's it became increasingly evident that development of an extensive carload freight business, with interchange of standard steam railroad equipment, was required.

A few of the lines originally ill equipped to handle heavy freight traffic had taken early steps to develop the necessary facilities. As early as 1906, for example, Illinois Congressman McKinley was building belt lines around principal cities on his Illinois Traction System to permit unrestricted carload freight operation, and his system ultimately became a major freight railroad. But not many other interurbans had equal foresight, and by the time the need for a heavy freight traffic became apparent, few of them had sufficient means to undertake the necessary improvements.

Many of the interurbans which had a capacity for carload freight operation all along, or managed to develop it, survived the interurban era as freight-only short line railroads, usually employing diesel-electric motive power. But for most interurbans freight traffic proved to be as ephemeral as passenger traffic, and when both vanished abandonment was the only recourse. 1

Almost all of the interurbans that have survived as freight-only carriers have abandoned electric equipment in favor of diesel-electric motive power. Iowa's Fort Dodge-Des Moines Line still employed both forms of power when this 70-ton General Electric diesel worked in the Des Moines River valley in 1955, but the railway has since taken down its trolley wire.
WILLIAM D. MIDDLETON.

Exit the Interurban

The sun set on the interurban at Tuck Station on British Columbia Electric's Steveston line. STAN F. STYLES.

Exit the Interurban

THE INTERURBAN was, of course, "done in" by the automobile, a form of transportation almost as old as the electric cars themselves. In a manner not unlike that in which the interurban had largely supplanted steam railroad local passenger service, the automobile in its turn captured the public fancy simply because it provided an even greater utility and convenience than the electric service it displaced.

In the automobile's infancy few, even among its most ardent advocates, had any notion of the monster industry it would one day create. The early autos were far too costly for any but the well-to-do; they were extremely unreliable; and the roads were abominable in any case. Clearly, autos were no more than a rich man's plaything. The electric cars, on the other hand, were sturdy, dependable vehicles that had proven their worth and were headed for a golden future which held unlimited promise. Electric transportation, it was widely felt, would soon become almost universal.

Occasionally, during the early days of motoring, the auto was even a source of extra revenue for the interurbans. In 1905 the general superintendent of the Lake Shore Electric Railway, noting the frequency with which farmers were hauling in disabled automobiles from the highway which paralleled the railway all the way from Cleveland to Toledo, established an "automobile ambulance" service, which employed a flat car drawn by a freight locomotive and equipped with the necessary apparatus for hauling stranded autos aboard. The service, which cost $15 and up, was said to be "much less embarrassing than having to resort to the horse to get back to town." The Buffalo & Lake Erie Traction Company was collecting $5 a head in a similar manner by providing a train of flat cars to haul motorists when roads became impassable along its line. Even as late as the '20's the Pacific Northwest Traction Company was doing a lively business hauling trucks, buses, and automobiles around gaps in the uncompleted Pacific Highway north of Seattle on the electric line's "land ferries," which consisted of flat cars drawn by a freight locomotive.

As early as 1905 the *Street Railway Journal* took editorial notice of the rapidly growing number of automobiles, but only to discount it as a threat of any consequence. And even 10 years later, when some interurbans were beginning to feel the effects of automobile competition, the *Journal*, still not sure there was anything to worry about, remarked, "Whether this condition will be permanent or whether it will practically disappear, as in the case of the bicycle, is hard to say."

Any lingering doubts were soon resolved. Automobile ownership soared and the traction industry found itself with a competitor that could no longer be disregarded. The urban transit industry was the first to feel the severe effects of widespread auto ownership, but a clamor from the new motoring public set in motion a road building program to get rural America "out of the mud," and the interurbans soon found that more and more of their onetime passengers were driving their own cars over a new network of hard-surfaced roads. A few of the smaller lines, which had been marginal propositions all along, promptly folded, but generally the first effect of the new competition was to bring to a halt the heretofore spectacular growth of the interurbans. Total U. S. interurban mileage, which had grown steadily to a peak of about 18,100 miles in 1917, leveled off and then began a gradual decline, although occasional new construction continued for another 10 years. The last new interurban line, for example — Texas' Houston North Shore Railway — opened as late as 1927. But after 1917 the abandonments always came faster than the new construction.

Interurban car construction, another indicator of the industry's health, gradually declined from an average of more than a thousand cars annually during

With the end of over 40 years of service not far away, a lonely Illinois Terminal interurban waited quietly in a January 1955 snowstorm at the Champaign depot. WILLIAM D. MIDDLETON.

the years prior to 1910 to a low of 128 new cars built during 1919.

If business was not quite as good as it had once been, most of the interurbans were still in good shape, and throughout the '20's the stronger systems that had been soundly conceived to begin with were able to wage a determined battle to regain their passenger traffic. Millions were spent on track and power improvements and on line relocations to provide faster service. Older rolling stock was modernized, and as many lines installed brand-new equipment, interurban carbuilding enjoyed a brief resurgence, reaching a peak of over 500 cars annually in 1924. Imaginative new services were started, and freight traffic, which the interurbans had been giving increasing attention, grew to unprecedented levels.

Dr. Thomas Conway's prescription for the successful interurban included consolidation, high-speed equipment, new traffic promotion ideas, and publicity. After one of his new Cincinnati & Lake Erie interurbans defeated an airplane in a race staged for newsreel cameras in 1930, a bannered car toured Dayton streets inviting the public to see films of the race at a local theater. C&LE later adopted such innovations as free taxi service to and from the depot, but the lure of the automobile was irresistible and the system lasted only until 1939. MAYFIELD PHOTOS INC.

Despite its aged equipment, the Atlantic City & Shore Railroad tried to keep right up with the times in 1940 by providing its interurbans with hostesses on the run between Atlantic City and Ocean City. Ann Hackney, "the world's first trolley hostess," prepared to board her Shore Fast Line wooden car in 1942. CENTRAL STUDIOS, ATLANTIC CITY.

A remarkable pair of Pennsylvania interurbans, Lehigh Valley Transit and West Penn Railways, survived into the '50's as typical examples of the passenger interurban of old. In 1950, LVT's Liberty Bell Limited No. 1030, a former Indiana Railroad high-speed car, careened down Lehigh Mountain near Allentown on its way to Norristown. Abandonment was a year away. WILLIAM D. MIDDLETON.

A bright orange West Penn interurban rambled across the high bridge at Brownsville. The broad-gauge system lasted until the mid-'50's, despite a lack of commuters and carload freight. DAVID A. STRASSMAN.

For a time the rejuvenation had encouraging results. A good example of the thoroughgoing overhaul given many properties was that of the Cincinnati & Dayton Traction Company, which had been in almost continuous receivership for 10 years when it was reorganized in 1926 as the Cincinnati, Hamilton & Dayton. Headed by Dr. Thomas Conway Jr., the new management refinanced and completely rebuilt the property. Track was rebuilt with new rails and ties, drainage was improved, and the power distribution system completely rebuilt. New shops were erected, new passenger cars were placed in service, and a large fleet of freight equipment was acquired for a new fast freight and express service.

The publicity-conscious Conway management introduced the newly overhauled CH&D with a gala celebration near Dayton on June 22, 1927. Nearly 400 prominent citizens, public officials, and railwaymen attended a banquet at the new car shops, then adjourned to a nearby natural amphitheater where nearly 30,000 were awaiting the public celebration. There was a night flying exhibition and an elaborate fireworks display, and a band played while seven old cars were burned. The climax of the occasion came when the lights were turned on in the new fleet of cars to the accompaniment of horns and gongs.

Thus, with much fanfare, the CH&D regained its competitive position and was soon solidly back in the black. Other lines enjoyed similar comebacks and many electric railwaymen, for a few brief years, looked to the future with renewed confidence. Predicted Britton I. Budd, president of Samuel Insull's North Shore and South Shore interurbans at Chicago, in 1927, "Well-located interurban lines, instead of being obsolete, are in reality entering upon the period of their greatest usefulness." His prediction, although it proved correct in the special case of his own lines, turned out to be a rather bad guess about the future of the interurbans.

The first interurban came close to being the last. Portland's Oregon City line, opened in 1893, lasted until early 1958. Former Pacific Electric car 4018 rolled across a much-photographed trestle at Milwaukie, Ore., in 1955. WILLIAM D. MIDDLETON.

The Milwaukee Rapid Transit & Speedrail Company was an ill-fated attempt to modernize the remaining interurban routes of the old Milwaukee Electric system with the economies of lightweight cars and one-man operation. A head-on collision of two excursion trains in 1950, the last big wreck of the interurban era, brought financial difficulties and abandonment a year later. On a bright December day in 1950 Waukesha Limited car No. 60, a Cincinnati curved-side lightweight that had seen service on three Indiana and Ohio lines, sped through West Junction. WILLIAM D. MIDDLETON.

Pacific Electric transported the greatest passenger loads in its entire history during World War II, and continued to carry a flourishing rail passenger traffic into the early '50's. During rush hour at Amoco Tower, on the celebrated four-track main line of PE's Southern District, a Watts local on the outer track had just been overtaken by a fast moving Bellflower express. Early in 1961 the last PE interurban route — to Long Beach — was abandoned by its most recent operator, the Los Angeles Metropolitan Transit Authority. WILLIAM D. MIDDLETON.

Smoking brake shoes and motors testified to the heat of a July afternoon in 1955 as a North Shore local, en route from Chicago to Waukegan over the Shore Line route, braked to a stop at North Chicago Junction, only a week before the route was abandoned. Once the main line, the Shore Line continued to operate an extensive, if unprofitable, commuter business to the suburbs north of Chicago following completion of the high-speed Skokie Valley main line in 1925. Early in 1963 the remainder of the North Shore system was abandoned. WILLIAM D. MIDDLETON.

The great depression that began with the stock market crash of 1929 brought the interurbans' comeback to an end. As business activity stagnated, interurban freight and passenger revenues declined accordingly, and often there was too little left even for operating expenses, much less further improvements. For 40 major interurbans *Electric Railway Journal* reported 1930 net operating revenues that were down 46 per cent from the year before, while operating expenses decreased only slightly. Financial reports for 1931 were even worse. A survey of 23 interurbans revealed that operating revenues had dropped as much as 60 per cent below 1930 results, and while 10 of the lines had reported some net income in 1930, only 6 had anything left after operating expenses in 1931. Further drops in revenues as high as 40 per cent were reported in 1932. System after system went under, and by 1933 interurban mileage had been reduced to little over 10,000 miles, a decline of almost 6000 miles in 10 years. New interurban car construction reached an all-time low of seven cars in 1932, and then disappeared altogether.

Separate Chicago Aurora & Elgin cars from Aurora and Elgin had just been consolidated into a single Chicago express at Wheaton, Ill., on a summer evening in 1955. A few years later, with insufficient freight revenues to cover commuter traffic losses, the CA&E became the first of Samuel Insull's "super interurbans" to abandon service. WILLIAM D. MIDDLETON.

Even under the crushing effect of depression there were a few major efforts to modernize and to consolidate separate lines into strong systems. In Ohio in 1929, Dr. Conway, with his overhauled CH&D as a nucleus, assembled the new Cincinnati & Lake Erie system stretching from the Ohio River to Lake Erie, bought 20 new high-speed cars, and installed improved through services. In 1930 the Insull interests organized the statewide Indiana Railroad System, bought 35 new high-speed cars, spent thousands on line improvements, and inaugurated vastly improved service. In 1932 the Fonda, Johnstown & Gloversville in New York placed new Bullet cars on limited schedules that cut as much as half an hour from previous Gloversville-Schenectady timings, and enjoyed a 78 per cent increase in net revenues over those for 1931. Such efforts were widely hailed, and many thought the winning combination for the interurban had at last been found.

Still going strong in 1965, the Philadelphia Suburban Transportation Company was the only surviving interurban east of Chicago. A lightweight Brill suburban car, one of the last cars turned out by the once-great Philadelphia carbuilder, rolled through a rock cut at Smedley Park in 1956, en route from Media to 69th Street terminal. WILLIAM D. MIDDLETON.

A South Shore Line express from Gary, Ind., slid into Illinois Central's Randolph Street Suburban Station in Chicago in 1955. Lengthened and fitted with picture windows, foam rubber seats, and air conditioning, this equipment helped place the South Shore in the forefront of passenger interurbans, but tonnage freight traffic moving behind heavy electric motive power had a lot more to do with the South Shore's continued prosperity in 1965. WILLIAM D. MIDDLETON.

One of Dr. Conway's wind-tunnel-designed Bullet cars raced through Gulph Cut on the third-rail "super-interurban" Philadelphia & Western line, since 1954 a part of the Philadelphia Suburban system. WILLIAM D. MIDDLETON.

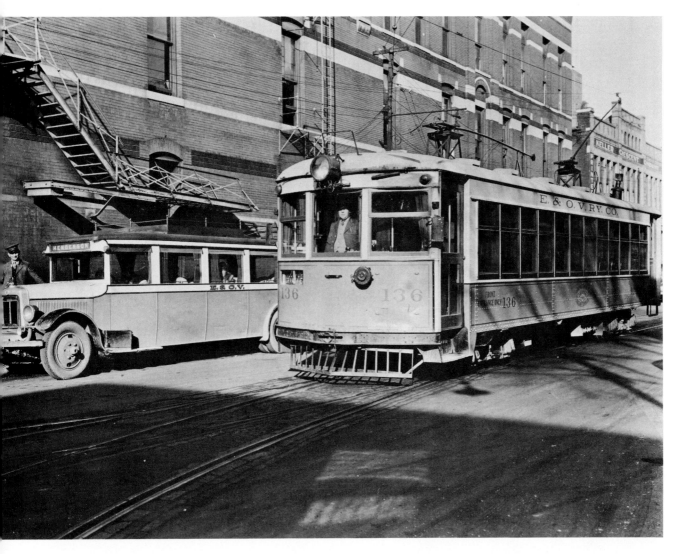

*A lightweight interurban car of the Evansville &
Ohio Valley Railway in Indiana was one of
the first to fall to the bus. In 1928 No. 136
posed beside its replacement on the Hender-
son (Ky.) run.* GEORGE KRAMBLES COLLECTION.

But such measures provided only a temporary
stay of execution. By 1932 piecemeal abandonments
had reduced Indiana Railroad mileage from 850 to
only 300, and the entire system was gone by 1941.
Dr. Conway's Cincinnati & Lake Erie lasted only
until 1939, and the high-speed cars that had shown
such early promise on the FJ&G were returned to the
builders in default of payments several years after
delivery.

The few interurbans that survived into the '40's
and '50's could generally be fitted into one of two
special categories. Some, which entered large metropolitan areas, found new usefulness as home-to-work
transportation for burgeoning bedroom suburbs. All
three of the major Insull interurbans at Chicago, for
example, became important commuter railroads.
Others which had become essentially electric freight
railroads continued to operate an interurban passenger service which was by this time no more than
a minor sideline. A few fortunate systems enjoyed
both a substantial freight traffic and a large commuter business. Los Angeles' Pacific Electric, with

both a tremendous suburban passenger business and
enough on-line industries to make the railway California's third largest originator of freight traffic,
was one of these.

A few remarkable interurban systems managed
to survive as purely passenger-carrying intercity
railroads. Notable among them was Pennsylvania's
Lehigh Valley Transit Company, which served the
populous communities of the Lehigh Valley and
had good connections for Philadelphia-bound passengers. When the Cincinnati & Lake Erie folded in
1939 LVT acquired the major part of C&LE's fleet
of high-speed, lightweight cars, completely refurbished them for its "Liberty Bell Route," and continued to operate an interurban passenger service
in the grand old manner until 1951.

407

A sober-faced group gathered in the main street of New Philadelphia, O., in 1929 for the departure of the last interurban car on the Northern Ohio Power & Light Company. STEPHEN D. MAGUIRE COLLECTION.

Those lines that survived the depression enjoyed a brief return to the bonanza traffic of an earlier era during the World War II years of gasoline rationing and the great industrial activity of national defense. The Southern California population explosion generated by an extraordinary defense industry growth, for example, provided the Pacific Electric system with more rail passengers (a peak of 109 million in 1945) than it had ever handled before.

With the end of the war the forces which had been at work on the interurbans resumed. More autos than ever before rolled off the assembly lines, and continuing declines in what passenger traffic was left combined with growing operating costs to force the abandonment of the remaining marginal passenger operations. Low fares and excessively high peak hour requirements served to make commuter traffic less and less attractive, regardless of its volume; and even those few systems that operated exceedingly large suburban traffics found remaining solvent more and more difficult. Within less than 10 years Pacific Electric had almost entirely converted its passenger operation to more economical, if less satisfactory, bus services, and in 1961 its last interurban route, by then part of a metropolitan transit authority, was discontinued. By early 1963 two of the three Insull interurbans at Chicago — the Chicago Aurora & Elgin and the North Shore Line —had quit entirely. Only the South Shore Line transported enough freight traffic to underwrite its passenger losses and continue operation.

Sometimes the interurban's last run was the occasion for a celebration every bit the equal of its inaugural trip. This crowd gathered at Thurmont, Md., one rainy day in 1954 to see the last trolley off on the Potomac Edison's interurban line to Frederick. H. N. PROCTOR.

A handsome 1903 Niles wooden interurban of classic lines, originally owned by the Toledo, Port Clinton & Lakeside Railway, approached Proprietors' Road on trackage of the Ohio Railway Museum at Worthington. JOHN MALLOY.

409

Excursionists boarded a restored Connecticut Company open car in 1959 for a ride over the Branford museum's line near East Haven, Conn. WILLIAM D. MIDDLETON.

Traction enthusiast E. J. Quinby, a former interurban motorman, took the controls of a well-restored open car on the Branford Electric Railway museum. WILLIAM D. MIDDLETON.

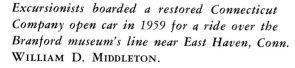

A former Connecticut Company open car rolled through a New England wood on the Connecticut Electric Railway trolley museum, whose rails are laid on the long-abandoned roadbed of a Hartford & Springfield Street Railway branch. WILLIAM D. MIDDLETON.

East of Chicago only a single system, the Philadelphia Suburban Transportation Company, favored with unusual circumstances that helped level off the peak demands of its suburban passenger business, continued to operate.

As the interurban, along with the urban trolley car, vanished from North America, its determined fans, who seemed to grow in numbers as the electric cars became increasingly uncommon, commenced to assemble its history in painstaking texts, countless photographs, maps, timetables, and other memorabilia. Their ultimate achievement was to preserve and operate the cars themselves, and the first such group formed for this purpose, the Seashore Electric Railway, was established at Kennebunkport, Me., in 1939. Others followed, and by 1961 there were more museum groups operating interurban cars than there were surviving interurban railways. Over two dozen groups had preserved well over 200 pieces of electric railway equipment, and more than a dozen of these were actually operating the cars or had definite plans to do so. The Seashore undertaking alone, the largest of the projects, had preserved no less than 71 items of traction rolling stock of every description.

In retrospect it is all too easy to write off the interurban railways as ill-conceived ventures, for clearly they failed to achieve the lasting position and universal application that was once so freely predicted for them, and only rarely did they reap the promised rich financial returns that once made them so popular with investors. But in their time the electric cars served well the transportation needs of a growing nation, and this essential contribution can never be overlooked.

It is worth noting, too, that the interurban railways were rendered obsolete not by a transportation development of superior technology but by one that provided only a greater mobility. As a mass transportation vehicle the electric railway possessed many of the same virtues in 1965 that it had in 1900. For it could still transport large numbers of people far more economically, and quite often more rapidly, than its petroleum-fueled successors.

As America's metropolitan planners, and not a few of the commuting public as well, were becoming increasingly aware, the private automobile, with its insatiable demand for highway and parking space, was a costly and far from satisfactory way of getting the suburban dweller between home and work. It is not unreasonable to suppose, for example, that the Waukesha commuter who once was whisked to

...terurban enthusiasts of the Iowa Railway Historical Museum have the 17-mile Southern Iowa
...ailway at their disposal for excursions with the group's former Waterloo, Cedar Falls & Northern
...ailroad parlor-buffet-observation car. WILLIAM D. MIDDLETON.

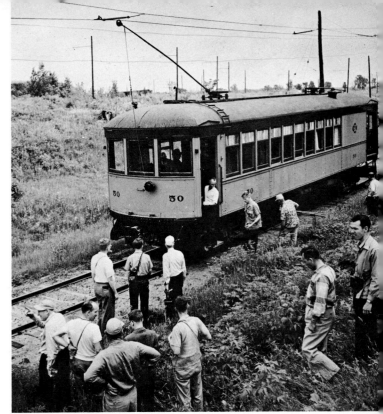

Iowa's Charles City Western Railway, which couldn't bear to part with its interurban after passenger service ended in 1952, refurbished car No. 50 with a pastel color scheme, draperies, and lounge furniture and offered it for charter trips over the freight-only line by trolley fans and nostalgic local residents. WILLIAM D. MIDDLETON.

downtown Milwaukee in as little as 35 minutes by interurban, and who must now spend considerably more time making the same trip by bus or maneuvering his automobile through congested streets, regards the disappearance of his electric railway with some regret.

Indeed, throughout the '50's there was a growing interest again being shown in the electric railway. Toronto completed its handsome new Yonge Street subway, Cleveland inaugurated a brand-new rapid transit system, and Chicago was extending its subway and elevated lines into new territory. San Francisco, Los Angeles, Montreal, and many other cities were making serious plans for construction of rapid transit systems. To be sure, the new electric railways bore little outward resemblance to the colorful interurbans of a half century before, but beneath their sleek and functional modernity the very same principles of clean, quiet, and efficient electric transportation were at work.

If the *Buckeye Specials, Hoosierlands,* and *Comets* that once raced importantly through the countryside in the glamorous days of the interurban era were gone forever, a new and different era of electric transportation was perhaps at hand. I

413

Interurban and Rural Railways
in the United States, Canada, and Mexico

*T*HIS *directory is based upon a 1922 Electric Railway Census by the Department of Commerce, with corrections, additions, and deletions by the author and others. Companies listed operated bona fide interurbans, rural trolley lines, or suburban electric lines with interurban characteristics. Companies which operated street railways only are excluded.*

Company names are normally those under which the railways were listed in 1922. Successor companies and previous names, when they were well known, are shown in italics. Steam railroad control or affiliation is shown in parentheses. Companies are entered under the state in which headquarters were maintained.

NOTES
*Company still electrically operated for passenger service in 1965.
†Company still electrically operated for freight service only in 1965.
All companies were operated by overhead trolley exclusively except as indicated below:
(1) Third-rail operation.
(2) Third-rail and overhead-trolley operation.
(3) Underground-conduit and overhead-trolley operation.
(4) Gas-electric operation.

NEW ENGLAND STATES

MAINE
Androscoggin & Kennebec Ry. Co., The
  Lewiston, Augusta & Waterville St. Ry.
Androscoggin Electric Co.
  Portland-Lewiston Interurban RR
Aroostook Valley RR Co. (CPR)
Atlantic Shore Ry. Co.
Bangor Ry. & Electric Co.
Biddeford & Saco RR, The
Cumberland County Power & Light Co.
  Portland RR
Rockland, Thomaston & Camden St. Ry. Co., The

NEW HAMPSHIRE
Berlin St. Ry.
Boston & Maine RR
  Concord Electric Co.
Claremont Ry.
Dover, Somerset & Rochester St. Ry. Co.
Exeter, Hampton & Amesbury St. Ry.
Manchester & Derry St. Ry.
Manchester & Nashua St. Ry.
Manchester St. Ry.
Nashua St. Ry.
Portsmouth Electric Ry.

VERMONT
Barre & Montpelier Traction & Power Co.
Bellows Falls & Saxton River Electric RR
Burlington Traction Co.
Mt. Mansfield Electric RR
Rutland Ry., Light & Power Co.
St. Albans & Swanton Traction Co.
Springfield Electric Ry. Co. (B&M)
  Springfield Terminal Ry.

Twin State Gas & Electric Co., The

MASSACHUSETTS
Attleboro Branch RR Co.
Berkshire St. Ry. Co. (NH)
Blue Hill St. Ry.
Boston & Worcester St. Ry. Co.
Bristol County St. Ry. Property
Concord, Maynard & Hudson St. Ry. Co.
Connecticut Valley St. Ry. Co.
Eastern Massachusetts St. Ry. Co.
  Bay State St. Ry. Co.
Fitchburg & Leominster St. Ry. Co.
Grafton & Upton RR
Holyoke St. Ry. Co.
Interstate Consolidated St. Ry. Co.
Lowell & Fitchburg St. Ry. Co.
Massachusetts Northeastern St. Ry. Co.
Medway & Dedham St. Ry. Co.
Middlesex & Boston St. Ry. Co.
Milford & Uxbridge St. Ry. Co.
Milford, Attleboro & Woonsocket St. Ry. Co.
Nahant & Lynn St. Ry. Co.
New Bedford & Onset St. Ry. Co.
Northampton Street Ry. Co.
Northern Massachusetts St. Ry. Co.
Norton, Taunton & Attleboro St. Ry. Co.
Plymouth & Brockton St. Ry. Co.
Plymouth & Sandwich St. Ry. Co.
Shelburne Falls & Colerain St. Ry. Co.
Springfield St. Ry. Co. (NH)
Union St. Ry. Co.
Ware & Brookfield St. Ry. Co.
Worcester Consolidated St. Ry. Co. (NH)

RHODE ISLAND
Newport & Providence Ry. Co.
Providence & Fall River St. Ry. Co.
Rhode Island Co., The (NH)
  United Electric Rys. Co.

CONNECTICUT
Bristol & Plainville Electric Co.
Connecticut Co., The (NH)
Danbury & Bethel St. Ry. Co.
Hartford & Springfield St. Ry. Co.
Shore Line Electric Ry. Co., The
Waterbury & Milldale Tramway Co., The

MIDDLE ATLANTIC STATES

NEW YORK
Albany Southern Ry. Co. (2)
Auburn & Syracuse Electric RR Co.
Buffalo & Lake Erie Traction Co.
  Buffalo & Erie Ry.
Chautauqua Traction Co.
Cortland County Traction Co.
Elmira, Corning & Waverly Ry. (Erie)
Elmira Water, Light & RR Co.
Empire State RR Corp.
Erie Railroad (Mt. Morris Div.)
Fonda, Johnstown & Gloversville RR Co.
Geneva, Seneca Falls & Auburn RR Co.
Hudson Valley Ry. Co. (D&H)
International Ry. Co.
Ithaca-Auburn & Lansing RR
Jamestown, Westfield & Northwestern RR Co.
Kaydeross RR Corp.
Keesville, Ausable Chasm & Lake Champlain RR (1)
Lima-Honeoye Electric Light & RR Co.
New Paltz, Highland & Poughkeepsie Traction Co.
New York & Stamford Ry. Co.
New York State Rys. (2) (NYC)
  Rochester & Sodus Bay Ry.
  Rochester & Eastern Rapid Ry.
  Oneida Ry.
  Utica & Mohawk Valley Ry.
New York, Westchester & Boston Ry. Co. (NH)
Niagara Gorge RR Co., The
Olean, Bradford & Salamanca Ry. Co.
Orange County Traction Co.
Paul Smith's Electric Light, Power & RR Co.
Penn Yan & Lake Shore Ry.
Putnam & Westchester Traction Co.
Rochester & Syracuse RR Co.
  Rochester, Syracuse & Eastern RR Co.
Rochester, Lockport & Buffalo RR Corp.
  Buffalo, Lockport & Rochester Ry.
Schenectady Ry. Co. (D&H-NYC)
Southern New York Power & Ry. Corp.
  Southern New York Ry.
Syracuse & Suburban RR Co.
Syracuse Northern Electric Ry.
Walkill Transit Co. (Erie)

NEW JERSEY
Atlantic & Suburban Ry. Co.
Atlantic City & Shore RR Co. (2)
Atlantic Coast Electric Ry. Co.
Bridgeton & Millville Traction Co.

Burlington County Transit Co.
Jersey Central Traction Co.
Millville Traction Co.
Monmouth County Electric Co.
Morris County Traction Co., The
North Jersey Rapid Transit Co.
Northampton-Easton & Washington
Traction Co.
Public Service Ry. Co.
Salem & Pennsgrove Traction Co.
Trenton & Mercer County Traction
Corp.
Trenton-Princeton Traction Co.
(RDG)

PENNSYLVANIA
Allegheny Valley St. Ry. Co.
West Penn Ry. Co.
Allen Street Ry. Co.
Allentown & Reading Traction Co.
Altoona & Logan Valley Electric Ry.
Co.
Bangor & Portland Traction Co.
Beaver Valley Traction Co., The
Bethlehem Transit Co.
Blue Ridge Traction Co.
Carlisle & Mount Holly Rys. Co.
Centre & Clearfield Ry. Co.
Chambersburg & Gettysburg Electric
Ry. Co. (PRR)
Chambersburg & Shippensburg Ry.
Co.
Chambersburg, Greencastle &
Waynesboro St. Ry. Co.
Citizens Traction Co., The
Cleveland & Erie Ry. Co.
Conestoga Traction Co.
Corry & Columbus Traction Co.
Cumberland Ry.
Eastern Pennsylvania Rys. Co.
Ephrata & Lebanon Traction Co.
Fairchance & Smithfield Traction Co.
Hanover & McSherrystown St. Ry.
Co.
Harrisburg Rys. Co.
Hershey Transit Co.
Indiana County St. Ry. Co.
Jefferson Traction Co.
Jersey Shore & Antes Fort RR Co.
Johnstown & Somerset Ry. Co.
Johnstown Traction Co.
Lackawanna & Wyoming Valley RR
Co. (2)
Lancaster & Southern
Lancaster & York Furnace St. Ry. Co.
Lehigh Traction Co., The
Lehigh Valley Transit Co.
Lewisburg, Milton & Watsontown
Passenger Ry. Co.
Lewistown & Reedsville Electric Ry.
Co., The
Lykens Valley Ry. Co.
Mauch Chunk & Lehighton Transit
Co.
Montgomery Transit Co.
North Branch Transit Co.
Northampton Transit Co.
Northern Cambria Ry. Co.
Northwestern Electric Service Co. of
Pennsylvania
Pennsylvania RR (Dillsburg branch)
Pennsylvania & Maryland St. Ry. Co.
Pennsylvania-New Jersey Ry. Co.
Philadelphia & Easton Transit Co.

*Philadelphia & West Chester
Traction Co.
*Philadelphia Suburban Transporta-
tion Co.*
*Philadelphia & Western Ry. Co. (1)
*Philadelphia Suburban Transporta-
tion Co.*
Phoenixville, Valley Forge &
Strafford Electric Ry. Co.
Pittsburgh Ry. Co.
Pittsburgh, Harmony, Butler & New
Castle Ry. Co.
Pittsburgh, Mars & Butler Ry. Co.
Pottstown & Reading St. Ry.
Reading Transit & Light Co.
Schuylkill Ry. Co.
Scranton Ry. Co.
Scranton, Montrose & Binghamton
RR Co.
Shamokin & Edgewood Electric Ry.
Co.
Shamokin & Mount Carmel Transit
Co.
Sharon & New Castle St. Ry. Co.
Slate Belt Transit Co.
Southern Cambria Ry. Co.
Southern Pennsylvania Traction Co.
Stroudsburg Traction Co., The
Sunbury & Sellinsgrove Ry. Co.
Titusville Traction Co.
Trenton, Bristol & Philadelphia St.
Ry. Co.
United Traction St. Ry. Co.
Valley Rys.
Warren & Jamestown St. Ry. Co.
Warren St. Ry. Co.
Waverly, Sayre & Athens Traction
Co. (Erie)
West Chester, Kennett & Wilmington
Electric Ry. Co.
West Chester St. Ry. Co., The
West Penn Ry. Co.
Wilkes-Barre Ry. Co., The
Wilkes-Barre & Hazleton Ry. Co.,
The (2)
York Rys. Co.

SOUTH ATLANTIC STATES

DELAWARE
Wilmington & Philadelphia Traction
Co.

MARYLAND
Cumberland & Westernport Electric
Ry. Co.
Kensington Ry. Co.
Potomac Public Service Co.
Hagerstown & Frederick Ry.
United Rys. & Electric Co. of
Baltimore
Washington, Baltimore & Annapolis
Electric RR Co. (3)
*Baltimore & Annapolis RR Co.
(B&O)*

DISTRICT OF COLUMBIA
Washington Ry. & Electric Co. (3)

VIRGINIA
Newport News & Hampton Ry.
Gas & Electric Co.
Norfolk Southern RR
Richmond & Chesapeake Bay Ry.

Richmond-Ashland Ry. Co.
Richmond-Fairfield Ry. Co.
Roanoke Ry. & Electric Co.
Virginia Ry. & Power Co.
Washington & Old Dominion Ry.
Washington-Virginia Ry. (3)
*Arlington & Fairfax Ry.
Washington, Alexandria & Mt.
Vernon Ry.*

WEST VIRGINIA
Appalachian Power Co.
Tri-City Traction Co.
Charleston Interurban RR Co.
Kanawha Traction & Electric Co.
*Monongahela West Penn Public
Service Co.*
Lewisburg & Ronceverte Electric Ry.
Co.
Monongahela Power & Ry. Co.
*Monongahela West Penn Public
Service Co.*
Ohio Valley Electric Ry. Co.
Parkersburg & Ohio Valley Electric
Ry.
Princeton Power Co.
Tri-City Traction Co.
Sistersville & New Martinsville
Traction Co.
Tyler Traction Co.
Wellsburg, Bethany & Washington
Ry. Co.
Wheeling Public Service Co.
Wheeling Traction Co.

NORTH CAROLINA
Piedmont Ry. & Electric Co.
Tidewater Power Co.

SOUTH CAROLINA
Charleston-Isle of Palms Traction
Co.
Columbia Ry., Gas & Electric Co.
Piedmont & Northern Ry. Co.

GEORGIA
Atlanta Northern Ry. Co.
Augusta-Aiken Ry. & Electric Corp.
Fairburn & Atlanta Ry. & Electric
Co. (4)
Georgia Ry. & Power Co.
Savannah Electric & Power Co.

FLORIDA
None

NORTH CENTRAL STATES

OHIO
Cincinnati & Columbus Traction Co.
Cincinnati & Dayton Traction Co.,
The
*Ohio Electric Ry. Co.
Cincinnati, Hamilton & Dayton Ry.
Co.
Cincinnati & Lake Erie RR*
Cincinnati, Georgetown &
Portsmouth RR Co., The
Cincinnati, Lawrenceburg & Aurora
Electric St. RR Co., The
Cincinnati, Milford & Blanchester
Traction Co., The
Cincinnati St. Ry. Co.
Cleveland, Alliance & Mahoning
Valley RR Co.

Inland Empire RR Co.
Spokane, Coeur d'Alene & Palouse Ry. (GN)
Lewiston-Clarkson Transit Co.
North Coast Power Co.
Olympia Light & Power Co.
Pacific Northwest Traction Co.
Pacific Traction Co.
Puget Sound Electric Ry. (2)
Puget Sound International Ry. & Power Co.
Seattle & Rainier Valley Ry. Co.
Seattle Municipal St. Ry.
Spokane & Eastern Ry. & Power Co.
Spokane, Coeur d'Alene & Palouse Ry. (GN)
Tacoma Ry. & Power Co.
Twin City Ry.
Vancouver Traction Co.
Walla Walla Valley Ry. Co. (NP)
Washington Water Power Co.
Willapa Electric Co.
†Yakima Valley Transportation Co. (UP)

OREGON
Oregon Electric Ry. Co. (SP&S)
Portland Ry. Light & Power Co.
Southern Oregon Traction Co.
Southern Pacific Co.
Portland, Eugene & Eastern Ry.
United Rys. Co. (SP&S)
Willamette Valley Southern Ry. Co.

CALIFORNIA
Central California Traction Co. (2) (SP-WP-ATSF)
Fresno Traction Co.
Glendale & Montrose Ry. (UP)
Market St. Ry.
Northwestern Pacific RR (1) (SP)
Pacific Coast Ry. Co.
Pacific Electric Ry. Co. (SP)
Peninsular Ry. Co. (SP)
Petaluma & Santa Rosa RR Co. (NWP)
†Sacramento Northern RR (2)(WP)
San Diego Electric Ry. Co.

San Diego Southern Ry. Co.
San Francisco, Napa & Calistoga Ry.
San Francisco-Oakland Terminal Rys. (2)
Key System
San Francisco-Sacramento RR Co.
Sacramento Northern RR (WP)
Southern Pacific Co.
Interurban Electric Ry.
Tidewater Southern Ry. (WP)
Visalia Electric RR Co. (SP)

CANADA

NEWFOUNDLAND
None

NOVA SCOTIA
Cape Breton Tramways
Pictou County Ry.

NEW BRUNSWICK
None

QUEBEC
Hull Electric Co. (CPR)
Montreal & Southern Counties Ry. (CNR)
Montreal Tramways
Quebec Ry., Light & Power Co. (CNR)

ONTARIO
Brantford & Hamilton Electric Ry.
Brantford Municipal Ry.
Chatham, Wallaceburg & Lake Erie Ry.
Grand River Ry. (CPR)
Grand Valley Ry.
Hamilton & Dundas St. Ry.
Hamilton, Grimsby & Beamsville Electric Ry.
Hamilton Radial Electric Ry.
Lake Erie & Northern Ry. (CPR)
London & Lake Erie Ry. & Transportation Co.
†London & Port Stanley Ry.

Mt. McKay & Kakabeka Falls Ry.
Niagara Falls Park & River Ry.
Niagara, St. Catharines & Toronto Ry. (CNR)
Nipissing Central Ry.
Sandwich, Windsor & Amherstburg Electric Ry.
Schomsburg & Aurora Ry.
Sudbury-Copper Cliff Suburban Ry.
Toronto & York Radial Rys.
Toronto Suburban Ry. (CNR)
Windsor, Essex & Lake Shore Rapid Ry.
Woodstock, Thames Valley & Ingersoll Ry.

MANITOBA
Winnipeg Electric Co.
Winnipeg, Selkirk & Lake Winnipeg Ry.

SASKATCHEWAN
None

ALBERTA
Calgary Municipal Ry.

BRITISH COLUMBIA
†British Columbia Electric Ry.

MEXICO

F.C. Electrico de Lerdo a Torreon
F.C. Electrico de Tampico a la Barra
F.C. Mexicano, Tejeria-Jalapa branch (mule power)
*Servicio de Transportes Electricos, Mexico City

CUBA

*F.C. Cubano de Hershey

PUERTO RICO

Caguas Tramway Co.

Principal Interurban Carbuilders

*F*OR *a more detailed discussion of carbuilders the reader is referred to "Railway Car Builders of the United States & Canada," written by E. Harper Charlton and published by* Interurbans, *from which this summary is drawn with the kind permission of the author and publisher.*

American Car Company, St. Louis, Mo., 1891-1931.
A leading street and interurban carbuilder, American was acquired by J. G. Brill in 1902 as a strategically located plant for Brill's western orders. Cars were built there under the American label until the plant's reorganization as J. G. Brill of Missouri in 1931, only a scant four months before the works closed its doors for good.

American Car & Foundry Company, 1899-
Formed by the merger of 13 older firms, ACF is still a leading railroad carbuilder. Much of ACF's interurban car construction was centered at its Jeffersonville (Ind.) plant, which included among its output many of the handsome heavy steel coaches, diners, parlor cars, and sleepers that graced Ohio and Indiana traction during the '20's, and a portion of the

Indiana Railroad's notable high-speed, lightweight car fleet of 1931.

Barney & Smith Car Company, Dayton, O., 1849-1923.
A general railway carbuilder, Barney & Smith built interurbans for many Midwest and other systems. The plant made the transition to steel carbuilding in 1913, and closed only 10 years later.

J. G. Brill Company, Philadelphia, Pa., 1868-1956.
Without question Brill was the leader in street and interurban car construction throughout the age of electric traction. Formed by John George Brill and his son G. Martin Brill, the firm pioneered many important advances in electric railway

cars and their equipment. In 1899 the company laid plans to consolidate its own activities with several other firms' into the Consolidated Street Car Company, which would have absorbed 90 per cent of the electric carbuilders in the U. S. These plans were later abandoned, but between 1902 and 1908 Brill acquired the American Car Company at St. Louis; G. C. Kuhlman Car Company at Cleveland; John Stephenson Car Company at Elizabeth, N. J.; Wason Manufacturing Company at Springfield, Mass.; and Danville Car Company at Danville, Ill., giving the company strategically located plants in most parts of the U. S. In 1912 Compagnie J. G. Brill was formed with a plant at Paris, France, which produced cars and trucks for electric lines throughout the Eastern Hemisphere. Brill cars were, in fact, to be found throughout the world.

Every conceivable type of car was built by Brill. Among a few of the most notable Brill designs were the patented Brill semi-convertible car, which was widely used throughout the U. S.; the heavy steel high-speed articulated cars built in 1926 for the Washington, Baltimore & Annapolis; and the lightweight, high-speed Bullet cars developed in 1930. Brill had patents covering virtually every component of car construction, from trucks to trolley wheels, and the firm pioneered "package" selling and assembly line production.

Brill declined along with the electric railways it supplied, and the last car came out of the Philadelphia plant in 1941, after which the firm turned its attention to buses and other products.

Canadian Car & Foundry Company, Limited, Montreal, Que., 1909-

A general railway carbuilder ever since its organization, Canadian Car was a leading builder of electric railway cars in Canada, and large volumes of street and interurban cars were built from 1909 until the last one rolled out of the plant in 1946. Now Canadian Car Company, Ltd., the plant still produces railroad equipment.

Cincinnati Car Company, Cincinnati, O., 1902-1931.

A subsidiary of the Cincinnati Street Railway, Cincinnati Car had its origin in Chester Park shops which built cars and trucks for the parent firm for its own use. Other Ohio companies asked to have cars built for them, and as the demand increased the separate carbuilding firm was formed.

Cincinnati cars were seen largely on systems in the Midwest and Southeast. Virtually every type of car, both wood and steel, was built during the

firm's 30 years in business, but the most notable among them were the famous curved-side lightweight cars built during the 1920's, and the fleet of lightweight, high-speed cars built in 1930 for the Cincinnati & Lake Erie Railroad. The latter represented virtually the last cars built by the firm, for only a year later Cincinnati completed its final order.

Columbia Car & Tool Works, Portland, Ore.

Columbia built only a modest number of cars for electric lines in the Northwest but is deserving of mention by virtue of having built the first cars, in 1892, for the Portland-Oregon City East Side Railway, generally regarded as the first interurban.

Danville Car Company, Danville, Ill., circa 1900-1913.

Danville, a short-lived firm, built a considerable number of street and interurban cars for Midwest and Western systems. The plant was acquired by J. G. Brill in 1908 but went out of business only five years later when the traction industry began the transition to steel equipment.

Harlan & Hollingsworth, Wilmington, Del., 1836-1905.

Established in 1836, Harlan & Hollingsworth was one of the oldest railway carbuilders. Purchased by Bethlehem Steel in 1905, the car works continued in operation until 1944. Among the most interesting interurban cars produced by the plant were the "Holland" sleeping cars built in 1903, which converted from a parlor car by day to a sleeper by night, and the unusual articulated units constructed by Bethlehem in 1935 for the Key System's Bay Bridge service between San Francisco and the East Bay cities.

Jewett Car Company, Newark, O., 1894-1918.

Jewett was one of several builders that produced in large numbers the handsomely proportioned "classic" cars that typified the wood car era on the Midwestern interurbans. Jewett changed over to steel construction and turned out a few groups of distinguished all-steel cars before it went into receivership and out of business in 1918.

Jones' Sons Car Company, Watervliet, N. Y., 1839-1922.

An early entrant in the electric carbuilding industry, the Jones firm began building street railway cars in 1864 and as early as 1886 was said to be building 300 streetcars a year. Jones cars went to many countries, but most of them were to be found on the streetcar and rural trolley lines

of New England and the East. Production of cars ended in 1912.

G. C. Kuhlman Car Company, Cleveland, O., 1892-1932.

Kuhlman built an extensive variety of street and interurban cars, including wood cars of classic pattern, heavy steel cars, and a considerable number of lightweights during the 1920's. J. G. Brill absorbed the Kuhlman firm in 1904, as part of its program to acquire plants at strategic locations. Production continued under the Kuhlman name until 1931, when the plant was reorganized as J. G. Brill of Ohio. Only a year later carbuilding ceased for good.

Laconia Car Company, Laconia, N. H., 1881-1928.

Cars by Laconia, one of the leading builders in New England, were found everywhere in the Northeast, and frequently in other parts of the U. S. as well. The company was also an important builder of steam road equipment. Along with a majority of the traction carbuilders, Laconia went out of business with the decline of the electric railway industry in the late 1920's.

McGuire-Cummings Manufacturing Company, Chicago and Paris, Ill., -1943.

Entering the electric railway field as a car truck builder in 1888, McGuire-Cummings was known as the McGuire Manufacturing Co. Later the company began building specialized equipment, and finally became a major producer of all types of electric railway equipment, as well as a considerable amount of steam railway rolling stock. A great volume of wood and steel interurbans bore the McGuire-Cummings label. Probably the most distinguished among them were the three steel parlor-buffet-observation cars built for limited service on the Waterloo, Cedar Falls & Northern Railroad in 1915. The company later became the Cummings Car & Coach Company, and built its last car in 1930.

Niles Car & Manufacturing Company, Niles, O., 1901-1917.

Although it built a few steel cars in its last years, the Niles firm was noted principally for the handsome wood cars it turned out during the peak years of interurban carbuilding. Niles called its cars "The Electric Pullmans," and among them were perhaps the largest wood interurbans ever constructed. Built for the Washington, Baltimore & Annapolis in 1907, these 62-foot cars weighed 44 tons.

419

Osgood Bradley Car Company, Worcester, Mass., 1833-1930.

A producer of railway cars since 1833, the Osgood Bradley plant, which operated until 1960 as part of Pullman-Standard, was the oldest carbuilding plant in the United States. Its 127 years of production included virtually every type of steam and electric railroad car. Osgood Bradley was associated with the Standard Steel Car Company after 1910, and became part of Pullman-Standard in 1930. P-S rapid-transit car production was concentrated at the Osgood Bradley plant until its closing in 1960.

Ottawa Car Manufacturing Company, Ottawa, Ont., 1891-1947.

One of the leading Canadian carbuilders, Ottawa built large numbers of street and interurban cars that operated in all parts of the Dominion. The plant closed in 1947, after building a final order of streetcars for the Ottawa Electric Railway.

Pressed Steel Car Company, Pittsburgh, Pa., 1896-1954.

A pioneer steel carbuilder from the time of its organization, Pressed Steel was exclusively a freight carbuilder until 1906, when it built some of the first steel passenger cars. The firm, principally a steam road carbuilder, also manufactured street and interurban cars, among them some of the earliest all-steel designs. Outstanding among its interurbans were 24 all-steel cars built in 1915 for high-speed service over Pacific Electric's première San Bernardino line. The legendary super-salesman "Diamond Jim" Brady was associated with Pressed Steel Car until 1902, when he walked out to join in forming the rival Standard Steel Car Company.

Preston Car & Coach Company, Preston, Ont., 1908-1921.

Another of the principal Canadian builders, Preston built electric railway cars, as well as occasional steam road equipment. In 1921, when the Toronto Transportation Commission restricted bidding on new cars to Canadian firms, J. G. Brill leased Preston Car & Coach and set up Canadian Brill Company, Ltd., which lasted hardly long enough to complete the 50-car Toronto order it obtained.

Pullman-Standard Car Manufacturing Company, 1867-

One of the leaders in American carbuilding, the Pullman organization began its carbuilding activities in 1867, when George Pullman founded Pullman's Palace Car Company. Various corporate changes have taken place in the intervening years but the name "Pullman" has been synonymous with sleeping cars and carbuilding ever since. Pullman entered the electric car field in 1891 and has continued in the business to the present time, building everything from 4-wheel streetcars to heavy M.U. coaches for steam road electrifications. Among distinguished Pullman interurbans have been some of Pacific Electric's finest steel interurbans, cars for Southern Pacific's Oregon electrification, high-speed steel equipment for the Insull interurbans at Chicago, and a portion of Indiana Railroad's 1931 fleet of high-speed aluminum cars.

St. Louis Car Company, St. Louis, Mo., 1887-

Exceeded only by Brill in volume, St. Louis Car was one of the greatest of the electric carbuilders, and it enjoys the distinction of being the only one of the firms once devoted largely to carbuilding for the electric railway industry that still remains in business. In 1960 the company was purchased by General Steel Castings Corporation. St. Louis has built electric equipment of every description, and a considerable amount of steam railroad rolling stock also, including carbodies for many of Electro-Motive's early gas-electric cars and several of its first diesel-electrics. Like Brill, St. Louis designed and built trucks and virtually every other major car component, as well as cars themselves. The noteworthy interurbans produced by St. Louis are almost too numerous to mention. Among the most recent were the two extraordinary 85-mile-per-hour streamlined *Electroliner* trains built for the Chicago North Shore & Milwaukee in 1941, and the three post-World War II electric streamliners for the Illinois Terminal Railroad, which were the very last interurbans built. Today St. Louis is turning out rapid transit cars and equipment for steam railroads.

Southern Car Company, High Point, N. C., 1904-1917.

In business only 13 years, Southern Car was nonetheless an important builder, and its street and interurban cars were found throughout the South, and at points as far away as New York and Puerto Rico. When Southern went out of business a new firm, the Perley A. Thomas Car Works, was established, which took over the plant and continued building streetcars until 1930.

John Stephenson Car Company, Elizabeth, N. J., 1831-1917.

Stephenson was one of the first U. S. railroad carbuilders. Originally located in New York, the firm built most of the city's first street railroad rolling stock. In the 15 years from 1876 to 1891 alone, Stephenson built 25,000 horse, cable, and electric cars. During the boom years of interurban construction many lines were equipped with handsome wood cars turned out by the Stephenson plant, including some of the earliest cars capable of really high speeds. In 1903, for example, a Stephenson car covered 35 miles on the new third-rail Aurora, Elgin & Chicago Railway in 34 minutes 39 seconds, including speed restrictions and stops.

The Stephenson plant was acquired by J. G. Brill in 1904, but production continued under the Stephenson name. The plant never tooled up for steel carbuilding, and closed in 1917.

Wason Manufacturing Company, Springfield, Mass., 1845-1931.

Wason was another of the carbuilders acquired by J. G. Brill in its expansion program shortly after the turn of the century. Wason electric cars were built in large numbers for lines in New England and other areas, and it was also a steam road carbuilder. Trucks and bodies for General Electric's line of gas-electric cars were almost always turned out by the Wason plant. The Wason name continued in use after the 1906 Brill purchase until 1931 when the plant, in common with the other remaining Brill subsidiaries, lost its identity and became J. G. Brill of Massachusetts. Within a year, also in common with the other Brill subsidiary plants, Wason went out of the carbuilding business for good. 1

Principal Types of Interurban Rolling Stock, Important Components, and Accessories

PASSENGER CAR TYPES

CLOSED CAR: The ordinary closed car, comparable in general arrangement to steam railroad coaches, with doors and enclosed vestibules at each end, was by far the most common type of interurban passenger car.

COMBINE CAR: With the provision of a compartment for mail, express, and baggage at one end of the car, a single unit enabled interurban operators to provide varied services.

CENTER-ENTRANCE CAR: With doors and steps at or near the center of the body, the center-entrance car usually had side plates that sloped down to the bottom of the steps, giving what was described as a "possumbelly" or "sow belly" appearance.

OPEN CAR: The most common variety of this summer car had transverse benches across the full width of the car, with longitudinal steps the full length of the car to permit boarding or alighting at any point.

COMBINATION OR "SEMI-OPEN" CAR: Divided between open and closed sections, this arrangement was popular in California, where weather changes were often sudden.

CALIFORNIA CAR: This variation, the original type of "semi-open" car, placed the closed section at the center.

CONVERTIBLE CAR: Equipped with removable side panels and windows, the "full convertible," which enjoyed only modest popularity, was an attempt to develop an open car suitable for year-around operation.

SEMI-CONVERTIBLE CAR: Window sash which could be removed, or which disappeared into wall or roof pockets, made the semi-convertible a practical car for both winter and summer operation, and it was built in great numbers for interurban lines in all parts of the U. S.

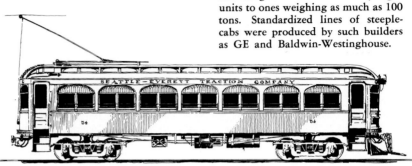

CLOSED

ARTICULATED CAR: Articulation, with two carbodies resting on a common truck, made possible a high-capacity unit which could still nego-

COMBINE

tiate the restrictive curvature common to most interurbans. Another type of articulated car, consisting of a short carbody suspended between two single-truck cars and often described as "two rooms and a bath," was used on a few street railways.

FREIGHT EQUIPMENT

BOX OR EXPRESS MOTOR: Essentially a motorized baggage car, with controls at one or both ends, the box motor was used for express or light freight service.

B-B STEEPLE-CAB LOCOMOTIVE: This locomotive, the most widely used locomotive type for interurban freight service, had a center cab of variable length, with sloping hoods at each end that housed a part of its air, electrical, and other equipment. These machines were usually equipped for multiple-unit operation, and ranged in size from very light units to ones weighing as much as 100 tons. Standardized lines of steeple-cabs were produced by such builders as GE and Baldwin-Westinghouse.

B-B BOX-CAB LOCOMOTIVE: Otherwise identical to the steeple-cab design, the box-cab locomotive had all of its equipment installed in a full-length cab. The arrangement was simplicity itself, but the design was never as popular as the steeple-cab, principally because visibility was not as good in switching operations.

B-B + B-B ARTICULATED LOCOMOTIVE: Several interurban lines with extremely heavy freight traffic built powerful locomotives of this arrangement, which employed four power trucks under a pair of articulated frames to operate through short radius electric line curves.

CURRENT COLLECTION

OVERHEAD SYSTEMS: A trolley pole, which was held against the wire

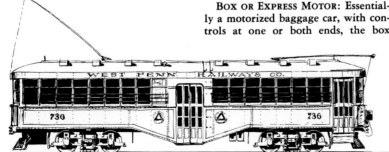

CENTER-ENTRANCE

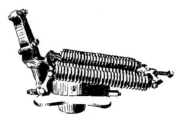

TROLLEY BASE

TROLLEY WHEEL

TROLLEY SHOE

RETRIEVER

by the tension of springs mounted in a swiveling trolley base, was the usual means of current collection for overhead systems. Originally the use of a large trolley wheel, 6 inches or more in diameter and cast from a variety of compositions, was favored for current collection. A trolley "harp" held the wheel and provided a positive means of electrical contact. In later years sliding shoes were developed which seemed to work better, and they were eventually substituted for wheels on most lines. In case of dewirement the flailing trolley pole often caused damage to the overhead construction, and some lines used various types of retrievers, which automatically pulled the pole down when the shoe or wheel became disengaged from the wire.

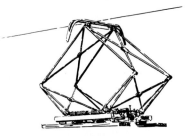

PANTOGRAPH

The amount of current that could be successfully drawn by a single trolley wheel or shoe was limited, and for heavy-duty lines on which large currents were required the panto-

graph system was preferred. The pantograph, employing one or two flat collectors which slid along the wire, was raised and held against the wire by springs and was lowered by air pressure.

The use of "pole bow" trolleys, which combined some of the features of an ordinary pole trolley and a pantograph, although common in Europe, was rare in North America. Either a flat collector or a roller was held against the wire by spring tension. Only one line, the Indianapolis & Cincinnati Traction Company, used this system for an extended period.

THIRD-RAIL SYSTEMS: Current collection from third-rail systems was usually by means of a truck-mounted iron collection shoe, which was held against the top of the power rail by its own weight. In protected third-rail installations, where the power rail was usually inverted, an "underrunning" shoe, held in place by spring tension, was used.

UNDERGROUND CONDUIT SYSTEMS: Sliding shoes on a truck-mounted "plow," which projected through the slot between the rails, collected current from the underground power rail. Two shoes were usually necessary, since most conduit systems had a separate return rail.

TRUCKS AND MOTORS

The double-truck car was virtually universal in interurban operation, and truck design largely followed the pattern of steam railroad passenger car practice. The typical interurban truck was a four-wheel design of the M.C.B. (Master Car Builders) type, with the car weight carried to the truck frame by a transverse bolster beam supported by leaf springs, and the load in turn carried to the axles through coil springs and equalizer bars. Trucks were usually built up from steel shapes and forged sections, although some builders used pressed steel assemblies, and in later years a few cars were built with cast steel trucks. Several of the major carbuilders, such as St. Louis and Brill,

BOW TROLLEY

OVERRUNNING SHOE

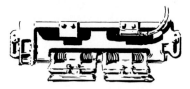

UNDERRUNNING SHOE

built trucks of their own design, which were often applied under the cars of other builders as well as their own; the Baldwin Locomotive Works and the American Locomotive Company both built widely used motor trucks; and a number of independent truck builders, prominent among them Peckham, Standard, McGuire, and Taylor, also built extensively used designs.

The wheelbase of interurban trucks usually varied between 6 and 7 feet. A longer wheelbase provided a smoother ride in high-speed operation, but the necessity for operation around sharp curves set a limit on the practical maximum wheelbase. Iron wheels and axles were often used on the earlier cars but steel soon became standard for this purpose. A wheel around 36 inches in diameter was ordinarily employed, although some roads used wheels as large as 39 inches for high-speed operation. Wheel flanges were usually smaller than M.C.B. standards because of the restricted flanges and specialwork prevalent on the street railways used for city entrances. The smaller flanges were more prone to chipping or breaking, and provided a smaller margin of safety against derailment at high speed. Because of the limita-

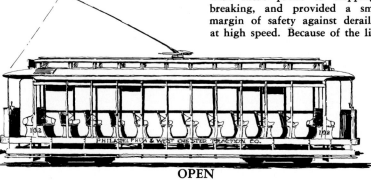

OPEN

tions of trolley curvature, the six-wheel "Pullman" type of passenger car truck was impractical for interurban service, and only a few cars were ever attempted with this type.

One of the most radical departures in interurban truck design was the modified arch bar cantilever (A.B.C.) truck developed in 1923 by the Cincinnati Car Company for use on its lightweight interurbans and streetcars. The equalizer bar of conventional practice was eliminated and the load was carried directly from the truck frame to the axles through coil springs. Various types of "snubbers" were used which counteracted the tendency of coil spring suspension to set up a dangerous rhythmic undulation (in some Cincinnati experiments test cars actually left the rails from this cause). Further refined in subsequent years, the Cincinnati A.B.C. truck was extremely successful in providing a smooth ride at high speeds. Much smaller and lighter than the usual M.C.B. trucks, the A.B.C. used wheels only 28 inches in diameter, and required the development of very compact motors.

Many early interurban cars employed only two motors, placing one on each truck or both on a single truck, but the requirement for

LIGHTWEIGHT TRUCK

HEAVYWEIGHT TRUCK

ample power to drive heavy cars at high speed soon made the four-motor car the most common type. Motors were either "inside" or "outside" hung, depending upon whether they were placed between or outside the axles, and were connected to the axles by gear drives. The inside-hung arrangement, which was almost universal on trucks designed for interurban service, required a longer wheelbase, which was needed for smooth operation at speed anyway. Motors normally varied from about 75 to 100 horsepower in large interurban car applications, but on occasion motors developing as much as 200 horsepower each were used for exceptionally large and fast cars.

BRAKES AND CONTROLLERS

Conventional air brake systems were almost always used by inter-

urban roads. At first, when single car operation was common, "straight air" systems, in which air was admitted to or exhausted from the brake cylinder directly by the motorman's valve, were used. Train operation required the use of "automatic" brake systems, with the brake cylinders directly controlled by a "triple valve" in each car, which in turn was controlled by varying the pressure in the brake pipe with the motorman's valve. An electric motor-driven compressor under each car provided the necessary air supply.

At least one interurban system, the West Penn Railways, made wide use of cars which had no air brakes at all, but used instead a magnetic track brake. This consisted of an electromagnetic brake shoe suspended between the wheels from springs mounted on the truck frame. To apply brakes the electromagnet was energized, which drew the brake shoe down against the rail. When air braking systems alone were found inadequate for the extremely high-speed cars developed by several lines in 1929-1930, they were supplemented by magnetic track brakes.

To control the flow of current to the traction motors on the earliest interurban cars, a "direct controller" was used, which passed the entire current through the motorman's controller. This type had several disadvantages. The electrical equipment required to control the heavy currents drawn by the powerful motors of

CAB INTERIOR

large interurban cars made the controller extremely bulky, and the presence of high-voltage, high-amperage currents on the platform presented a potential hazard to crew and passengers. Also, the direct controller was adaptable to single car operation only.

The invention of multiple-unit control — which was essentially a remote-control system — by Frank J. Sprague in 1898 eliminated the shortcomings of the direct-control system. The remote-control system employed only a small master controller at the motorman's position and a low-voltage, low-amperage control circuit that actuated, by means of magnet-

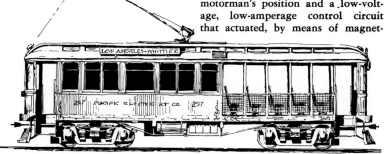

SEMI-OPEN

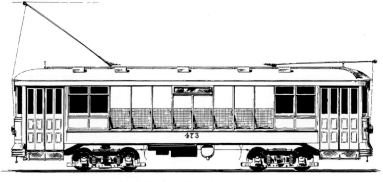

SEMI-CONVERTIBLE

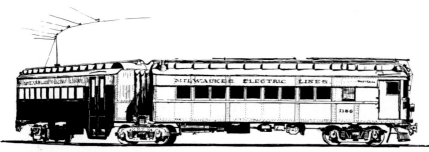

ARTICULATED

ic or pneumatic switches, the main controller which was located under the car. When operation of more than one car in a train was desired, the control circuits of the separate cars were simply connected by jumpers and the main controller of each car was then operated simultaneously with others in the train by the master controller in the lead car.

MISCELLANEOUS CAR EQUIPMENT

PILOTS AND FENDERS: Huge projecting timber pilots were often employed on the early cars, but when operation in trains was contemplated, pilots of more restrained size, recessed under the front of the car to permit coupling, became necessary. After the earliest years, steel and iron were almost always used for pilots. For winter operations in areas of heavy snows, pilots were sometimes covered with sheet metal to act as plows, or were sometimes replaced entirely by snowplows.

City ordinances in many areas, particularly in California, required electric lines to provide their cars with special fenders, which looked not unlike a large bed spring, designed to scoop up wayward pedestrians before they were run over by the cars.

ANTI-CLIMBERS: The projecting steel corrugations of this device, which was installed at each end of interurban cars, were supposed to interlock in the unfortunate event of a collision with another car, and prevent the floor of one car from riding over that of the other with a devastating telescoping effect.

COUPLERS: Interurban lines most often employed automatic couplings similar to those which were by then in general use on steam railroads. However, the short shank and limited swing of the standard steam road coupler made it impossible to use on the sharp curves of interurban lines, and special long-radius couplings were developed. Some lines developed special fully automatic couplings which made all of the necessary air, electrical, and control connections automatically.

HEADLIGHTS: Oil lamps were used on the earliest interurbans, but were

FRONT EQUIPMENT

soon replaced by massive electric arc headlights. One problem encountered with electric headlights was their failure whenever the power supply was interrupted, often at a critical moment. Some roads solved this problem by the use of a storage battery on the car. Another difficulty was the insistence by cities and towns that the bright arc headlights be dimmed. This was sometimes accomplished by means of a curtain device, which the motorman could pull over the headlight with a string, but most lines adopted combination arc and incandescent headlights and turned off the arc light when passing through cities or towns. Later, incandescent headlights were used almost exclusively. The "Golden Glow" headlight, which employed a special colored reflector that extracted from the headlight beam blue and violet rays, thought to have a blinding effect, was a patented type that was widely used.

WHISTLES, HORNS, AND BELLS: Interurbans usually had an air-operated horn or whistle which acted as a warning device. For operation through city streets some sort of air- or foot-operated bell or gong was provided for the same purpose.

DESTINATION SIGNS: Interurban cars operating over fixed routes sometimes had the names of their destination cities painted directly on the vestibule dash, but more often destinations were shown by metal or wooden signs hung on the front or sides of the cars, and sometimes illuminated at night by lights. Later on, an illuminated roller destination sign became the most common practice.

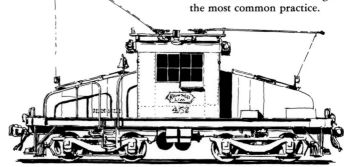

B-B STEEPLE-CAB

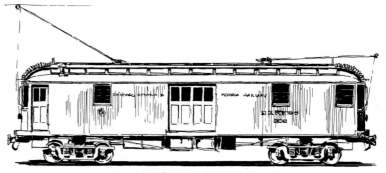

EXPRESS MOTOR

SANDERS: To prevent slipping on wet rail, most interurbans were equipped with some sort of sanders. A supply of sand, stored in a dry, well-protected box or container, was fed onto the rail by gravity or air pressure and was directed under the wheels by pipes.

HEATING SYSTEMS: Interurban cars were heated with either electrical resistance heaters or coal-fired hot water heaters, and a few cars had both types. The hot water heaters were more economical to operate, but took up more space and were not as clean as electric heat. An important advantage of a hot water system was the fact that a car could still be heated without a power supply.

FARE REGISTERS: Some interurbans employed a fare register, which the conductor could operate from any point in the car, to ring up fares as they were collected, but most relied on the same type of cash fare receipt used by steam railroads to account for fares received. When one-man car operation became common during the '20's the time-consuming handling of fare collections by the motorman often slowed up operation, and elaborate registers were developed that automatically computed the fare and printed a receipt. I

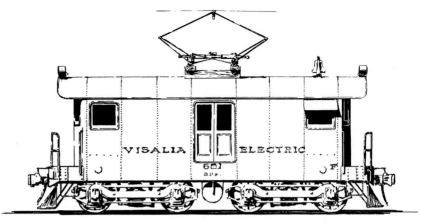

B-B BOX-CAB

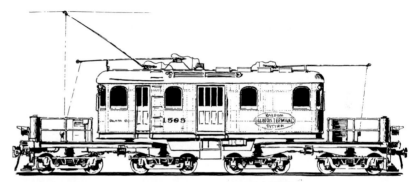

B-B+B-B ARTICULATED

Electrification and Current Collection

CURRENT AND VOLTAGE

DIRECT CURRENT: Low-voltage, direct-current motors, which were simple and rugged in construction, and possessed superior control and performance characteristics under the varying demands of electric railway service, were by far the most widely used type on both street and interurban railways. Because higher voltages presented greater hazards to the public and were generally frowned upon for street railway service, direct current systems of 550 to 600 volts became virtually universal for urban electric railways, and since interurbans frequently used the streetcar tracks to enter cities and were often operated by the same companies, 600-volt electrification became the most common type for interurban railways as well.

Low-voltage direct current did have some disadvantages in interurban operation, however. Since a larger current is required to transmit a given amount of energy at a lower voltage, transmission of 600-volt current over any distance resulted in either excessive voltage drop and power loss, or extremely heavy trans-

mission line requirements. Consequently, the spacing of substations, which converted the high-voltage alternating currents used for efficient long distance transmission to the low-voltage direct current fed to the trolley wire, could rarely exceed 10 to 12 miles. Even then, under severe operating conditions the actual voltage available to an interurban car sometimes dropped to as little as 250 volts, and often less than 50 per cent of the power generated was actually delivered to the car.

Higher voltage direct current systems of 1200 to 1500 volts were also common, and since the current required for a given amount of power decreased in inverse ratio to the voltage, transmission losses were reduced and substation spacing could be substantially increased. When operation over 600-volt streetcar lines was necessary, the high-voltage cars either were operated at half speed or used relatively simple changeover devices. Occasionally even higher voltages of 2400 to 3000 were used on interurban systems, and on at least one occasion an experimental direct current electrification at 5000 volts was made.

Basic substation equipment consisted of transformers to reduce the voltage of the alternating current from the transmission lines, and either motor-generator sets or synchronous or "rotary" converters to convert alternating to direct current. A motor-generator was nothing more than an alternating current motor driving a direct current generator, while the rotary converter performed an identical function but incorporated both motor and generator into a single unit. In later years mercury arc rectifiers were developed which did the same job more efficiently. Occasionally banks of storage batteries were included in substations to provide for peak loads which exceeded the capacity of the conversion equipment, or to act as an emergency power source in case of power failure. Many interurban systems also employed portable substations, which incorporated all of the necessary equipment into a box car that could be moved about the system to take care of seasonal or other peak load requirements.

In earlier years of the interurban era, substation equipment was such that it required an operator in continuous attendance, but later reliable controls were developed which permitted automatic operation.

425

ALTERNATING CURRENT: The use of high-voltage, single-phase alternating currents for electric railways, which largely eliminated the need for frequent substation installations and the problems of voltage drop and power loss inherent in low-voltage direct-current systems, presented, in theory at least, a much more satisfactory system of electrification, and enjoyed a brief period of popularity shortly after the turn of the century when a number of interurbans were thus electrified, usually with either 6600- or 13,000-volt systems. Alternating current motors were less satisfactory in performance or efficiency, and the necessary heavy transformers and complicated control systems added greatly to the weight of rolling stock. Many lines found the equipment more difficult and costly to maintain as well. The complexity of A. C. equipment was further increased when operation into cities over 600-volt D. C. systems was necessary. The single phase A. C. motors normally used could also be operated on direct current, but separate control and current collection systems were required. Such were the practical disadvantages that in later years many of the A. C. interurbans were converted to D. C. operation, usually at great expense and necessitating extremely intricate construction schedules to avoid interruptions to service. When the Pittsburgh & Butler Street Railway, for example, converted from alternating current to 1200-volt D. C. operation in 1914 it was able to realize a 15 per cent saving in power costs, and reduce the weight of each of its motor cars by 6 tons through elimination of the bulky A. C. equipment.

DISTRIBUTION AND CURRENT COLLECTION

DIRECT SUSPENSION: Overhead wire distribution systems were used by the majority of interurban systems. The most common type was the "direct suspension" system consisting of a single hard drawn copper wire supported at intervals of 80 to 125 feet from either metal brackets or insulated span wires suspended between poles on opposite sides of the track. Originally soldered "ears" were used to attach the wire to its supports but later a grooved wire was developed to which a mechanical clamping ear could be attached. Parallel feeder wires were used to feed current to the trolley wire. On single track lines, double overhead wires, spaced about 6 inches apart, were occasionally employed, one for traffic in each direction, which eliminated the need for overhead switches or frogs at turnouts and replaced some of the feeder copper requirement.

CATENARY: The sag between supports and the varying flexibility of direct suspension sometimes caused dewirement of the trolley wheel or shoe, and for high-speed operation catenary systems were often used, in which the trolley wire was hung from a "messenger" wire by hangers of varying length. The spacing of supports was usually increased to intervals of about 150 feet with catenary systems. A few lines used catenary spans of as much as 300 feet. The more uniformly level catenary system was especially desirable when pantograph collection was employed.

OVERHEAD SUPPORTS: Wood poles were usually used to support overhead construction, but some of the more elaborate installations employed substantial steel structures. When the supporting structure was also used to carry high tension transmission lines for a parent power company, as was sometimes the case, the resulting installation was impressive indeed. Within cities more ornamental metal poles were often used.

THIRD RAIL: For heavy-duty, high-speed interurbans third-rail systems were often used. A steel power rail was used, usually mounted about 6 inches above and 20 inches out from the running rail and supported on insulators placed on the ends of extra long ties spaced every 6th to 10th tie.

Third-rail systems had the advantage of a greater conductivity than was possible with a trolley wire, and could be more easily made level and true. However, because of the danger to human life, they could be used only on private right of way and most third-rail interurbans had to install alternate overhead wires where operation in city streets or in populated areas was involved. Still other disadvantages were the necessity for gaps in the third rail at road crossings and switches and the extreme vulnerability of the bare rail to sleet, which stuck to the rail like varnish and had to be removed with special scrapers or brine. The use of a protected third rail, which employed a metal or wood cover, helped eliminate the sleeting problem and reduced the potential hazard to life. Third-rail lines still required a pole line to support feeders, and were usually more costly to install than an overhead system.

Third rails were normally used only for low-voltage D. C. systems, but at least one line, the Michigan Railway, had a 2400-volt third-rail system, later cut to 1200 volts, on its high-speed Kalamazoo-Grand Rapids and Battle Creek-Allegan lines. Extremely elaborate protective measures were required, however, to insure the safety of the public.

UNDERGROUND CONDUIT: A variation of third-rail current collection was the underground system, consisting of power rails mounted in a conduit beneath the track, which eliminated the unsightly overhead construction. The system was extremely costly and resulted in intricate specialwork at switches and crossings. It was used in the U. S. only by street railways in Washington, D. C., and New York City, and the several interurban lines that entered Washington were the only ones that ever used it.

CURRENT RETURN: Except on a few street railways, which employed a second overhead wire, and the underground conduit systems, which had a separate return rail, the running rails were universally used to complete the return circuit to the powerhouse. This required careful bonding between each length of rail, usually by means of copper wire. When bonding systems were not carefully maintained the current had a habit of wandering off and following other conductors, such as water pipes, gas mains, and telephone cables, creating electrolytic corrosion and other complicated problems. In one instance, in 1930, on the Milwaukee Electric's interurban line between Racine and Kenosha, where many rail bonds were missing, it was found that the return current was striking off across a celery marsh for half a mile to the North Shore Line's rails, which it followed to Racine, then jumped to the city car rails and followed these to the Milwaukee Electric powerhouse.

POWER SUPPLY

In the early years of interurban construction, the provision of a company-owned power generating plant was the usual practice. In many cases the interurban companies also sold power to communities or individual users, and the sale of power by interurban companies was occasionally the first form of rural electrification. The first electric range installed in an Ohio farm home, for example, was powered by current purchased from the Scioto Valley Traction Company. Indeed, many interurbans were no more than subsidiaries of large power companies, although Government trustbusters were to frown upon this practice in later years.

Because of the varying power demands at different times of the day, most interurbans found that generation of their own electricity was less economical than purchase from public utility companies, and most later discontinued the operation of their own plants in favor of purchased power. 1

Electric Railway Museums in the United States and Canada

NEW ENGLAND

MAINE

SEASHORE ELECTRIC RAILWAY, Kennebunkport, operated by the New England Electric Railway Historical Society, was founded in 1939 and is the original, as well as the largest, electric railway museum. The museum collection includes 43 city cars, 11 interurbans, and 26 freight or work cars, and represents a nearly complete selection of important car types and builders throughout the history of North American electric traction. Among the outstanding interurban cars preserved are lightweight, high-speed cars from both the Indiana Railroad and the Cincinnati & Lake Erie. Over a mile of track is presently operated and construction of 3 additional miles is under way.

The museum is open daily from late June through Labor Day, and on week ends during the remainder of the year. Cars are operated daily during the summer.

CONNECTICUT

BRANFORD ELECTRIC RAILWAY ASSOCIATION INC., Short Beach, founded in 1945, operates one of the most successful of all trolley museum projects. The museum collection includes 28 city and suburban cars, 4 interurbans, and 15 freight or work units, representing almost all important car types and periods. Outstanding among the interurban cars are a former Connecticut Company parlor car, still completely furnished, and a Cincinnati & Lake Erie high-speed car.

A mile of track, part of the abandoned Connecticut Company Short Beach line, is presently operated. Service over another half mile of track is suspended until reconstruction of a hurricane-damaged trestle. The museum is open daily, and cars are operated from 1 p.m. to 6 p.m. on Sundays from April through November, and during the same hours on Saturdays and holidays from May 30 through Labor Day. Cars may also be chartered by advance arrangement.

CONNECTICUT ELECTRIC RAILWAY ASSOCIATION INC., Warehouse Point, founded in 1941, or its individual members own 16 city cars, 1 interurban, and 10 work or freight units. Equipment is operated over a mile of track laid on the roadbed of the abandoned Rockville branch of the Hartford & Springfield Street Railway. In the future track will be laid over 3 miles of right of way owned by the group, and picnic facilities are planned at the site of Piney Ridge Park, once operated by the Hartford & Springfield.

Cars are operated Sunday and holiday afternoons from July through October, with private charter operation by advance arrangement.

MIDDLE ATLANTIC STATES

NEW YORK

RAIL CITY MUSEUM INC., Sandy Creek, opened in 1955, is principally a steam railroad museum, which also owns 2 streetcars and 2 electric work cars. In addition, 2 wood interurban cars from Ontario lines, owned by the Syracuse Chapter, NRHS, are located at the museum.

Steam equipment only is operated. The museum is open daily during July and August, and on week ends during June, September, and October.

PENNSYLVANIA

ARDEN SHORT LINE ELECTRIC RAILWAY, Washington, operated by the Pittsburgh Electric Railway Club, was founded in 1954. Car ownership includes 5 city cars, 3 interurbans, and a freight locomotive. Of particular interest is former West Penn Railways car No. 832, the only intact surviving example of the famous Cincinnati Car Company curved-side lightweight car.

The museum has completed 3700 feet of track, most of it on the right of way of the abandoned Pittsburgh Railways Washington interurban line. Construction of an additional 600 feet is planned for 1961, and operation of cars may begin late in 1961. Track is laid to the 5'-2½" Pennsylvania broad gauge, with 500 feet of dual broad- and standard-gauge track.

The museum is open to the public on Saturdays from 10 a.m. to 4 p.m.

SOUTH ATLANTIC STATES

MARYLAND

MARYLAND HISTORICAL SOCIETY, Baltimore, owns a collection of 8 historical Baltimore streetcars, donated by the Baltimore Transit Co. At present the cars are in storage but attempts are being made to locate a suitable site for permanent exhibition and, perhaps, operation of the cars. An additional car is on display at a city playground.

NORTH CENTRAL STATES

OHIO

OHIO RAILWAY MUSEUM, Worthington, founded in 1948 by the Central Ohio Railfans Association, has been operating electric cars since 1952. Equipment includes 3 city cars, 3 interurbans, and a wide variety of miscellaneous electric and steam railroad rolling stock. Interurban equipment includes a 1905 Niles combine typical of the graceful wooden cars of the early interurban years, and one of the Cincinnati & Lake Erie Railroad's famed lightweight, high-speed cars of 1930.

One mile of track, laid on the roadbed of the abandoned Columbus, Delaware & Marion Electric Co., is operated, and another mile will be constructed in the future. A steam locomotive is also operated.

The museum is open Saturday afternoons and Sundays, and cars are operated on Sundays from 2 p.m. to 5 p.m. from May 1 to November 1.

MICHIGAN

FORD MUSEUM, Dearborn, has 3 streetcars, including a former Fort Collins (Colo.) Birney car and a Peter Witt car.

ILLINOIS

ILLINOIS ELECTRIC RAILWAY MUSEUM INC., North Chicago, was founded in 1953. Six city cars, 5 interurbans, and a variety of elevated and work equipment are owned by the museum. Notable among them are a former Indiana Railroad lightweight, high-speed car; a coach and parlor car from the Milwaukee Electric; and several Illinois Terminal cars. Equipment is temporarily stored until a suitable site for an operating museum is located.

The present storage site at the Chicago Hardware Foundry, North Chicago, is normally open on Saturdays, and the cars may be seen Sundays by appointment.

ELECTRIC RAILWAY HISTORICAL SOCIETY, Chicago, founded in 1952, owns 8 street railway cars from Chicago which are temporarily stored near Downers Grove, Ill. Future plans call for operating trackage, possibly in conjunction with the Illinois Electric Railway Museum.

The cars may be seen Sunday afternoons, and usually on Saturdays.

ILLINI RAILROAD CLUB, Champaign, owns 2 former Illinois Traction System business cars built in 1910 for the use of Congressman William B. McKinley, founder and president of the system. Not equipped with motors, the cars are used for annual club excursions behind diesel power.

Stored at Champaign, they may be inspected on appointment with club members.

IOWA

IOWA RAILWAY HISTORICAL MUSEUM INC., Centerville, was founded in 1958 by the Iowa Chapter, NRHS. The museum owns former Waterloo, Cedar Falls & Northern parlor-buffet-observation car No. 100, which is stored at the carbarn of the Southern Iowa Railway. Two annual trips, in June and October, plus charter trips during the summer, are operated by the museum over approximately 16 miles of electrified SIRy track. In addition, SIRy equipment, which includes a streetcar as well as electric freight equipment, is operated on excursions.

WATERLOO, IA., has a former Waterloo, Cedar Falls & Northern streetcar on display in Cedar River Park. The car originally operated in Knoxville, Tenn.

MISSOURI

NATIONAL MUSEUM OF TRANSPORT, Barretts Station, St. Louis, founded in 1945, owns an extensive collection of steam and electric railway equipment. Electric car ownership includes 13 city and 8 interurban cars, as well as 2 cable cars, a Brooklyn rapid transit car, and an interurban freight locomotive. Of unusual historical significance among the interurban car collection is the famous test car *Louisiana*, originally constructed in 1904 for high-speed tests in Indiana and later operated as a Purdue University test car. Also noteworthy are 2 streamlined Illinois Terminal passenger units, and a four-truck Illinois Terminal freight locomotive.

Equipment is stored on track laid on an abandoned Missouri Pacific right of way which includes two tunnels. Operation of equipment is not contemplated, but the museum will have displays of many forms of transportation equipment and a large transportation library.

The museum is open daily from 10 a.m. to 8 p.m., May 15 to September 15, and from 10 a.m. to 5 p.m., September 15 to May 15.

NEBRASKA

PIONEER MUSEUM, Minden, owns a former Fort Collins (Colo.) four-wheel Birney streetcar.

SOUTH CENTRAL STATES

KENTUCKY

CINCINNATI RAILWAY HISTORICAL SOCIETY owns the former Cincinnati, Newport & Covington single-truck parlor car *Kentucky*, built in 1892, which is on display at the William Behringer Museum, Devou Park, Covington, Ky.

The museum is open between 1 p.m. and 8 p.m. daily except Monday, from Easter to October.

KENTUCKY RAILWAY MUSEUM INC., Louisville, was opened in Eva Bandman Park in 1958. Devoted largely to steam railroad equipment, the museum's collection also includes a Milwaukee streetcar.

The museum is open on week ends from Memorial Day to Labor Day.

TEXAS

WITTE MEMORIAL MUSEUM, San Antonio, has a former San Antonio streetcar on display.

MOUNTAIN STATES

COLORADO

COLORADO RAILROAD MUSEUM, Golden, has a display of historical narrow-gauge and standard-gauge cars and locomotives from Colorado railroads. Included in the collection are a four-wheel Birney streetcar from Fort Collins and a Denver & Intermountain interurban car, both preserved by the Rocky Mountain Railroad Club. Future plans contemplate the construction of operating track and electrification.

The museum is open daily.

PACIFIC STATES

WASHINGTON

PUGET SOUND RAILWAY HISTORICAL ASSOCIATION, Seattle, owns a streetcar, a British Columbia Electric interurban, and a line car, in addition to a variety of steam railroad equipment. An operating museum is under construction at Snoqualmie, Wash.

OREGON

GLENWOOD ELECTRIC RAILWAY, Glenwood, operated by the Oregon Electric Railway Historical Society, was founded in 1957. Car ownership includes two former Australian streetcars, and a Key System articulated Bay Bridge unit.

Located on the site of the yards of an abandoned logging railroad, the museum has an old depot, water tower, and other buildings, among them former enginehouses used to store equipment. Cars will be operated over both standard-gauge and 3'6"-gauge divisions, to be constructed on abandoned roadbeds of the logging line and an SP&S branch.

The museum is open week ends during the summer, and may be viewed by appointment at other times.

WILLAMETTE VALLEY ELECTRIC RAILWAY ASSOCIATION INC., Portland, owns 2 streetcars and 4 interurbans, among them the Oregon Electric open-platform observation car *Champoeg* and the British Columbia Electric *Duke of Connaught*. Equipment is stored at present and may be seen only by prior arrangement. Future plans call for operation.

CALIFORNIA

ORANGE EMPIRE TROLLEY MUSEUM, Perris, was founded in 1956. Car ownership includes 43 streetcars, interurbans, and miscellaneous pieces of work, freight, and steam road equipment, chiefly from the Pacific Electric Railway and the Los Angeles Railway. Notable among them are a double-deck Irish tram, one of Pacific Electric's famous 1000-class wooden interurbans, an aluminum car originally operated by the Northwestern Pacific Railroad, and a Key System articulated Bay Bridge unit. The first 1000 feet of the museum's operating track and overhead were placed in operation during 1960, and ultimate plans call for construction of about 5 miles of track. All mainline track will be dual-gauge to permit operation of 3'6"-gauge Los Angeles Railway cars.

The museum is open daily, and cars are operated for the public on Sunday afternoons.

TRAVEL TOWN, located in Griffith Park, Los Angeles, and owned by the City of Los Angeles, has on display 2 city cars, a San Francisco cable car, a Pacific Electric box motor, and historic PE locomotive No. 1544, the *Electra*, which was originally operated by the North Coast Railroad and was employed in rubbish removal service following the San Francisco earthquake of 1906.

The exhibit is open daily.

RAILWAY HISTORICAL SOCIETY OF SAN DIEGO owns a former San Diego Electric Railway PCC car which is located on the grounds of the Southern California Exposition and San Diego County Fair at Del Mar. A future operating museum is planned.

PACIFIC RAILROAD SOCIETY INC., Los Angeles, owns a former Los Angeles Railway funeral car, the *Descanso*, which is located at Summit, in Cajon Pass north of San Bernardino.

LOS ANGELES COUNTY FAIR GROUNDS, Pomona, has on display the Pacific Electric Railway's elegant business car No. 1299. It may be seen during the fair the last two weeks in September.

PACIFIC COAST CHAPTER, RAILWAY & LOCOMOTIVE HISTORICAL SOCIETY, San Francisco, owns a collection of historical railroad equipment, including several San Francisco streetcars, a two-car train of former New York "El" cars, and a Key System articulated Bay Bridge unit, which will be displayed at the San Francisco Maritime Museum.

BAY AREA ELECTRIC RAILROAD ASSOCIATION, Berkeley, or its members own 9 city cars, 4 interurbans, and 5 pieces of work or freight equipment. Among the interurban car ownership are included a Salt Lake & Utah observation trailer and a Sacramento Northern combine. Equipment is presently in storage but the organization plans to establish an operating museum.

CANADA

QUEBEC

CANADIAN RAILROAD HISTORICAL ASSOCIATION INC., Montreal, owns 12 historical items of railway equipment, among them 5 city streetcars, a suburban car, 2 interurbans, and an electric locomotive, from all parts of Canada.

The group is participating in the development of a Canadian transportation museum, which will include both operating steam and electric railway sections. A site was selected at St. Constant, Que., and work started late in 1960.

MONTREAL TRANSPORTATION COMMISSION owns a collection of 14 historical electric railway cars, most of them from the Montreal area, and including the first streetcar to operate in Montreal. This equipment will probably be placed in the proposed Canadian transportation museum near Montreal.

ONTARIO

HALTON COUNTY RADIAL RAILWAY, Rockwood, sponsored by the Ontario Electric Railway Historical Society, was founded in 1953. Equipment includes two Toronto streetcars and a Montreal & Southern Counties interurban.

The museum is located on the roadbed of the abandoned Toronto Suburban Railway, and operating track is planned for future years. The museum is normally open on week ends during the summer. I

Bibliography

THE following summary is derived largely from "The Literature of the Street Railway," by Foster M. Palmer, which appeared in the Winter 1958 issue of the Harvard Library Bulletin, and has been extracted with the kind permission of the author.

Among the most important sources of information concerning the history of interurban railways are the several trade periodicals which were published throughout the interurban era.

ELECTRIC RAILWAY JOURNAL was the leader among them. It began in 1884 as the *Street Railway Journal*, then became *Electric Railway Journal* in 1908. The title *Transit Journal* was adopted in 1932 and continued until publication ended in 1942. The JOURNAL is a voluminous source of technical and historical matter concerning electric railways. Of particular interest are its special issues which were published on the occasion of the annual American Street Railway Association convention and contained detailed articles devoted to the street and interurban railways of the convention city or special reports on electric railway practices.

ELECTRIC TRACTION was second in importance only to the *Journal*. First published in 1905 as the *Interurban Railway Journal*, it became the *Electric Traction Weekly* in 1906, and finally just ELECTRIC TRACTION in 1912. During the '20's the magazine sponsored the famous interurban speed competition. Still published, it is now known as *Mass Transportation*.

STREET RAILWAY GAZETTE, later the *Electric Railway Gazette*, appeared in 1886 and was published for a decade before merging with *Electrical World*.

STREET RAILWAY REVIEW, founded in 1891, became *Electric Railway Review* in 1906 and was merged with the *Electric Railway Journal* two years later.

Catalogs and other promotional literature published by carbuilders and electric railway equipment suppliers provide many details of cars and equipment, as well as a considerable amount of general information. Almost every builder issued periodic catalogs which detailed representative cars in the company's line, and such major suppliers as General Electric and Westinghouse issued special publications devoted to modern cars of many builders, in addition to catalogs of their own lines of locomotives and equipment.

MODERN TYPES OF CITY AND INTERURBAN CARS AND TRUCKS, John Stephenson Co., 1905, is an outstanding example of the carbuilder's catalog which includes interior and exterior photographs of representative car types, freight equipment, car construction details, and trucks.

ELECTRIC RAILWAY DICTIONARY, Rodney Hitt, McGraw Publishing Company, 1911, is a comprehensive encyclopedia of the equipment of electric railways published near the peak of the interurban era. It is comparable in format to such steam railroad publications as the *Car Builders' Cyclopedia*. A reproduction of principal portions of the DICTIONARY was published in 1960 under the title *Street Cars and Interurbans of Yesterday* by Owen Davies, Chicago.

DEVELOPMENT & PROGRESS OF THE ELECTRIC RAILWAY INDUSTRY, Westinghouse, 1923, described modern electric railway practices and offered a brief outline of electric railway history.

BRILL MAGAZINE, published for promotional purposes from 1907 to 1927 by the leading carbuilder, is a rich source of interurban information. In addition to giving details of new Brill cars and equipment, the magazine regularly featured articles devoted to such topics as leading interurban centers and systems, and biographies of prominent electric railway officials.

Throughout the several decades of their prodigious growth, electric railways were considered to have an almost limitless future; and their design, construction, and operation were the subject of a number of engineering texts, reports, and similar works, which now constitute an excellent source of information concerning the technical details of interurban railroading.

ELECTRIC RAILWAY TRANSPORTATION, Blake & Jackson, McGraw Hill, 1917, was typical of a number of electric railway engineering and operation textbooks.

ELECTRIC TRACTION FOR RAILWAY TRAINS, Edward P. Burch, McGraw-Hill, 1911, was another typical textbook, with a particularly good summary of electric railway history.

REPORT OF THE ELECTRIC RAILWAY TEST COMMISSION, 1904, presented the results and conclusions of a group organized by the officials of the St. Louis Louisiana Purchase Exposition, which conducted a series of high-speed tests on the Union Traction Company of Indiana.

PROCEEDINGS and other publications of the American Street Railway Association, organized in 1882, are an important source of technical information. The organization became the American Street and Interurban Railway Association in 1905, the American Electric Railway Association in 1910, and finally the American Transit Association in 1933. Beginning in 1923, a committee of the Association chose the recipients of the Charles A. Coffin prize, awarded annually to leading electric railways, and the exhibits submitted by the candidates were the basis for *Electric Railway Practices* (1923-30/31). These volumes constitute a valuable source of information on leading interurban railways during this period.

Reports and publications of the Interstate Commerce Commission and the many state regulatory bodies contain statistical and other information related to electric railways.

SPECIAL REPORTS: STREET AND ELECTRIC RAILWAYS, issued by the Bureau of the Census in 1902 and 1907, and later similar publications are a source of economic and statistical information concerning interurban railways.

POOR'S MANUAL OF THE RAILROADS OF THE UNITED STATES from 1868 to 1913 and POOR'S MANUAL OF PUBLIC UTILITIES from 1913 to 1918 contained electric railway corporate and financial information.

MOODY'S MANUAL included similar information from 1901 until 1924, when it was succeeded by *Poor's*, which was merged in 1940 with the *Standard Corporation Records.*

MOODY'S ANALYSIS OF INVESTMENTS, which became *Moody's Manual of Investments* in 1926, is still another source of such information.

MCGRAW TRANSIT DIRECTORY, originally a section of the *Street Railway Journal*, listed every street railway in the U. S., its officers, and other basic information.

RAND MCNALLY'S COMMERCIAL ATLAS, published annually from 1911 to date, is an excellent source of detailed information on interurban routes.

THE CENTURY DICTIONARY AND CYCLOPEDIA, forming *The Century Atlas*, in its 1911 edition included maps of electric railways in the New England, Middle Atlantic, and Central states.

Timetables and other promotional literature published by individual interurban companies often provide details of their operations. The elaborate timetable folders issued by some of the larger systems often contained considerable material about the various services and equipment offered, as well as schedules. In the early years of the century, many interurbans issued lithographed folders containing handsomely colored panoramic maps, in addition to descriptions of recreational, scenic, and historical attractions along the way, designed to stimulate traffic. Booklets detailing the attractions available on electric lines were another variation. Among typical examples were:

WAYSIDE SCENES, published by the Philadelphia & Easton Electric Railway;

A LITTLE TRIP THROUGH HISTORY, issued by the Lehigh Valley Traction Company;

SUMMER BOARDING & TENT LIFE ON THE BUTLER SHORT LINE, offered by the Pittsburgh & Butler Street Railway; and

SEEING LANCASTER COUNTY FROM A TROLLEY WINDOW, which stimulated tourist travel over Pennsylvania's Conestoga Traction Company.

In areas where interconnected electric networks existed, many trolley touring guide books were published. More of them appeared in New England, perhaps, than in any other location.

OFFICIAL STREET RAILWAY GUIDE FOR NEW ENGLAND was one of a number of such guides published by Robert H. Derrah of Boston.

TROLLEY TRIPS ON A BAY STATE TRIANGLE was typical of the series of guides published by Katherine M. Abbott of Lowell, Mass.

TROLLEY WAYFINDER, the "Official Street Railway Guide of New England," was issued by the New England Street Railway Club.

TROLLEY TRIPS THROUGH NEW ENGLAND, an offering of the Trolley Press at Hartford, was one of still another New England series.

THE EAGLE TROLLEY EXPLORING GUIDE, which described many trolley outings in the New York area, as well as surrounding states, was published annually for a number of years by the *Brooklyn Eagle.*

INTERURBAN TROLLEY GUIDE, published at Chicago, outlined possible tours on Midwestern interurban lines.

In recent years several books of considerable interest concerning electric railways have appeared.

FARES, PLEASE!, John A. Miller, D. Appleton-Century Co., 1941, covered all forms of local transportation. A paperback reprint was published in 1960 by Dover Publications, Inc.

TROLLEY CAR TREASURY, Frank Rowsome Jr. and Stephen D. Maguire, McGraw-Hill, 1956, is a well-illustrated popular history of street and interurban railways.

THE ELECTRIC INTERURBAN RAILWAYS IN AMERICA, George W. Hilton and John F. Due, Stanford University Press, 1960, is a history of the interurbans with particularly good coverage of their economics, which includes a complete set of maps of U. S. and Canadian interurbans and individual histories of over 300 companies.

During the past quarter century, as the electric railway has all but vanished from North America, a number of railroad fan organizations have been formed, which have helped to assemble and preserve much of the history of the electric railway, and their great variety of periodicals and historical publications have assumed increasing importance.

HEADLIGHTS, a monthly publication of the Electric Railroaders' Association at New York since 1939, although devoted largely to news, often contains much in the way of historical matter.

TROLLEY SPARKS has been published since 1944 by the Central Electric Railfans' Association at Chicago. In recent years it has taken the form of a profusely illustrated annual album devoted to electric railways of a particular Midwestern state.

INTERURBANS, published at Los Angeles as a periodical from 1943 to 1948, has also issued an intermittent series of *Specials* from 1944 to date which are largely devoted to West Coast electric lines but have occasionally ventured as far afield as the Midwest and Canada, and which represent some of the best of the railroad fan publications. Of particular interest is the column "Tapping the Field," by Felix E. Reifschneider, which appeared in the monthly *Interurbans* and discussed many of the details of electric railway equipment.

BULLETINS, published at Chicago by the Electric Railway Historical Society, have included many excellent histories of individual traction lines, as well as reproductions of important articles from *Brill Magazine* and catalogs of a number of car and equipment manufacturers which are otherwise almost unobtainable.

PACIFIC RAILWAY JOURNAL, San Marino, Calif., has published in recent years several issues devoted to interurban railways, notable among them a beautifully reproduced Pacific Electric album by Donald Duke in 1958.

THE WESTERN RAILROADER, San Mateo, Calif., has published a number of articles or special issues devoted to the electric interurbans of the West.

A great many other individuals, regional fan groups, and chapters of such organizations as the National Railway Historical Society have issued many publications devoted to local electric railways.

TRANSPORTATION, issued since 1946 by the Connecticut Valley Chapter of the NRHS at Warehouse Point, Conn., which has covered in great detail the histories of many New England traction properties, is notable among such publications.

RAILROAD MAGAZINE, published at New York, has contained occasional electric railway news and feature articles since the late '30's, and has carried a regular Electric Lines Department, edited by Stephen D. Maguire, since the early 1940's.

TRAINS MAGAZINE, published at Milwaukee, has also carried occasional electric railway features since its inception in 1940. ⊥

KALMBACH PUBLISHING CO.

book editor / DAVID P. MORGAN
continuity / ROSEMARY ENTRINGER
design / DAVID A. STRASSMAN
layout / LA VERNE F. BLEIFUSS
sketches / GEORGE A. GLOFF

printing and binding / RAND MC NALLY & CO.

The interurban era is past but some of the more resourceful aficionados have acquired their own rolling stock. The Iowa Railway Historical Museum operates a former Waterloo, Cedar Falls & Northern combine on tracks of the Southern Iowa Railway out of Centerville. Camera stops are one of the most popular features of fan excursions.
WILLIAM D. MIDDLETON.